YOUR 90 DAY
FINANCIAL BREAKTHROUGH

THE POWER COACH™
MADELINE ALEXANDER

FOR THE WEAPONS OF OUR WARFARE ARE NOT CARNAL
BUT MIGHTY IN GOD FOR PULLING DOWN STRONGHOLDS
2 CORINTHIANS 10:4 (NKJV)

YOUR 90 DAY FINANCIAL BREAKTHROUGH

90 POWER PROMISES AND THE WEAPONS OF OUR WARFARE
TO WIN IN YOUR FINANCES NOW

THE POWER COACH™

MADELINE ALEXANDER

CREATIVE COMMUNICATIONS GROUP INTERNATIONAL
HOUSTON, TX

to have such an incredible sister and friend. I could not do this work without you. I love you very much!

To my brother, *Rob*, and my sister, *Jackie*, thank you for continually speaking life to my purpose and potential from early childhood until now, and helping me to become a better and stronger person. Thank you for all you have sown into my life. This is our time of breakthrough! I love you both very much!

To *Josiah, Jack, Marc, Paul, John, Jonathan, Åse, Jaana, Carol (Bunny), Kenneth, Kevin M., Kevin E.,* and all of my extended family members, again, thank you so much for your love, encouragement, and support. I love you all very much. You are a major part of this breakthrough. The best is yet to come!

My life is wholly and unquestionably devoted to my *Heavenly Father*, my *Lord and Savior Jesus Christ*, and the *Holy Spirit*. I pray my walk is worthy of the calling on my life. May my life be a living testimony to Your unconditional love and amazing grace! I am humbled and honored that You have called me to this work. Thank You for giving me the words to encourage, educate, empower, and emancipate others to live in the fullness of salvation. *Lord Jesus*, I live each day to worship You, honor You, and help others to know You through the power of Your resurrection! I love You with all of my heart.

Now to Him who is able to do exceedingly, abundantly above all that we ask or think, according to the power that works in us, to Him be glory in the church by Christ Jesus to all generations, forever and ever. Amen.

Ephesians 3:20-21 (NKJV)

praise

"Few people can make you hunger to know more about a subject like Madeline. Her comprehensive biblical research, practical wisdom, and powerful presentation inspire us to life-changing choices and actions — all to God's honor and praise. I have for many years as Pastor and friend been impressed by Madeline's deep love for Jesus and devotion to ushering people into life as He intends it. It seems to me she has no greater joy. Without hesitation, I am honored to recommend *Your 90-Day Financial Breakthrough* to all!"

PASTOR MARSHALL TOWNSLEY
Believers Center of Albuquerque
Albuquerque, NM
www.believerscenter.com

"What a timely and much needed resource, first, for the Body of Christ, and then for anyone who may be experiencing challenges in their finances. It is filled with biblical principles along with practical application of how to control your finances rather than your finances controlling you. If you're looking for a quick-fix on how to get rich, this may not be the book for you, but if you're willing to discipline yourself for 90 days, apply the principles, pray, and allow the Holy Spirit to direct you, then this book is for you. Madeline has ministered in our Church and her profound yet practical way of sharing the Word of God is life-changing. I personally believe that her book, *Your 90-Day Financial Breakthrough*, has come to the Kingdom for such a time as this!"

PASTOR GEORGE MERRIWEATHER
Northeast Community Fellowship Church
Portland, OR

"Once again, I am absolutely inspired by this powerfully anointed woman of God, chosen for this generation to unravel insightful biblical truths, designed to penetrate the hearts of God's people, birthing profound wisdom. This book is truly designed to equip you with key principles to total financial freedom, no matter what your current state may be. *Your 90-Day Financial Breakthrough* provides bold new prayers and practical tools to help you move forward and ascertain total financial victory. I tip my hat to The Power Coach™ Madeline Alexander as she omnivorously sits under the superintendent guidance of the Holy Spirit, and melodiously comprises how to break through every barrier of lack — spirit, soul, and body."

APOSTLE **D.E. HAMILTON**
Infallible Word of Faith Ministries
Houston, TX

special thanks

I would like to thank the following people who contributed to the completion of this work. Your talents and contributions are greatly appreciated and valued. Thank you.

CREATIVE DIRECTOR, INTERIOR DESIGN & TYPESET
Allison Young
Oak Owl Design and Illustration
oakowldesign@gmail.com

COMMERCIAL PHOTOGRAPHY
Dwayne Hills
Dwayne Hills Photography
www.dhillsphotography.com

COVER CONCEPT & DESIGN
Kir at www.gnibel.com

PRINT & PUBLICATION
Joel Turner
America's Press
www.americas-press.com

HAIR DESIGN
Brandye Rhone
DUO II Beauty Bar, Houston TX
www.vagaro.com/DuoBeautyBar

acknowledgments

Each new book is a unique and life-changing journey. Writing *Your 90-Day Financial Breakthrough* has radically changed my life and expanded my ministry vision. I am deeply thankful to everyone who has stood with me, interceded for me, and covered me in prayer as I studied, prepared, and completed this writing. I am eternally grateful to every person who has battled with me for breakthrough, as I press forward to bring breakthrough to others. I love and appreciate you greatly!

To *Samantha Norris* and *Giselle Hampton,* thank you for your sisterhood, unfailing love, and support. You are *always* there for me. I know the Lord will pour out upon your lives such blessings that you will not have room enough to receive them! I thank God daily for your powerful prayers, faithful friendship, selfless service, and enormous encouragement. I love you both!

To *Charmie Smith, Kelly Cogswell, Chantell Aden,* and *Rosalyn Caldwell,* thank you for your amazing friendship, faithful intercession, and faith-filled belief in me. Your daily prayers have given me supernatural strength, protection, and power. Your encouragement has given me tremendous endurance. I love you dearly. I do not have words to express my gratitude for your love, generosity, and commitment. May the Lord open the windows of Heaven to you. As you have sown so bountifully, may you reap bountifully! You are a major part of this victory and I praise God for you.

To my faithful friends, *Delores Cante, Wayne Lawrence, Wayne Stephens, Greg Allen, Cleo Dunigan, Marvin Dillard, and Wanita Mitchell,* thank you for your unconditional love and unwavering support over many years! You have been a great source of care and encouragement to me. Thank you for believing in me and seeing my vision with your eyes of faith. I love and appreciate you so much. May your blessings be pressed down, shaken together, and running over!

To my goddaughter *LaTorria Jones,* I am so proud of you, and I love you very much! May the Lord grant you the desires of your heart!

To *Pastors Marshall* and *Cindi Townsley,* thank you for over 25 years of faithful friendship and heartfelt pastoral care. You are my pastors for life! I am so thankful to experience the unquestionable and unconditional love of Jesus Christ through you. You are the epitome of true shepherds. I pray that many more members of the Body of Christ could experience true pastoral care in the same manner as what you have given to me. I love and appreciate you both so much. Praying that the Lord will bless you indeed, and enlarge your territory!

To my spiritual mother, *Pauline Terry,* thank you for embracing me as your own daughter, and discipling me in Christ. Thank you for teaching me to memorize the Word of God, and demonstrating how to battle for breakthrough. I love you very much! May salvation come to every person whose name you have spoken before the Lord.

To my pastors and extended families at *Lakewood Church*, Houston, Texas, Pastors Joel and Victoria Osteen, and the *Believers Center of Albuquerque*, Albuquerque, New Mexico, Pastors Marshall and Cindi Townsley, I am deeply thankful the Lord placed me in the Body with you! Planted in the house of the Lord we shall flourish in the courts of our God!

partners

I would like to extend a special heartfelt thank you to the following Lifetime Founding Partners, the charter members of *Partners with The Power Coach*™. Through your unwavering support, we are sharing the message of financial breakthrough and spiritual deliverance across the nation and around the world. Thank you for your commitment to change and transform lives for the Kingdom. You are amazing! I deeply appreciate your passion and faithfulness. Thank you for being a generous blessing to others.

LIFETIME FOUNDING PARTNERS

Alice R. Edwards . .(Believers Center of Albuquerque, Albuquerque, NM)

Allison Young . . . .(Believers Center of Albuquerque, Albuquerque, NM)

Eunice Young. . . . .(Believers Center of Albuquerque, Albuquerque, NM)

Carol Spellman . . . . (Bibleway Apostolic Church, Chesapeake, VA)

Charmie Smith . . . . (The City Church, Seattle, WA)

Chantell Aden . . . . (Overcomer Covenant Church, Auburn, WA)

Kelly Cogswell. . .(Maple Valley Presbyterian Church, Maple Valley, WA)

Theresa Hooks. . . . . (Champions Centre, Tacoma, WA)

Sonia Williams . . . . (Life Church, Ft. Worth, TX)

Samantha Norris. . . . . (Lakewood Church, Houston, TX)

Min. Rosalyn Caldwell . . . . (Lakewood Church, Houston, TX)

Charles & Latrinia Clark. . . . . (Lakewood Church, Houston, TX)

Darla Litton . . . . (Lakewood Church, Houston, TX)

Giselle Hampton . . . . (The Church Without Walls, Houston, TX)

Wayne Lawrence. . . . . (The Church Without Walls, Houston, TX)

Elex Gauthia Henry . . . . (The Church Without Walls, Houston, TX)

Tijuana Latham. . . . . (The Church Without Walls, Houston, TX)

Dea. Marcelio Tatum. . (CRM City Fellowship Church, The Woodlands, TX)

Min. Lou Richardson . . .(CRM City Fellowship Church, Sugar Land, TX)

Min. Wanita Mitchell . . . . . (CRM City Fellowship Church, Houston, TX)

Johnny Tyson, Jr. . . . . . .(Living Word Fellowship Church, Houston, TX)

Min. Jotina Buck. . . . (St. Luke Missionary Baptist Church, Humble, TX)

Charles Kimmons . . . . .(Northeast Community Fellowship Church, Portland, OR)

Edna Kimmons. . . . .(Northeast Community Fellowship Church, Portland, OR)

Shelia Noland. . . . . (Northeast Community Fellowship Church, Portland, OR)

Suzan Bafford . . . . (Mission Community Church, Gilbert, AZ)

Crystal Bradford. . . .(Greater Mount Calvary Holy Church, Washington, DC)

Rhiana Wilks . . .(Greater Mount Calvary Holy Church, Washington, DC)

Diane Williams . . . . (Trinity AME Zion Church, Washington, DC)

Denise Whitehead. . . . . . (First Corinthian Baptist Church, Harlem, NY)

Sandy White . . . .(Elim Christian Fellowship, Buffalo, NY)

Debra Edmundson . . . . (World Changers Church – New York, NY)

Susan A. Hill . . . .(World Changers Fellowship Church, Macon, GA)

Min. Alexis M. Chatman. . . . . . (Faith Christian Center, Jacksonville, FL)

Tonjala Eaton . . . .(Liberty Faith Christian Church, Bessemer, AL)

Willie Johnson. . . . . (The Dwelling Place, Fayetteville, AR)

Cornelius Boomer . . . .(Kingdom Life Ministries, Holts Summit, MO)

Marvin Dillard. . . . .(Jubilee Church of God In Christ, Memphis, TN)

Fay Angus . . . . (Uniondale, NY)

Beverly Burns . . . .(Washington, DC)

Delores Cante . . . . (Tacoma, WA)

Irene Cruz . . . . (Guam, USA)

Cleopas Dunigan. . . . . (Memphis, TN)

Shawna Hill . . . .(Great Falls, MT)

Nicole Jenkins. . . . . (New York, NY)

Roseal Johnson, Jr.. . . . . (Houston, TX)

Zeno & Tammy Latin . . . .(Portland, OR)

Leslie Neinast . . . . (Wichita, KS)

Colin Thompson . . . . (Galveston, TX)

Joy Voith . . . . (Goodlettsville, TN)

Christine Wilson . . . .(Philadelphia, PA)

Bonita White . . . .(Fairburn, GA)

THE POWER COACH™
MADELINE ALEXANDER

about the author

The Power Coach™ Madeline Alexander is America's premier rapid results success coach and leading authority on lasting breakthrough experiences. She is the author of "Your 90-Day Financial Breakthrough — *90 Power Promises and the Weapons of Our Warfare to WIN in Your Finances Now*" and the top-selling inspirational series, "How to Break Through Barriers and Achieve Power Results — *Create Your Power Mindset for Success In 30 Days or Less* (Vol. I) and Power Mindset II: *CHOOSE TO BE A CHAMPION* (Vol. II).

Madeline delivers dynamic keynotes and transformational seminars for churches, corporations, colleges and universities, and youth organizations nationwide. An anointed minister of the gospel, and acclaimed motivational speaker, Madeline's pioneering, inspiring, and life-changing messages leave congregations strong, courageous, and mission-minded! Her no-nonsense, truth-telling style, contagious passion, and powerful energy cut to the core of real issues in the shortest period of time.

Inventor of the revolutionary Power Coaching System™, Madeline specializes in removing the barriers that are stopping you, your church, or your business from taking action and achieving extraordinary results.

Madeline is also the founder of the national Power Coach™ Financial Network (PCFN) business consortium, dedicated to bringing economic recovery and financial empowerment to one million families nationwide through business ownership.

Madeline is active in world relief efforts through ChildFund and World Vision.

Madeline resides in Houston, Texas.

table of contents

Part III: 90 Days of Prayer
for Financial Breakthrough

∞⟨ ⟩∞

∞⟨ ⟩∞

introduction

Whether you are soaring, stagnant, or struggling right now, God has a new level of financial blessing, increase, and abundance ahead for you! It is my desire to help you break through every barrier, pull down every stronghold, overcome every obstacle, and remove the spiritual resistance that is opposing you financially, so that you can experience everything the Lord has in store for you, and fulfill your mission assignment on the earth.

If you have ever felt that your financial battles are particularly intense, you are right. If you could pull back the veil and see clearly into the spiritual realm, you would quickly understand the battle that is raging over your finances. You would understand the magnitude of what is at stake for you and your family right now. You would grasp the eternal significance of your words, actions, choices, and responses. That is exactly my intention with this book. With the help of the Holy Spirit, I want to give you a glimpse into the spiritual realm, and equip you with the weapons of our warfare to win in your finances now. Rest assured, you have the victory and it is time for you to walk in it!

This book is not a personal finance manual. This is a spiritual warfare book, designed to equip you to battle for your financial breakthrough, and enforce the fullness of the victory Jesus has already won for you at the cross. True liberation begins with a spiritual liberation. Lasting freedom has its foundation in spiritual freedom through Jesus Christ. A power mindset always precedes a prosperous manifestation. Everything in the natural realm begins and is continually held together in the spiritual realm. When your spirit is liberated and your mind is renewed, and you take dominion and subdue all opposing forces in the spiritual realm, you will see permanent, radical change in your life. My desire is to help you radically renew your money mindset with the Word of God so that you will 1) clearly understand the promises of God regarding your finances, 2) change your actions in the natural realm, and 3) elevate your response to the spiritual opposition that is behind the financial challenges in your life and WIN.

As we begin this journey of breakthrough, I want you to understand upfront this book will not co-sign on carnal desires to increase financially for purely selfish gain. This is not a cherry-picked listing of the scriptures that promise the blessings of God, devoid of the balance of obedience, responsibility, generosity, stewardship, and self-control.

In this writing, we will concentrate on understanding and walking in the fullness of your financial inheritance. Your Heavenly Father wants you well and whole financially — able to sufficiently provide for yourself and your family, prepare for the future, pass on an inheritance, build the Kingdom, and give generously to those who are in need. He wants you to be thoroughly equipped for every good work, not living under the stress and strain of debt and lack, but abundantly supplied to the point of overflow. He wants you to have more than enough for every need. He wants you to enjoy your life and the blessings He has provided for His children.

God's Word has numerous promises, commands, directives, strategies, and instructions for you as His child regarding your finances. We will first study the principles of wealth as outlined in the scripture so that you have a full understanding of your blessing, birthright, and your responsibilities when it comes to wealth, prosperity, and abundance. We will also study the opposition that will come against you as a child of God, as the enemy attempts to stop you from possessing your Promised Land of soul prosperity and financial wealth.

Then together, we will master, meditate, and memorize 90 of your covenant promises regarding your finances. You must know the promises of God to enforce them. We are going to learn 90 power promises — one scripture per day, for 90 days.

Wealth is a powerful blessing and useful tool that the Lord has for you! Make no mistake — your Heavenly Father desires to bless you abundantly! He wants you to be financially well and whole; however, to whom much is given, much is required. In addition to the blessings, you must also fully understand the warnings of wealth from scripture. Your Heavenly Father will not injure you by bestowing a blessing upon your life that you do not have the maturity to handle properly.

As I was writing this book, I felt a deep burden to provide balance. I want you to understand and embrace the blessings of the Lord and use your faith boldly to receive them all. Be encouraged and excited about what is to come for you! I also want you to understand the responsibility that comes with the blessing of wealth. This book will challenge you to go to higher levels in your faith, obedience, prayer life, warfare, generosity, and financial stewardship.

I want you to be sober and vigilant as you begin this journey of breakthrough. Some of the concepts in this book will be challenging. You may need to re-read a chapter a few times to grasp it fully. I encourage you to read for comprehension. Take your time. Read carefully, highlight the text, look up each of the scriptures in your own Bible, and most definitely pray and ask the Holy Spirit to help you understand each concept and apply it to your life. Start where you are and apply the scriptures one step at a time. Each power promise that you learn will produce change and growth in your life. It is not by your human strength. You can do it by the power of God at work within you. You already have the victory. Right now, I am joining my faith with yours in prayer. Write your name on the lines below and read this prayer out loud.

Father, in the name of Jesus, I pray in agreement for my friend, _____ . Father, Your Word says that if any two of us agree on earth concerning anything that we ask, it shall be done by our Father in Heaven. Right now Father, I ask that You protect the time that _____ will invest daily in reading this book, starting now. I pray they will not be distracted, delayed, or detoured from consuming this word.

Holy Spirit, I ask that You explain each scripture and every concept so they can grasp it, understand it, and believe it by faith. I pray that they may come into full obedience to Your Word. I declare and decree that every need is met according to Your riches in glory in Christ Jesus. Lord, You are their Shepherd, and they shall not lack. What we bind on earth shall be bound in Heaven, and what we loose on earth shall be loosed in Heaven. Right now, I bind every demonic attack set in motion against _____ . I cancel every scheme, fiery dart, and planned manifestation of lack in the mighty name of Jesus. No weapon formed against them will prosper.

I pray that _____ is transformed by the renewing of their mind, that they may prove what is that good, pleasing, and perfect will of God.

Right now we agree for financial wellness and wholeness. I pray that _____ may prosper and be in health, even as their soul prospers. Let Your perfect will be done now in their life and may their plans be established and succeed! In the mighty name of Jesus we pray, Amen.

PART I

Understanding Financial Wellness:
God Wants You Well Now

1 | home invasion

Resting in the comfort of your home, you awaken to find that armed robbers have laid siege; a home invasion is in progress. You and your spouse's purse and wallet lay scattered on the floor, all of the money removed. Your jewelry has been rifled through; all precious gems have been stolen. You see a person carrying off your flat screen television. Right behind him are two invaders, carrying off your computers and other home electronics. Two more individuals are carrying away the safe in your home with all of your valuables. Your car has been stolen from the garage. Your furniture has been smashed and destroyed, as the robbers search for any remnant of remaining valuables.

Now you see others, more ominous than the first, carrying off your children one by one, bound and gagged. Yet another is dragging away your spouse, tied up tightly with a hood over their head. Everything in your home is being systematically stolen, demolished, and destroyed.

Nothing is holding you back – you can take action. You have loaded weapons to protect yourself at your immediate disposal. Your cell phone is readily accessible. You can call 911 at any time.

What are you going to do? Are you going to roll over and go back to sleep? Will you silently hope the invaders do not take everything you own, and secretly pray that your family will somehow be alright? Will you say to yourself, *"I probably didn't deserve those nice things anyway. It's probably God's will that this happened to me."* Will you ponder if you should do anything at all? Of course not!

As soon as you awakened and saw your home under siege and your family in danger, you would take IMMEDIATE, AGGRESSIVE ACTION to stop the invaders and the crimes in progress. You would do whatever it took to stop it. You would call 911 to get immediate help from law enforcement. You would fight to the finish to protect your children and spouse. You would use every natural means and power of the law to get your family, your money, and your possessions back. You would not stop until your family was safe from harm, everything was returned to you, and the criminals were punished to the full extent of the law.

Unfortunately, this scenario plays out every day in the spiritual realm. Hosea 4:6 (NKJV) tells us, *"My people are destroyed for lack of knowledge."* Many believers have no idea that their lives are under a full attack; a home invasion is already in progress. Their homes have been invaded and raided by the enemy, and their covenant provision, promises, and protections are being stolen. The spiritual bandits of financial lack, sickness and disease, and anger, strife, and division are all present. Health, strength, longevity, vitality, prosperity, healthy relationships, love, peace, joy, unity, connection, happiness, and harmony are being stolen. Dreams, goals, mission, vision, purpose, and lasting legacy are being stolen. Land, homes, businesses, inheritances, ideas, inventions, promotions, raises, bonuses, meaningful work, rewarding work, recognition, and advancement are being stolen. Provision, riches, wealth, abundance, overflow, and increase are being stolen. Sadly, many believers, though good people, do not recognize the stolen items as their own, rightful possessions, purchased and paid for in full, at the cross.

In John 10:10 (NKJV) Jesus tells us, *"The thief does not come except to steal, and to kill, and to destroy. I have come that they may have life, and that they may have it more abundantly."* Abundant life is a promise that God has given to us through our Lord Jesus Christ. The enemy comes to steal, kill, and destroy all that the Father has given to us. He does not have a lawful right to do any of these things. He is violating spiritual laws. Jesus soundly defeated the enemy at the cross. Your provision, protection, and promises have been paid for in full. Any uprising against believers in the Body of Christ is an act of trespass.

The enemy cannot legally cross over the blood line that sanctifies you and sets you apart. It is an unlawful invasion. Your life is under siege. However, if you do not know your covenant promises, you will be prone to allow the trespass and allow the enemy to perpetrate his illegal attack against you.

Today, the Lord is saying to us all...**WAKE UP**! A home invasion is in progress! The enemy is systematically carrying off your health, your wealth, your family, and your future. If this happened in one grand conflict, we might pay more attention to it and take action. However it happens slowly and subtly at first, gradually gaining momentum until the full assault is in progress.

You may be passed over for promotion at work, a business idea is stolen, or you may lose a major sales contract for your business. Unexpected bills and expenses keep consuming your savings; you just can't get ahead no matter how hard you work. A mortgage, second mortgage, student loans, and medical bills make a pleasant future seem implausible, and leaving an inheritance for your children is virtually impossible. You may think to yourself, *"How will I ever get over this mountain of debt?"*

Angry outbursts and strife may plague your relationship with your spouse, or perhaps you've coolly and complacently settled into roommate status. Your children are yielding to outside influences, their behavior is rough and rebellious, and you see your close relationships eroding away. The dreams you once had for your life just don't seem all that possible now, but you aren't really up to it anyway. You may be overweight, sluggish, tired, stressed, or just plain overwhelmed. High blood pressure, high cholesterol, obesity, diabetes, and daily aches and pains have settled in. Perhaps you have gotten a serious diagnosis of a chronic or terminal disease. This is not how life was supposed to go for you.

You may be at the beginning of your career, just out of college, trying to get your life underway. You can't find the right job to jumpstart your career. Basic needs like a good car, a nice starter home, and a bright future that is not saddled with student loan debt are turning out to be harder than you thought. Escaping through carousing, clubbing, and casual sexual relationships is creating more heartbreak and health threats than expected. You play it like you are living the life, doing your dream, but deep down, dissatisfaction and discouragement are already setting in.

You may be succeeding financially, but struggling with your health. Perhaps you are prospering, but at the expense of your marriage and family. Or you may be physically healthy, but seriously struggling or stagnant financially. A balanced life with holistic success in all areas seems more like a pipedream than God's promise.

None of this is God's plan or intention for your life! The covenant blessings of abundant life are YOURS. Jeremiah 29:11 (NIV) tells us, *"For I know the plans I have for you,"* *declares the Lord, "plans to prosper you and not to harm* *you, plans to give you hope and a future."* God has a divine design for your life that includes His purpose, His protection, His provision, and His promises. He has an abundant, blessed, fulfilling life for you. It is never too late, and it is never too early to get on track with the blessed, abundant, overflowing life in the Lord. It is time to command the enemy to stop wreaking havoc in your life. Mediocrity is not God's plan. Struggling in your finances, your health, or in your relationships is not God's best for you as a believer. God has given you every weapon you need to stop the invasion. It is illegal activity. You are in Christ. The enemy has no legal access to you. Do not tolerate the trespass!

2 Corinthians 10:3-6 (NKJV) declares, *"For though we walk* *in the flesh, we do not war according to the flesh. For the* *weapons of our warfare are not carnal but mighty in God* *for pulling down strongholds, casting down arguments and* *every high thing that exalts itself against the knowledge of* *God, bringing every thought into captivity to the obedience* *of Christ, and being ready to punish all disobedience when* *your obedience is fulfilled."*

The Word of God is our law enforcement. Any covenant blessing that God has given to you by His Word, you have a right to enforce and defend. If it is in the scripture you can enforce it. You must know what your covenant blessings are to protect them. Being whole and healthy in your finances, in your physical health, and in your relationships are essential parts of God's salvation package for you. Do not allow the enemy to steal any of it. A call to Jesus is the ultimate 911 call. He is never too busy, and He will arrive on the scene immediately with a host of warring angels to defend and protect you. The name of Jesus has all power and authority, and enables you to protect and enforce the blessings of God for your life and for your family.

It is vital that you know the Word of God and understand God's promises so you can protect them. Also, you must not leave access points to your life open to the enemy. If you leave the doors and windows wide open all around your home, thieves will see you as easy prey and will have unrestricted, repetitive access to your home and possessions. Many believers do not know the promises of God, and leave access points wide open to the enemy.

If you leave your doors open through sin, poor choices, bad habits, and disobedience, the enemy has easy access to your life. It is important that you shut and lock the windows and doors to your life to eliminate points of access. You will do this by understanding the Word of the Lord and obeying it. God has grace, forgiveness, and mercy readily available for your mistakes and missteps! Where you are weak, God is strong. He has your back. Your protections are not based on your obedience alone, but obedience to the Word of God is vital, and it is actually an act of spiritual warfare!

It is time to secure your life and put a "NO TRESPASSING" sign over your door in the spiritual realm. There are five steps you must take to stop the trespass of the enemy on your life.

Know the promises. You must know the promises of God so you can enforce them. It is important to meditate, master, and memorize the promises of God in His Word. We will learn 90 of His promises for your financial well-being over the next 90 days.

Shut down access. Next, shut down any access points that give the enemy easy or lawful entrance to your life, including actions that are contrary to the Word of God, disobedience, and poor choices. You can repent, which means to change your mind, and start on a new course of action. God is gracious and kind and He will immediately forgive you and cleanse you (1 John 1:9). Repentance shuts down the enemy! Submit to God, resist the devil, and he must flee (James 4:7). Making the decision to submit and resist *immediately* shuts down the actions of the enemy!

Bind the enemy. Command the enemy to cease and desist. What we bind on earth will be bound in heaven. What we loose on earth will be loosed in heaven (Matthew 18:18). You have been given delegated authority in the name of Jesus Christ to command the enemy to STOP. He cannot persist in illegal activity that violates the scriptural protections when you use your authority to command Satan and all demonic forces to cease and desist. You can arrest him in his process to steal, kill, and destroy.

Call in law enforcement. Learn to call upon the name of Jesus. All power and authority is in His name! God has given you many powerful weapons to enforce the victory Jesus has already secured for you at the cross. All authority in heaven and on earth has been given to the Lord Jesus. At the name of Jesus, every knee must bow. Philippians 2:9-11 (NKJV) tells us, *"Therefore God also has highly exalted Him and given Him the name which is above every name, that at the name of Jesus every knee should bow, of those in heaven, and of those on earth, and of those under the earth, and that every tongue should confess that Jesus Christ is Lord, to the glory of God the Father."*

Command the payback. Command the enemy to return what was stolen from you. You have the authority in Jesus not only to command the enemy to stop, to cease and desist, but also to RETURN that which has been stolen from you and PAY the additional penalties due for stealing from you. You can enforce scriptural punishments in the name of Jesus. We will cover this process in more detail in a later chapter.

Most of the enemy's destruction comes in three primary areas. When you learn to defeat the enemy's Trifold Attack, you will be well on your way to living the whole, healthy, and abundant life that the Lord has promised and secured for you. You already have the victory! It is time to enforce it. Don't tolerate the trespass!

2 | the enemy's trifold attack

*T*he thief does not come except to steal, and to kill,
and to destroy. I have come that they may have
life, and that they may have it more abundantly.
John 10:10 (NKJV)

If you think about the challenges you are facing right now
today, almost all of them are in one of three areas: your
money, your **health**, and your **relationships**. The enemy
wants to steal your money, kill you physically, and destroy
your relationships, so that he may ultimately destroy your
relationship with God. Once you are able to enforce the
promises of God in these three areas, most of what you are
battling on a daily basis will be resolved. Your wealth, health,
and relationships are the primary targets of the enemy's war
against you. Remember that Satan is a defeated foe. Jesus
has already won the victory in these areas, and in every area
of life. You must be able to stand your ground and ENFORCE
the victory.

Jesus encourages us in John 16:33 (AMP), *"I have told you
these things, so that in Me you may have [perfect] peace and
confidence. In the world you have tribulation and trials and*

distress and frustration; but be of good cheer [take courage; be confident, certain, undaunted]! For I have overcome the world. [I have deprived it of power to harm you and have conquered it for you.]"

Ninety percent of the enemy's attacks on the Body of Christ are focused on these three areas, which I will call the Trifold Attack. The attacks are:

- Poverty and Lack

- Sickness and Disease

- Sexual Immorality and Relationship Fracture.

POVERTY AND LACK

The first attack is **Poverty and Lack**. This attack is designed to STEAL your material blessings to ensure you do not have the finances necessary to meet your daily needs, provide for your family, persevere in emergencies and trials, secure your future, fulfill your mission assignment on the earth, and fund the work of the church for the Kingdom of God to save souls for all eternity. The money and financial blessings the enemy steals from you are used to fund the devil's own criminal and immoral enterprises to destroy lives. The enemy wants to starve the Kingdom of God of all resources necessary to share the gospel, help those in need, and most importantly, reconcile people to God.

The enemy's strategy is to destroy your life by taking away your basic needs, paralyzing your ability to move forward, and oppressing you in a system of debt bondage that is a form of slavery. The stress of financial oppression opens the door to sickness and disease and relationship problems, the other two components of the Trifold Attack. The enemy hopes to wear you down through difficulties, discouragement, and disillusionment so you will give up on your commitment to serve the Lord, and ultimately curse God.

We see this motive clearly in Job 1:9-11 (NLT), which tells us, *"Satan replied to the LORD, 'Yes, but Job has good reason to fear God. You have always put a wall of protection around him and his home and his property. You have made him prosper in everything he does. Look how rich he is! But reach out and take away everything he has, and he will surely curse you to your face!'"*

Also see Malachi 3:13-15 and Zephaniah 1:12 for additional insight.

SICKNESS AND DISEASE

The second attack is **Sickness and Disease**. This attack is designed to KILL the body so that your life on earth is cut short, your mission assignment is aborted, and you die disconnected from the Lord, spending eternity separated from the Father who loves you. If you die prematurely, you will not be able to 1) reconcile your life to God through Jesus Christ our Savior, and 2) rescue others from the grips of Satan, including your family, friends, and loved ones. If you are not able to fulfill your purpose, other souls will be lost to the evil one.

Every day that you are alive and well, serving the Lord, caring for your family, and building the Kingdom of God, you are a constant threat and daily frustration to the evil one. When you eat well, exercise, and rest, you are actually extending your life, which is a form of spiritual warfare!

Sickness and disease are a direct affront to the cross. Jesus has already paid the price for you to be well. Health, wellness, and long life are all part of your salvation. Sickness in your body is an offense to the cross. Any and every attack of sickness and disease is a direct insult to the cross, and a trespass you do not need to tolerate. Meditate on the following scriptures regarding the promise of divine health.

Worship the Lord your God, and his blessing will be on your food and water. I will take away sickness from among you, and none will miscarry or be barren in your land. I will give you a full life span.
Exodus 23:25-26 (NIV)

With long life I will satisfy him, And show him My salvation.
Psalm 91:16 (NKJV)

But He was wounded for our transgressions, He was bruised for our guilt and iniquities; the chastisement [needful to obtain] peace and well-being for us was upon Him, and with the stripes [that wounded] Him we are healed and made whole.
Isaiah 53:5 (AMP)

Jesus went throughout Galilee, teaching in their synagogues, proclaiming the good news of the kingdom, and healing every disease and sickness among the people.
Matthew 4:23 (NIV)

But if the Spirit of Him who raised Jesus from the dead dwells in you, He who raised Christ from the dead will also give life to your mortal bodies through His Spirit who dwells in you.
Romans 8:11 (NKJV)

He personally bore our sins in His [own] body on the tree [as on an altar and offered Himself on it], that we might

die (cease to exist) to sin and live to righteousness. By His
wounds you have been healed.
1 Peter 2:24 (AMP)

Sexual Immorality
and Relationship Fracture

The third attack is **Sexual Immorality and Relationship Fracture**. This attack is designed to defile and DESTROY your relationship with God. The enemy seeks to separate you from the Lord and your fellow man. If he can bring division and strife into your relationships, it is easier to isolate you. Once isolated, you are easy prey for destruction. 1 Peter 5:8 (NKJV) tells *us, "Be sober, be vigilant; because your adversary the devil walks about like a roaring lion, seeking whom he may devour."* Who is the easiest prey to devour? It is the one separated and isolated from the flock. By maintaining close, intimate, and accountable relationships with God, your family, your friends, and other believers, you are implementing a form of relationship covering and protection. The devil uses sexual sin to get you off track with your relationship with God because it is pleasurable, so it is by far the easiest sin and deviation from the Word with which to tempt you. Sexual sin is the only sin that you commit within your own body.

1 Corinthians 6:18-20 (NIV) tells us, *"Flee from sexual immorality. All other sins a person commits are outside the body, but whoever sins sexually, sins against their own body. Do you not know that your bodies are temples of the Holy Spirit, who is in you, whom you have received from God? You are not your own; you were bought at a price. Therefore honor God with your bodies."*

The enemy has a special hatred for us as human beings because we are the only created being in which God chooses to dwell. Your Heavenly Father not only comes close to you, He has chosen to send His very Spirit to dwell inside of you! When you have a relationship with God, He actually lives in you and sits upon the throne of your heart. Satan was cast out of Heaven because he strongly desired and coveted the worship due only to God at His throne. When we cooperate with the enemy's plans through sexual sin, we are cooperating with degrading and defiling the very temple where God dwells.

The enemy enjoys defiling and degrading the temple and destroying the worship that should be happening within your heart. It is the ultimate "in your face" move against the Lord to use your body in a perverse and ungodly manner. Over time, this hardens your heart and sears your conscience, and you become less sensitive to the voice of the Lord. It is easier now to separate you permanently. The Lord's ban on sexual immorality is not an old, antiquated command that is out of place in today's modern society. He is protecting the sacred sanctuary of your body, the temple of the Holy Spirit, where He desires to dwell with you. Do not allow the enemy to defile the very temple of God through sexual sin in your body.

Relationship fracture is all about severing your relationships to isolate and destroy you. The enemy knows a house divided cannot stand. Therefore, he seeks to bring all forms of anger, strife, bitterness, wrath, and unforgiveness into your relationships to SEVER your relationships with others, and eternally SEPARATE you from God for destruction. He has an extreme hatred for the marriage relationship, because it is a human picture of Christ's relationship with His Bride, the Church. The enemy wages a relentless war to separate and bring division between couples in marriage, parents and children, families, friendships, churches, and communities. Much of our pain, heartache, and anguish in this life comes from rampant relationship damage: shattered marriages, fatherless children, dysfunctional families, and damaged individuals. Hurts, betrayals, and offenses in friendships and relationships are commonplace. Through deep, soul injuries coming through damaged relationships, the enemy strives to alienate you from others and ultimately from God Himself. Spiritual death, due to a destroyed relationship with God, is a far worse fate than even physical death, because it separates you from God for all eternity. Spiritual destruction is the enemy's ultimate goal with the Trifold Attack. He desperately wants to destroy your eternal relationship with God.

THE ENEMY'S STRATEGY

To maximize effectiveness, the enemy concentrates on three areas: your money, your health, and your relationships. By waging the Trifold Attack of Poverty and Lack, Sickness and Disease, and Sexual Immorality and Relationship Fracture, the enemy attempts to destroy your life and relationship with God, and he renders much of the Body of Christ ineffective by keeping the members in bondage in these three areas.

The Trifold Attack – Figure 1

MOTIVE	MODE OF ATTACK	METHODS
STEAL	Poverty and Lack	Debt/Devour
KILL	Sickness and Disease	Disease/Death
DESTROY	Sexual Immorality and Relationship Fracture	Defile/Divorce/ Divide

The attacks of Poverty and Lack, Sickness and Disease, and Sexual Immorality and Relationship Fracture all work together in a vicious cycle that continually strengthens and increases the effectiveness of each individual component.

The Trifold Attack – Figure 2

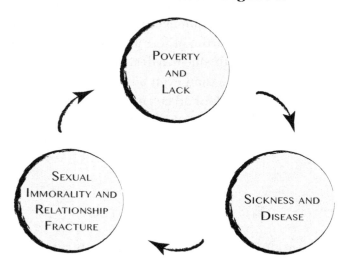

- Financial challenges are a leading cause of relationship problems and divorce.

- Stress from financial issues can open the door to sickness and disease.

- Poverty is linked to poor health and the lack of adequate health care.

- Unexpected medical expenses can quickly bankrupt a family.

- Sexual immorality opens the door to sickness and disease and destroys marriages and families.

- Toxic relationships create emotional and physical sickness.

God has already provided the solution. You must enforce the victory already won for you at the cross. Remember, all power has been stripped from the enemy. The devil is a defeated foe. Colossians 2:15 (AMP) tells us that, *"[God] disarmed the principalities and powers that were ranged against us and made a bold display and public example of them, in triumphing over them in Him and in it [the cross]."*

Therefore, the devil uses lies, deception, and illegal activity – stealing, killing, and destroying – to inflict pain and suffering on you, and ultimately attempt to destroy your relationship with God. His only hope is that you do not know:

- The **power** of God – that you underestimate the power of God's Word and His name

- The **promises** of God and therefore he can deceive you out of your blessings

- How much **authority** you have to enforce the Word of God through the name of Jesus Christ, and

- Jesus has already won the **victory** at Calvary. Satan has been stripped of his authority and power over you.

If you do not know these things, the enemy can wreak havoc in your life through deception. He doesn't have a right to do it, but if you do not know that, he can still operate as if he has a legal right to do damage to your life. He cleverly disguises the damage as natural circumstances that appear to be unavoidable.

Wreaking Havoc Worldwide

The devil is NOT omniscient (all knowing), omnipresent (present everywhere), or omnipotent (all powerful). Only God alone has these three divine attributes. Satan is not everywhere attacking all people simultaneously. The enemy is not all powerful. Jesus holds ALL power and authority. The Bible tells us that Jesus stripped Satan and all demonic forces of all authority and made a public spectacle of them.

Then Jesus came to them and said, "All authority in heaven and on earth has been given to me."
Matthew 28:18 (NIV)

And having disarmed the powers and authorities, he made a public spectacle of them, triumphing over them by the cross.
Colossians 2:15 (NIV)

Satan is a defeated foe. So how is he able to carry out his crimes against the Body of Christ, the body of believers? The answer is **deception**.

The enemy uses a number of tactics in the following categories.

- Cunning Plans
- Plots
- Wiles
- Lies
- Temptation
- Diversion
- Crafty Devices
- Schemes
- Deceptions
- Trickery
- Seduction
- Division

If he is not omnipresent, how is the devil able to wreak havoc in so many lives simultaneously? The devil is shrewd, sneaky, and astute. He is calculating. He conspires. He uses **strategies** and **systems**. Let's review five of his most effective strategies and systemic attacks.

Mental Barriers. Through circumstances, situations, and difficult occurrences in your life, the enemy implants barriers in your mindset to keep you in bondage and oppression. This is a form of self-imprisonment. If you have deeply ingrained, limiting beliefs about your life, he does not need to do very much to stop you – you will stop yourself and keep yourself stuck. This is why it is so important that you renew your mind (Romans 12:2) and renew the spirit of your mind (Ephesians 4:23) to eliminate the impact of limiting beliefs, negative and traumatic events, and negative words spoken over you.

Generational barriers. Generational barriers are sin and iniquity that get passed down through your family lineage to the third and fourth generation (Exodus 20:5). The enemy exploits this to ensnare generations of families.

Institutional oppression. He infiltrates and perverts systems that affect millions of people at one time (Exodus 1:11, Numbers 10:9, 1 Peter 5:9).

Demonic forces. He uses the demonic beings — the one third of the angels that were cast out of Heaven with him to execute his plans and schemes (Revelation 12:3-9). He uses them to wage war against you and all of the body of believers.

When the enemy was cast down to the earth, he was able to convince a third of the angels to stand in mutiny to the Lord. He has an army of such, although they were soundly defeated by Michael the Archangel and the other angelic beings. Revelation 12:7-9 (AMP) tells us, *"Then war broke out in heaven; Michael and his angels went forth to battle with the dragon, and the dragon and his angels fought. **But they were defeated, and there was no room found for them in heaven any longer.** And the huge dragon was cast down and out—that age-old serpent, who is called the Devil and Satan, he who is the **seducer (deceiver)*** *of all humanity the world over; **he was forced out** and down to the earth, and **his angels were flung out along with him**."*

The enemy still has influence over a third of the angelic beings, now demons, that are operating on the earth. Although they are a defeated militia, they still attempt to attack and deceive. The enemy has organized the fallen angels into a system of ranks, like what you would see in the military. The Bible tells us in Ephesians 6:11-12 (NKJV), *"Put on the whole armor of God, that you may be able to stand against the wiles of the devil. For we do not wrestle against flesh and blood, but against **principalities**, against **powers**, against the **rulers of the darkness** of this age, against **spiritual hosts of wickedness** in the heavenly places."*

I want you to notice there are ranks within the enemy forces. The Trifold Attack is executed by ruling, high-ranking demons. These are the most cunning, deceitful, destructive, and lethal demonic forces next to Satan himself. As we begin the process of bringing down financial strongholds, and bringing forth financial breakthrough to you and to your family, it is important that you understand this is a process of **warfare**. Breakthrough and spiritual warfare are not to be taken lightly. You must understand what you are up against.

Breakthrough is violent. You must be prepared to violently oppose the ruling demonic forces who want to keep you deceived and in bondage. They will take notice of your uprising and they will attempt to oppose you.

Jesus Christ has already won the complete victory for you. God is on your side. What you and I will do is ENFORCE the victory that Jesus has already won. Our job is to stop the illegal activity that is robbing you of the blessings of God, up to and including your salvation, and the salvation of your family, friends, loved ones, and others entrapped in darkness.

Remember, the enemy's Trifold Attack is executed by ruling, ranking demons. These ruling demons are not little imps with pitchforks. These are lethal demonic forces that are NOT to be feared, but they are not to be played with either. These ruling demonic forces work independently as well as together. You must understand what you are battling and use all of the spiritual weapons that the Father has given to you through the authority of Jesus Christ and the Holy Spirit to enforce your victory every day. Remember, in Jesus you already have the VICTORY!

The following table will help you understand the ruling demons, their strategies, and weapons.

The Trifold Attack – Figure 3

STRATEGY	TARGET	ATTACK	RULING DEMONS/ PRINCIPALITIES	PRIMARY WEAPONS
Steal	Money	Poverty and Lack	The Devourer	Delay/Divert
			The Strongman	Devour
				Debt/Debt Slavery
Kill	Body	Sickness and Disease	Spirit of Infirmity	Sickness
			Deaf and Dumb Spirit	Disease
			Spirit of Heaviness	Stress
			Spirit of Fear	Depression
Destroy	Relationships	Sexual Immorality and Relationship Fracture	Perverse Spirit	Fornication
			Spirit of Whoredoms	Adultery
			Spirit of Jealousy	Licentiousness
			Lying Spirit	Anger/Strife
				Division/Divorce
				Bitterness/ Unforgiveness

Oftentimes when people pray, their prayers are ineffective because 1) they are not praying the Word of God which holds all power, 2) they are not praying in the name of Jesus which holds all authority, and 3) they are not combating the right target.

Matthew 18:18 (NIV) instructs us as follows: *"Truly I tell you, whatever you bind on earth will be bound in heaven, and whatever you loose on earth will be loosed in heaven."* To increase the effectiveness of your prayer life in spiritual warfare, it is important to **bind** the attacking spirit and **cancel** the planned manifestation (the weapon formed against you). Often what we are praying against is the manifestation (the fruit) instead of the spirit that is the cause of the matter (the root). The enemy executes schemes, sets traps, and devises plots against you. You can arrest the spirit at work, and simultaneously cancel the plans set in motion against you. Using the shield of faith you can extinguish every fiery dart (planned manifestation) the enemy shoots at you (Ephesians 6:16). No weapon formed against you shall prosper (Isaiah 54:17)!

In the area of financial breakthrough against **Poverty and Lack**, we must bind the ruling spirit, the Devourer, and cancel all manifestations that are set as schemes against you. When you tithe, your Heavenly Father promises to rebuke the Devourer for you (Malachi 3:8-12), so you can concentrate on identifying and canceling any manifestations that show up in your life.

The following chart depicts some of the most common manifestations the Devourer employs against you.

The Trifold Attack – Figure 4

MANIFESTATIONS OF POVERTY AND LACK		
Shortage	Lack	Poverty
Debt	Interest	Long-term Loans
Debt Slavery	High Interest Rates	Usury/ Predatory Lending
Fines/Fees	Hidden Fees	Undisclosed/Unfair Contract Terms
Demands	Judgments/ Garnishment	Liens
Repossession	Foreclosure	Bankruptcy
Under- Employment	Unemployment	Disenfranchisement
Hostile Work Environment	Harassment	Discrimination
Firing	Layoffs	Company Shutdowns/ Job Outsourcing
Low Wages	Mistreatment	Oppression
Lost Raises	Lost Bonuses	Lost Promotions
Slow Sales	Slow-paying Clients	Write-Offs
Employee Theft	Fraud	Embezzlement
Legal Wrangling	Delayed Permits/ Contracts	Lost Permits/Contracts
Tickets	Breakdowns	Accidents
Unexpected Bills	Unplanned Medical Bills	Catastrophic Illness

In the area of **Sickness and Disease**, you must **bind** the Spirit of Infirmity, the Spirit of Fear, and the Spirit of Heaviness which are the ruling demons that are at work in physical and mental illness, and **cancel** all assigned manifestations that could show up in your life. The following chart depicts some of the common manifestations of sickness and disease.

The Trifold Attack – Figure 5

MANIFESTATIONS OF SICKNESS AND DISEASE		
Ailment	Sickness	Disease
Accident	Injury	Damage
Allergy	Allergic Reaction	Illness
Attack	Infirmity	Chronic Disease
Aches	Pain	Degenerative Disease
Aging	Decay	Terminal Disease
Fear	Fright	Phobia
Worry	Anxiety	Panic
Discouragement	Depression	Despair
Grief	Mourning	Isolation
Rejection	Loneliness	Hopelessness
Sadness	Sorrow	Suicide

As a practice, I bind the Spirit of Infirmity and cancel the above manifestations of physical infirmity on a daily basis as a part of taking Holy Communion each morning. Praise, worship, singing, and rejoicing in the Lord are your primary weapons against the Spirit of Heaviness. The enemy plots to return at a later time, so to combat that, stay sober and vigilant and maintain your protection every day. The enemy is relentless in his attack. We must be relentless in our warfare. If you are already experiencing a named disorder like the flu, diabetes, depression, or cancer, bind that specific manifestation that the enemy is attempting to put on you. The name of Jesus is above every name!

In the area of **Sexual Immorality and Relationship Fracture**, bind the Perverse Spirit, the Spirit of Whoredoms, the Spirit of Jealousy, the Spirit of Bondage, and the Lying

Spirit. There are numerous manifestations in this arena, many beyond the following listing. Cancel the following manifestations that the enemy will attempt to assign to your life.

The Trifold Attack – Figure 6

MANIFESTATIONS OF SEXUAL IMMORALITY AND RELATIONSHIP FRACTURE		
Unrestricted Desire	Lust	Covetousness
Sexually Loose	Licentiousness	Promiscuity
Lust	Fornication	Adultery
Captivity	Addiction	Oppression
Idolatry	Harlotry/Prostitution	Whoredom
Sexual Abnormality	Sexual Perversion	Sexual Deviancy
Suspicion	Jealousy	Rage
Cheating	Betrayal	Infidelity/ Unfaithfulness
Argument	Feud	Estrangement
Unforgiveness	Grudge	Bitterness
Angry Outburts	Rage	Wrath
Retribution	Retaliation	Revenge
Upset	Offended	Insulted
Hurt	Wounded	Injured
Anger	Strife	Malice
Lies	Accusation	Slander
Insinuation	Lies	Strong Delusion
Twisted Words	Misinterpreted Words	Perverted Words/ Gospel
Wedge	Split/Break Up	Severed Relationship
Friction	Fighting	Fractured Relationships
Division	Separation	Divorce
Seething Anger	Hate	Murder

As you can see, there are a number of schemes used in each of the areas of Poverty and Lack, Sickness and Disease, and Sexual Immorality and Relationship Fracture. If you submit to God, bind the demonic spirits, and cancel the planned manifestations, you can move forward more effectively in your Kingdom purpose. Pray to become more aware of the enemy's specific strategies that are employed against you.

If you have an abundance of money but you have lost your spouse, your family, or your health in the process, the enemy has stolen from you. If you are struggling financially and can never seem to get ahead in any area, you are in a battle with the Devourer, a very cunning demonic force that has infiltrated our banking and financial systems worldwide. If you are wealthy but you have no relationship with God, the enemy has perpetrated the ultimate fraud against you. You are temporarily rich, and eternally bankrupt. God loves you too much to allow you to stay in any of these conditions!

It is also very important to ensure that your actions in the natural realm are aligning with your prayers in the spiritual realm. For example, in combating Poverty and Lack, your financial choices and decisions are critical. Your spending, saving, and investing habits must align with what you are praying and believing for in the Word of God. If you are praying for increase, yet you are squandering the resources that you have now, your prayers will be ineffective. When you are faithful over little, God will make you ruler over much (Matthew 25:21).

If you are praying for healing and to walk in divine health, yet you are smoking cigarettes, overeating, and not exercising consistently, your prayers will be hindered. God still loves you and will heal you, but you are leaving the doors and windows of your spiritual home wide open for invasion. If you are praying for healing in your relationships, but you are prone to angry outbursts, difficult to communicate with, or unforgiving, your prayers will be hindered. The Bible calls an angry person a fool (Proverbs 29:11), and unforgiveness will lead to a root of bitterness in your heart (Hebrews 12:15). You can destroy your relationships with your own actions. The Bible says a foolish woman tears down her own house (Proverbs 14:1)!

When you enforce your covenant promises, remember that you do not have to fight the battle! You have already won! Remind yourself daily that the enemy is a defeated foe. You must stand your ground and enforce the victory Jesus has already won on your behalf. Jesus is your Victory. Victory lives in you. The enemy is relentless and cunning, but you are triumphant. Meditate on the following scriptures to prepare for your breakthrough.

There is no wisdom, no insight, no plan that can succeed against the Lord.
Proverbs 21:30 (NIV)

What then shall we say to these things? If God is for us, who can be against us?
Romans 8:31 (NKJV)

Yet amid all these things we are more than conquerors and gain a surpassing victory through Him Who loved us.
Romans 8:37 (AMP)

For I am persuaded beyond doubt (am sure) that neither death nor life, nor angels nor principalities, nor things impending and threatening nor things to come, nor powers, Nor height nor depth, nor anything else in all creation will be able to separate us from the love of God which is in Christ Jesus our Lord.
Romans 8:38-39 (AMP)

*Now thanks be to God who always leads us in triumph in
Christ, and through us diffuses the fragrance of His
knowledge in every place.*
2 Corinthians 2:14 (NKJV)

*In the Messiah, in Christ, God leads us from place to place
in one perpetual victory parade.*
2 Corinthians 2:14 (MSG)

*Fight the good fight of the faith; lay hold of the eternal life
to which you were summoned and [for which] you confessed
the good confession [of faith] before many witnesses.*
1 Timothy 6:12 (AMP)

*Little children, you are of God [you belong to Him] and have
[already] defeated and overcome them [the agents of the
antichrist], because He Who lives in you is greater (mightier)
than he who is in the world.*
1 John 4:4 (AMP)

3 | don't tolerate the trespass

One afternoon, I was speaking with a friend of mine after church. She was experiencing a few symptoms of sickness, and I was asking her what she was doing about it. "Are you praying the healing scriptures over yourself and your family?" *"No."* "Are you taking Holy Communion on a daily basis?" *"No, not yet."* "Are you binding the enemy and commanding him to be gone from your home?" *"No, not really."*

We had had this conversation before, regarding a chronic health condition (high blood pressure), and recurring illnesses that were affecting her family members. Yet to me, she still seemed somewhat passive about it – this is the beginning of the Trifold Attack! To her, the sickness symptoms were a nuisance but not anything to really get fired up about. *"This too shall pass."*

I felt a strong, RED ALERT going off in my spirit, and I remember I immediately told her, "DON'T TOLERATE THE TRESPASS!" God has promised us divine health and healing in His Word. It is part of your covenant blessing as a believer and as a child of the Most High God. Any sickness whatsoever is unacceptable – it is trespassing on God's property. Complacency at the onset of smaller illnesses relaxes our attitude of warfare against the presence of sickness and disease. We become desensitized to sickness, making it easier for the enemy to escalate and introduce more serious illness, chronic disease, and ultimately terminal disease into our lives. We should be just as aggressive in our response to a cold as we would be to cancer. Both are an invasion, a trespass into the life of a child of God. She and a friend were listening and I felt this time I was getting her attention.

I went on to explain to her that by maintaining a sober and vigilant attitude when it comes to any sickness, we train ourselves to always respond by faith, activate the Word of God, and combat the enemy. Each stomach ache, flu bug, allergy, or minor injury gives us an opportunity to practice our response to the presence of the enemy. I gave her a list of scriptures to read on healing and we immediately prayed on the spot to bind the enemy and cancel the manifestations of the sickness symptoms she was feeling.

This aggressive response to illness is my common practice. Most of my life, I have been a healthy, strong, and energetic person, with no major illnesses or diseases, but earlier in my life, I was sickly. I was anemic as a baby. In early adulthood, I was prone to catch every cold and flu bug that was making the rounds every year. Each winter, I would have a tough bout with bronchitis and other respiratory problems. Strep throat was a frequent visitor, and would leave my throat raw and painful for weeks. As a singer, I knew it was odd that I *always* seemed to get this vicious strep throat *every* year! It made it difficult for me to minister. Summer was plagued with allergy and hayfever symptoms. All year round, I battled digestive problems, beginning as far back as junior high and high school. As an adult, the digestive issues worsened. Ulcers, bleeding ulcers, painful digestion, ulcerative colitis (bleeding ulcers in the colon), were my battleground. Each year, I would undergo more and more tests, and I would be prescribed new medications with no definitive diagnosis or recommendations other than to de-stress my life.

When I became a Christian, my spiritual mother, Pauline Terry, who discipled me in the Lord, observed my battles with sickness and began to teach me about divine health and healing. I had no idea divine health was part of my salvation, and that I did not have to stay sickly! That was great news! Any parent with a sick child is caring and concerned, and wants that child to be well and whole immediately. God the Father is no different toward us, His children! He wants us to be well and whole.

I began to learn the scriptures on healing. I learned that I didn't have to keep enduring these annual ailments, and I didn't have to struggle with chronic illness in my digestive tract. Divine health was just as much a part of my salvation as eternal life. So I began to diligently pray for healing. I practiced a faith attitude and resisted sickness at every opportunity. I learned the scriptures on health and healing. I changed my expectations. I began to speak the Word of God over my health. I maintained healthy eating habits and an exercise regimen to cooperate physically with what I was praying for spiritually.

I experienced a dramatic transformation in my health, which made a HUGE difference in my life. I began to experience healings in my body. The stomach ulcers were healed. I did not contract those annual winter illnesses at the frequency I had all of my life. The allergy symptoms stopped. The bouts with strep throat stopped. When I did experience symptoms of sickness, I believed God would work through the treatments provided by my physicians to heal me. I believed for rapid recovery from any setback of sickness, injury, or accident. The change in my life was dramatic and permanent. Over the years, walking in divine health and expecting healing became my way of life. Every occurrence of sickness was an opportunity to resist the enemy, enforce my authority as a believer, and win.

About six years ago, after hearing Dodie Osteen's testimony of being healed from terminal cancer, I greatly expanded my knowledge of the healing scriptures and intensified my prayer life. I began to memorize more scriptures from the Word of God on healing. I learned the powerful benefits of taking Holy Communion on a daily basis, and speaking forth the Word of God to protect my health and well-being EVERY DAY. I experienced years of good health, completely free of colds, flu, strep throat, and bronchitis. I expanded my use of natural supplements to help my body heal itself in alignment with the Word of God. I began to bind the Spirit of Infirmity and cancel all the manifestations of chronic illness in my digestive system. I developed a list of manifestations that I knew were the schemes of the enemy, and I began to cancel them out in prayer every day. (See Chapter 2, The Trifold Attack, Figure 5 – Manifestations of Sickness and Disease.)

I began to declare the presence of good health, strength, power, vitality, energy, youth, and longevity over my life every day. I no longer needed medications for digestive issues. I remember my first week of eating meals without the aftermath of the chronic stomach pain that I had dealt with for over 30 years of my life. What a blessing to be pain free! I remember getting my first "clean" check-up with no stomach ulcers, bleeding, or colon issues. I brought my weight down to the level I was in high school and college. I prayed continually for myself, my family, and my friends. Declaring divine health and healing on a daily basis every morning became my way of life. That has been my daily practice now for years.

I expanded my faith to cover new areas of health and longevity. I discovered that much of what we call "aging" is actually sickness and disease that can be combated with the healing scriptures and healthy lifestyle habits. Now, I declare daily that my youth is renewed like the eagles! I feel and look younger, stronger, more vital, and more energetic than ever. I am mastering my warfare in this area of the Trifold Attack.

This is my manner of living to this day. Any form of sickness for me is a very rare experience that is not tolerated as normal. I recognize it as an attack of the enemy, and a trespass across the bloodline of the Lord Jesus Christ. I am sober, vigilant, aggressive, and focused in my warfare against the attack of sickness and disease on a daily basis.

Any time anyone asks me for prayer for themselves or a loved one, I share my testimony and transformation in this area. I share the specific scriptures I use daily for warfare, and I teach them the benefits of declaring the Word of God over their lives every day. I teach the benefits of partaking in Holy Communion, and I encourage them to begin to take it daily, much as they would a daily vitamin supplement, and in times of illness, on a recurring schedule like an antibiotic. If I am battling the manifestation of sickness symptoms, I increase my warfare and frequency of Holy Communion, believing for rapid recovery and complete restoration of my health. I pray that the Lord guides my physicians, giving them divine knowledge to effectively prescribe the right treatment. I use natural means to help my body heal itself and get well, and I intensify my spiritual warfare.

Through this process, I learned the following:

- My Heavenly Father wants me to be well and whole physically. He has provided protection for divine health, and specific, healing processes to combat sickness in the Word of God.

- Jesus Christ has already secured my victory over sickness and disease at the cross. By His stripes I am already healed.

- Empowered by the Holy Spirit, I have to enforce the victory already gained for me by 1) resisting the enemy, 2) combating sickness and disease as an act of spiritual warfare, and 3) cooperating with God's plan for physical wellness through my actions and choices. Sickness is a trespass and cannot be ignored or tolerated.

Here is the key point: divine health and healing were part of my salvation benefit from the MOMENT I was born again and became a Christian. However, I did not experience them until I 1) learned of my covenant promises for divine health and healing, 2) mastered, meditated, and memorized the specific scriptures from the Word of God in this area, and 3) enforced my covenant victory with the authority of Jesus Christ to stop the trespass of the enemy.

Early on in my Christian walk, although I was saved, the enemy could still terrorize me with sickness because I didn't know any better than to take it. When Miss Pauline began to teach me otherwise from the Word of God, my faith grew. Faith comes by hearing, and hearing by the Word of God (Romans 10:17). When my level of faith grew to the point that I had a warring spirit, I began to fight aggressively on a daily basis with a much more intensive level of warfare. When I began declaring my complete healing and freedom

YOUR 90-DAY FINANCIAL BREAKTHROUGH

from various manifestations of infirmity, the chronic illnesses had to cease. According to your faith, be it unto you!

To understand this principle, read the following scriptures: Matthew 9:29, Matthew 15:28, Mark 5:34, Mark 10:52, Luke 7:50, Luke 8:48, Luke 17:19, and Luke 18:42. Your level of faith determines your level of enforcement! I went from no enforcement, to partial enforcement, to daily, vigilant enforcement.

There is no question in my mind from studying the scriptures that sickness and disease are tools of the enemy and God the Father wants you well now! Remember, any parent with a sick child wants that child to be well and whole immediately. Your Heavenly Father is no different toward you, His child. His will and desire is that you are well and whole in EVERY area of your life. You cannot fulfill your mission assignment on the earth if your body is debilitated by sickness and disease.

No matter how big of a vision you have for your life, you will not be able to fulfill it if you are chronically tired, sick, and diseased. Your body is the temple of the Holy Spirit. There are so many scriptures on this topic, once you become well versed in them, your faith will skyrocket for divine health and wellness. Your salvation begins now, and healthy living is part of your salvation package. The covenant promise is yours now. You must learn it, declare it, and enforce it.

Now that you know my testimony and the principles behind it, let's return to the story. I had seen many victories against this component of the Trifold Attack, Sickness and Disease. I wanted my good friend to experience the same thing. When my friend shared she wasn't feeling well, but she wasn't aggressively combating the problem, I went into RED ALERT, war mode.

I remember saying, "DON'T TOLERATE THE TRESPASS!" I continued, "Jesus has already endured that sickness and paid the price for you to be well at the cross. By His stripes – the wounds that He endured in His body – you are healed (1 Peter 2:24). The enemy has no legal right to cross that bloodline. If you are in Christ, you are protected. Jesus has won the victory over sickness but you have to enforce it. You have to attack that sickness aggressively and relentlessly at the very first sign. Don't leave the door open for it to worsen or grow into something else." I reviewed the healing scriptures, the instructions on Holy Communion, and a prescription for spiritual warfare for breakthrough in her health.

A New Battleground

The next day in prayer, I was talking to the Lord about some financial challenges I was dealing with and needed help with. For example, I was working on some consulting contracts that were experiencing long, repeated delays and setbacks. I was having problems getting payment for work I had already completed for normally reliable clients. A few of my scheduled speaking engagements were cancelled, postponed, or had fallen through. I was encountering what seemed like insurmountable obstacles getting a faith-based financial empowerment training program off the ground successfully. Book sales were being held up, and other challenges kept coming up repeatedly that were affecting my personal provision and my ability to move forward with the ministry.

I was thinking of these challenges as ordinary business issues, but I immediately heard the Spirit of the Lord saying strongly in my spirit, *"DON'T TOLERATE THE TRESPASS! This is coordinated, calculated opposition from the enemy – he is* blocking your resources; he is stealing from you!" That got my attention. He said to me in my spirit, "You immediately attack any presence of sickness, but you allow the presence of the enemy in your finances. It is the same type of attack and requires a similar response."

I got quiet and listened. "You understand divine health and healing are part of your salvation and you enforce that victory vigorously with all that is within you every day. You know your Heavenly Father wants you well now. You know and have memorized the promises of God, you declare the Word of the Lord over your life daily, you bind the attack of the devil, you stand in faith, you call on Jehovah Rophe, the Lord Who Heals, and you are relentless and unyielding in your fight of faith for your covenant promises of health and healing. But you do not have the same aggressive, warring response to trial when the enemy launches an attack against your finances."

"You have not memorized as many of the promises of God on finances, you are not speaking the Word of God daily over your finances, you are not calling forth your covenant blessings of wealth and prosperity on a daily basis, you are not binding the ruling demons executing schemes against you and canceling their planned schemes, you are not calling on Jehovah Jireh, the Lord Who Sees and Provides on a daily basis, and, although you are an heir of God and joint heir with Christ, you are not relentless and unyielding in your fight of faith for your covenant inheritance of financial protection, wealth, prosperity, overflow, and abundance. You are a tither and giver, and YOU SHALL NOT TOLERATE THE TRESPASS!"

The Holy Spirit began to show me all the areas where I was being complacent under financial attack. Although my career had been very successful, He began to show me missed opportunities from the past in my years in corporate America: the times I was passed over for promotions that I had clearly earned but did not receive, the raises, bonuses, and recognition I had earned but did not receive in full, the times I was blocked for advancement to new opportunities by managers who did not want to see me elevate, and the unfair and oppressive treatment I endured under difficult bosses.

After leaving corporate America to begin my own business, He showed me the unfair and unscrupulous business deals I had experienced, and the lost contracts I should have been awarded, but did not obtain. He showed me delays, distractions, diversions, and detours that kept me off track from achieving my highest business goals and ministry objectives.

The Holy Spirit showed me my tolerance for interest-bearing loans and mortgage debt. Interest is a major strategy the enemy uses to consistently and systematically eat away at our finances. Interest is the penalty the world's system imposes on lack – it is the penalty we pay for not having enough to meet the need in full at the time of purchase. Borrowing money through credit cards, car loans, and mortgages eats away resources that could be used for better things, and puts us in a position of servitude to the lender! This is nothing to get comfortable with! He showed me little things like unexpected bills, fees, and expenses that, like locusts, were eating up finances I needed for my life and for the ministry. I thought about big impact projects I could not begin, and ministry work I could not complete because I didn't have the finances readily available to fund the new projects or plan for major expansion.

I felt these restrictions and limitations, but I was accepting them as the normal course of business, not a CALL TO

WAR against the presence of the enemy through lack. The presence of debt, shortage, and lack did not sound the "RED ALERT" in my spirit in the same way that the presence of sickness or disease in my body would have alerted me. I was not responding aggressively to this component of the Trifold Attack.

I definitely believed in the promises of financial blessing in the Word of God. I had been, and continue to be, a faithful tither and giver since I became a Christian over 25 years ago. In my time in corporate America, and particularly at Microsoft, I was so abundantly blessed financially I didn't need to battle for financial blessing and increase. I was very thankful for the provision and I sowed into the Kingdom of God wisely, but I didn't know how to battle for additional resources because I didn't have to do it. I used sound personal finance principles like paying down the principal for my homes to eliminate interest, and purchasing vehicles on a cash basis without financing. However, I wasn't stretching my faith and believing God for increase according to my covenant blessing to do more. I wasn't fighting the enemy with the same daily intensity, conviction, and determination to protect my wealth as I was for my health. I didn't really need to. The abundant blessing of my comfortable, corporate job had lulled me into a complacent attitude.

Transitioning to entrepreneurship and full-time ministry ushered in a new era. My work changed to directly oppose the plans and schemes of the enemy: to change lives and bring souls into the Kingdom of God. I had to truly trust God as my Source. I began encountering demonic opposition and spiritual warfare in the financial arena the likes of which I had never seen before. I was stirring things up in the spiritual realm. I was on the enemy's radar. A complacent attitude would not do!

I grabbed my prayer journal and begin to immediately write down what I was hearing in my spirit from the Holy Spirit. I was hearing a prophetic word specifically for my life and ministry, but I was also hearing a broader, all-encompassing prophetic word that the Lord was declaring corporately, for all of His people, the Body of Christ. I would like to share with you the specific word I received from the Holy Spirit. Meditate on it for your own life.

"DON'T TOLERATE THE TRESPASS! Don't allow the presence of the enemy! Don't be complacent in trial! Get a warring spirit – the spirit of the overcomer. 'This may be where I am now, but I'm not staying here! I'm not staying in debt, in lack, in poverty, in sickness, and in disease. I'm not staying here – in bondage, and in oppression. I'm not staying in anxiety, worry, doubt, and unbelief! I'm not staying here! I will go to war!' Jesus is your Rescue and your Ransom. He has already freed you. Stand! Fight! Don't tolerate the presence of the enemy! Have no tolerance for barely getting by! Have faith that God wants you in overflow! Have faith that God wants you to live in His abundance!

God wants you blessed in His prosperity to establish His covenant and build the Kingdom. Fight the good fight of faith! Do not accept anything short of overflow. You are called to be thoroughly equipped for every good work. Children, be warned: do not get bloated on the blessings. You must be willing to give and help others. Study the canker worm. Joel 1 and 2. Study the Devourer. Malachi 3. Study 1 Peter. GO TO WAR. Declare war on debt, lack, and all interest-bearing loans. There is a canker in your finances. It is malignant. It is a spreading sore. Infested. Corrupted. Likened to a destroying locust; it is a spreading, infectious disease. Teach my people. There are many sick and feeble among you."
(End of prophetic message.)

I sat there pondering what I had heard in my spirit. I often receive instructions like this from the Holy Spirit with specific scripture references I need to study to understand the word that has been given. I was struck by the mixture of references to illness (infectious disease) and infestation (as of pestilence through the locust) in the same message. I knew I had captured it correctly, but I didn't understand the end of the message on the canker until I began to study it thoroughly.

Once I studied the scriptures the Lord had given me, my entire frame of reference changed regarding financial health, prosperity, God's covenant blessing of wealth, and its divine purpose within the Kingdom of God. I had a radical paradigm shift that not only changed my personal focus, but it shifted my entire ministry assignment in the Body of Christ. This book was birthed in my spirit that day: *Your 90-Day Financial Breakthrough.*

From that initial eye-opening, life-changing, bondage-breaking Bible study, the Lord took me into a detailed study of the scriptures on prosperity, wealth (the blessings and the warnings), the purpose and plan for God's abundance, God's cycle of blessing, and the impending warfare with the evil one to combat poverty, lack, and debt within the Body of Christ.

Through much prayer, study, application, and confirmation, I am now equipped to share with you the revelations I received from the Holy Spirit on breaking financial barriers and achieving financial breakthrough. Let me share the mysteries I discovered. I pray you are challenged, changed, encouraged, and transformed!

4 | the canker: understanding the devourer

As I began this work, the Lord directed me to study a set of scriptures on the canker to help me better understand our adversary, the Devourer, and the tactics he uses against us. We have a tendency to underestimate the extent of the devil's strategy, which gives strength to his deceptions and schemes. Let me show you what was revealed to me so that you can take authority over the Devourer in your life.

The prophet Joel saw the horrors of an actual locust invasion in his time. He lived through the devastation and the Lord used this picture in his prophetic word to Israel regarding their disobedience to the Lord, the coming judgment, and the redemption and restoration God would bring to Israel. In his description in Joel 1:3-4, we see four different types of locusts.

Tell ye your children of it, and let your children tell their children, and their children another generation. That which the palmerworm hath left hath the locust eaten; and that *which the locust hath left hath the **cankerworm** eaten; and that which the cankerworm hath left hath the caterpiller eaten* ***Joel 1:3-4 (KJV)***

The precise identification of the four species or stages of locusts mentioned here is uncertain, but we can ascertain certain characteristics that will help us better understand the Devourer that we face.

Locust Type and Definition – Figure 1

LOCUST TYPE	HEBREW WORD	DEFINITION
Palmerworm	*gazam*	to cut short; cutting stripping, gnawing locust
Locust	*arbeh*	to multiply; a swarming multitude, immense increase, take over
Cankerworm	*yelek*	licking locust – devourer; eats everything in its path; grass, shrubs, bark of trees; bringing barrenness until nothing green is left
Caterpillar	*chasil*	to consume, to eat up; wasting and consuming all that comes in its way

The prophet Joel is describing an actual locust invasion that was God's judgment upon Israel as a result of their disobedience and rebellion. It is also a prophetic foretelling of four hostile invasions against Israel by oppressing kingdoms. (Many Bible scholars believe this represents the Assyrian, Chaldean, Macedonian and Roman empires, or possibly four successive invasions of the Chaldeans).

I believe the Lord is giving us an Old Testament type and picture of the spiritual warfare we encounter with the enemy, the Devourer, when we are outside of the covering of God's covenant, disobedient and rebellious to God's Word, or simply under an unwarranted and unlawful spiritual attack. I believe the Lord is giving us a descriptive picture of the characteristics of the hostile enemy we are battling so we can understand it and resist it. We are not at war with locusts or hostile empires, but we are at war with a hostile spiritual kingdom of demonic forces led by Satan. God has given us the victory!

From Joel 1:4, we can summarize the following characteristics of our enemy, the **Devourer**, as one who cuts short, swarms over, devours, produces barrenness, wastes, and consumes. We see a continual and continuous eating away, and relentless devastation until there is nothing left. This is the nature of the enemy we fight. We cannot have a lax or complacent attitude toward the Devourer!

A REVEALING WORD STUDY

In the book of Joel, Chapter 2, we see the restoration of the Lord after Israel had repented.

*Be glad then, ye children of Zion, and rejoice in the Lord your God: for he hath given you the former rain moderately, and he will cause to come down for you the rain, the former rain, and the latter rain in the first month. And the floors shall be full of wheat, and the vats shall overflow with wine and oil. And I will restore to you the years that the locust hath eaten, the **cankerworm**, and the caterpiller, and the palmerworm, my great army which I sent among you.* **Joel 2:23-25 (KJV)**

The word **canker** is the Hebrew word *yelek* which means licking locust or **devouring** locust. In Latin, the word **canker** comes from the same Latin root word from which we get the word **cancer!** It means **to devour**. It means an erosive or spreading sore; gangrene; to corrupt with malignancy.

What the Bible calls "canker" we would call "**cancer**" in our modern language!

The presence of shortage, struggle, lack, debt, and poverty in our finances is of the same severity as cancer in our bodies. It is not to be tolerated!

I want to share some additional definitions with you, to help you gain a complete picture of the nature of our enemy, the Devourer. This word study will be very helpful to us in our preparation for spiritual warfare and financial breakthrough. Further study of the word **cancer** (see Merriam-Webster's Dictionary) reveals the following.

Cancer is a malignant tumor of potentially unlimited growth that expands locally by invasion and systematically by metastasis.

Something that is **malignant** by definition is evil in nature, influence, or effect; injurious, passionately and relentlessly malevolent; aggressively malicious; tending to produce death or deterioration; tending to infiltrate, metastasize, and terminate fatally.

To be **malevolent** means having, showing, or arising from intense often vicious ill will, spite, or hatred.

To be **malicious** means to be given to, marked by, or arising from malice. **Malice** is a desire to see another suffer that may be fixed and unreasonable; intent to commit an unlawful act or cause harm without legal justification or excuse.

To metastasize means a change of position, state or form; the transfer of a disease producing agency from the site of the disease to another part of the body.

THE DEVOURER

Therefore, by putting this complete word study all together, in the word **canker** we see two vivid pictures of our enemy the **Devourer**: 1) a devouring **pestilence**, as to an overwhelming swarm of locusts, that cuts short, spreads, swarms over, devours, produces barrenness, wastes, and consumes until complete devastation is accomplished, and 2) a devouring deadly, malignant **disease**, as to **cancer,** that expands locally by invasion and systematically by metastasis; is evil in nature, influence, or effect; injurious; passionately and relentlessly showing or arising from an intense, often vicious ill will, spite, or hatred; and aggressively desiring to see another suffer to an extent that is fixed and unreasonable; marked by an aggressive intent to commit an unlawful act or cause harm without legal justification or excuse; tending to produce death or deterioration; tending to infiltrate, metastasize, and terminate fatally.

Take a moment to read that complete definition of the Devourer once again. That is an extraordinarily accurate description of the devil himself! Read it again slowly and absorb the power of the definition of the Devourer. Thanks be to God, the enemy is defeated! In Christ, we are fully protected from this enemy!

God has revealed to us through the scripture, with careful study of the **canker** and the **devourer,** an accurate picture of the evil we are up against. Further research of the scripture confirms this exact, twofold portrait of the Devourer as both a devastating pestilence and deadly disease. Let's review two translations of Malachi 3:11 to see this twofold nature of the Devourer.

*And I will rebuke the **devourer [insects and plagues]** for your sakes and he shall not destroy the fruits of your ground, neither shall your vine drop its fruit before the time in the field, says the Lord of hosts.*
Malachi 3:11 (AMP)

*Your crops will be abundant, for I will guard them from **insects and disease**. Your grapes will not fall from the vine before they are ripe," says the LORD of Heaven's Armies.*
Malachi 3:11 (NLT)

A **plague** is a disastrous evil or affliction: **calamity**; a destructively numerous influx <a *plague* of locusts>; an epidemic **disease** causing a high rate of mortality.

The presence of the Devourer, and the resulting erosion and devastation of your finances, is considered a pestilence and plague to the Lord. He has zero tolerance for it, and neither should you! Struggling, shortage, toiling, poverty, lack, insufficiency, barrenness, devastation, debt, and debt servitude — these are the results of the presence of the Devourer and are considered pestilence and disease to the Lord. It is not of God. It is unacceptable in the life of a believer. **It is financial cancer**.

GOD WANTS YOU WELL NOW!

God wants you financially WELL, and He wants you well NOW! Believing for God's abundance and prosperity does not mean you are selfishly seeking material gain. Understand that it is God's will for you to be financially well, financially whole, and financially protected from the Devourer. It is part of your salvation package to be well and whole. God does not want you to be subjected to financial cancer. God wants to heal you and restore you to wholeness. Believing for God's abundance and prosperity means you are seeking financial wellness, wholeness, and protection from the Devourer. It does not mean you have a love of money, or that you are greedy for gain. Do not be deceived! You have covenant promises of prosperity for your protection and provision. There is no reason to not ask for, believe for, and expect the Lord to prosper you. God wants you to be well financially, and to be well and prosper in all areas of your life. 3 John 2 encourages us, *"Beloved, I pray that you may **prosper in all things** and be in health, just as your soul prospers."*

When God has dominion over your finances, the Devourer is absent. When the Devourer is absent, wealth, riches, abundance, and overflow are present. Therefore, when God has dominion over your finances, wealth, riches, abundance, and overflow are present.

Look again at the restoration of Israel in Joel 2:23-25 (KJV), which tells us, *"Be glad then, ye children of Zion, and rejoice in the Lord your God: for he hath given you the former rain moderately, and he will cause to come down for you the rain, the former rain, and the latter rain in the first month. **And the floors shall be full of wheat, and the vats shall overflow with wine and oil. And I will restore to you the years that the locust hath eaten**, the cankerworm, and the caterpiller, and the palmerworm, my great army which I sent among you."*

When God restored and blessed Israel, He put them into a place of **overflow** and **abundance**. Their floors were full of wheat, and their vats – their storage places of provision – were in overflow. He reversed the curse of the canker. Overflow and abundance are blessings from the Lord. You can see from this text the actual rewinding of the curse, as the locusts are listed in reverse order!

Now let's look again at Malachi 3:10-11 (NKJV), which instructs us as follows: *"'Bring all the tithes into the storehouse, That there may be food in My house, And try Me now in this,' Says the LORD of hosts,* **'If I will not open for you the windows of heaven And pour out for you such blessing That there will not be room enough to receive it. "And I will rebuke the devourer for your sakes,** *So that he will not destroy the fruit of your ground, Nor shall the vine fail to bear fruit for you in the field,' Says the Lord of hosts."*

When the people of Israel were under the covering of God's blessing, not only did He put them into overflow and abundance, but He promised to handle the Devourer on their behalf! You do not need to fight the battle – when you understand your covenant promise and walk in obedience to the scripture, **God will rebuke the Devourer for you!**

In both the books of Joel and Malachi, we see a clear picture of overflow and abundance when the threat and presence of the Devourer is removed. Both prophets speak to the blessing of God in terms of overflow. God's presence brings overflow – more than enough – into our lives. Absence of the Devourer means the presence of abundance.

The presence of the Devourer in your finances means illness, likened to the severity of **cancer**. It is a spreading deadly plague, and an infectious outbreak in the Body of Christ. There is a cancer of debt, debt slavery, shortage, lack, poverty, insufficiency, and oppression in the Body of Christ that is an unlawful trespass of the evil one. God wants you to be restored and revived. He wants you healed and made whole. God wants you to be free of the devouring locust and the deadly cancer of financial lack metastasizing into other areas of your life, destroying your health, your peace of mind, your

78

family, and your relationships. God wants you to experience financial wholeness so that you are able to liberally provide for yourself and your family, prepare for the future, provide an inheritance for your children's children, be prepared for the unexpected, build the Kingdom of God, and give generously to the needs of others.

How do we eliminate the presence of the enemy, the Devourer, with his manifestations of debt, lack, insufficiency, and struggle, and move into the abundance and overflow of God's provision? What shall we do?

God's blessing, favor, protection, abundance, and overflow are communicated throughout the scripture and are part of our salvation benefit from the moment we are born again. However, much like my physical healing, we will not walk in the fullness of our financial health and wholeness until we 1) learn the covenant promises related to wealth, prosperity, and abundance, 2) master, meditate, and memorize the specific scriptures from the Word of God in this area, and 3) enforce our covenant victory with the authority of Jesus Christ to stop the trespass of the enemy, the Devourer.

To overcome this financial cancer, we will follow the same prescription the Lord gave me for overcoming sickness and disease in the physical body. If you have faced or ever face a difficult diagnosis in your health, you will go into RED ALERT mode. We are not in fear, for God has not given us a spirit of fear, but of power, love, and a sound mind (2 Timothy 1:7). We must wake up and snap out of complacency, and get serious about combating the presence of the enemy. We must get a warring spirit. Now that we have a deeper picture of the Devourer himself, and how serious it is to remove this threat, we can begin your financial breakthrough.

We must learn the **principles** of financial health and wellness from the Word of God. The Lord has specific instructions, directives, commands, warnings, restrictions, and safeguards regarding wealth that we must understand and follow to stop the devastation of the Devourer and participate in the blessings of abundance that God has for us. If we do not follow God's principles, we cannot expect Him to release His provision. If we follow God's principles, we can believe for and expect God's abundance to come to our lives.

We must understand the **process** of receiving God's blessing on our lives. There is a process for how the Lord blesses us and a proper response to the blessing. We must understand the cycle of blessing and cooperate with it. Just as a farmer must understand the cycle of farming and the process of sowing and reaping in order to consistently reap a healthy, bountiful harvest, we must do the same thing financially. If we don't cooperate with the cycle of blessing, we cannot expect a bountiful harvest.

We must learn the **promises** of God related to wealth, prosperity, abundance, and overflow. If we do not know our covenant blessings we cannot enforce them, and we are easily deceived by the enemy. The Lord warns us in Hosea 4:6 (NKJV), *"My people are destroyed for lack of knowledge."*

We must use the **power** of God through the authority of the Lord Jesus Christ to enforce the victory Jesus has already gained for us at the cross and stop the schemes of the enemy meant to destroy and devour our blessings. We must understand the warfare component and do our part.

We must implement the **plan** and strategy the Lord has designed for us in His Word to be blessed financially. There are practical, natural steps to financial wealth, prosperity, and abundance we need to implement in our lives. Let's begin your financial breakthrough!

5 | God wants you well now

And God is able to make all grace (every favor and earthly blessing) come to you in abundance, so that you may always and under all circumstances and whatever the need be self-sufficient [possessing enough to require no aid or support and furnished in abundance for every good work and charitable donation].
2 Corinthians 9:8 (AMP)

No matter where you are financially right now, God has a higher level of wellness, wholeness, and financial abundance prepared for you. God is able and He desires to cause every favor and earthly blessing to come to you in abundance. Whether you are struggling, stagnant, or soaring right now, there is a greater place of blessing, increase, and overflow for you. There is a larger and more significant assignment for you to fulfill, to be a blessing to others.

There is a natural progression in the process of financial wellness. First, your Heavenly Father wants to ensure all of your needs are abundantly supplied. In 2 Corinthians 9:8 (AMP), we see that God wants you to **always, under all circumstances**, and **whatever the need** be self-sufficient requiring no aid or support. He does not want you to stay in a state of shortage, debt, or lack in your life. Every financial need you can think of, in every situation and circumstance, God is willing and able to supply!

This blessing is yours, not because you have earned it, and it is not because you deserve it. You do not have to attain a certain socioeconomic position or worldly status in society to be counted worthy of this blessing. God wants to bless you because you are His child, and it is solely by His grace, His unmerited, unearned favor, that you are blessed in this manner. That amazing grace comes to you in abundance through your faith in Christ Jesus. **Every need is met** — that is the first part of your Heavenly Father's definition of financial wellness for you!

Take a moment and make a list of all of your needs — everything you can possibly think of, write it down. Start with the basics of your home and utilities, ample food, reliable, safe transportation, furniture, appliances, clothes, medical and dental insurance, life insurance, etc. Consider your health and safety needs. Now go beyond the basics and make a list of every additional need you can think of. Think about your educational and career needs. Think about the needs of your business and ministry. Think about your rest, recreation, and restoration needs.

Think about being out of debt **completely**. Consider owning everything you have free and clear: no credit card debt, car loans, student loans, installment debt, line of credit, second mortgage, or mortgage payments. At a minimum, you are at zero — in the black. You are no longer in the red — you are not indebted or indentured to anyone! Think about being in a position where you do not have to borrow or take out loans to meet your needs — you are self-sufficient, requiring no aid or support.

You do not need financial aid to complete your education – your needs are met. You do not need a bank loan for reliable transportation – your needs are met. You are not paying a penalty of three times the market value of your home in interest payments over a 30-year mortgage – your needs are met. Your home is paid in full. You own and hold the title deed for your home! I believe that being debt free is a basic necessity. God wants you to lend and not borrow (Deuteronomy 28:12). He wants to ensure you are not placed in a position of servitude to anyone or any institution (Proverbs 22:7).

In addition to being debt free, now think about having six to twelve months of cash reserves set aside to care for all of your needs and your family's needs in case of an emergency. Think about a savings and investment plan for your future. Think about having multiple income sources, so that if one source is affected, your livelihood is still protected.

Now, think about your family. Write down every possible financial need you may have to generously provide for your spouse and your children (1 Timothy 5:8). Think about their health and wellness needs. Fast forward and consider the college education expenses coming up in the future for your children. Consider what you would like to save for each of your children as an inheritance, to give them a strong head start in their lives (Proverbs 19:14). Now consider your extended family – what are their needs? Think about elder care for your parents and helping out other family members who may be in need. Contemplate leaving a generous inheritance for your children and your grandchildren (Proverbs 13:22). Any need that comes to mind, write it down now.

Philippians 4:19 (AMP) encourages us, *"And my God will liberally supply (fill to the full) your every need according to*

His riches in glory in Christ Jesus." If your needs are unmet, then lack is present. There is no lack or insufficiency in your Heavenly Father! The Lord is your Shepherd and you shall not lack (Psalm 23:1). No good thing will God withhold from those who walk uprightly (Psalm 84:11)! Your needs are met. Always. In all circumstances. Whatever the need.

In addition to meeting your needs, God promises that He will also give you all good things for you to enjoy. Your Heavenly Father wants you to enjoy your life! (See 1 Timothy 6:17-19.) Just as you desire to be good to your children, Your Heavenly Father desires to be good to you. He has already given the most precious gift He could ever bestow upon you – His own Son. Romans 8:32 (AMP) challenges us by asking, *"He who did not withhold or spare [even] His own Son but gave Him up for us all, will He not also with Him freely and graciously give us all [other] things?"*

If you focus on keeping your desires in alignment with His will, Your Heavenly Father will rejoice in giving you the desires of your heart. Your God is a more-than-enough God! He will go beyond meeting your basic necessities to blessing you with a rich and rewarding life. God will not come up short if you place a demand on His riches in glory. His finances aren't stretched thin by your needs. He is not in scarcity, nor does He have a limited supply of anything. He is El Shaddai, He is the Lord God Almighty who is more than enough to meet your every need. He is Jehovah-Jireh, the Lord Who Sees and Provides!

What do you desire to ask of the Father in order to provide a rich, rewarding, and enjoyable life for yourself, your family, and your loved ones?

Beyond meeting your every need and providing a rich and rewarding life for you to enjoy, your Heavenly Father has a greater assignment for you. Financial wellness goes beyond just you and your family. He wants you to participate in the Kingdom of God in an even greater way than you are today. This is the second part of God's definition of financial wellness and wholeness. Your Heavenly Father desires to bless you so that you may be a generous blessing to others.

The Lord has an exciting promotion for you. He wants you to be a conduit of His loving care. You are His ambassador of generosity and kindness on the earth. You are His representative of care and concern to the needy. You are His holy presence of compassion to the poor. Your Heavenly Father wants you to be financially well and whole so that you are not consumed with your needs, but concerned for the needs of others.

Returning to 2 Corinthians 9:8 (AMP), we see that God not only wants you to be self-sufficient, but also *furnished in abundance for every good work and charitable donation.* To be financially well and whole means you can give at every opportunity. You can respond to His voice. You can move when the Lord prompts you to move. Your life is elevated to the blessed place of being the hands, feet, and heart of Jesus on the earth. What a powerful testimony the Church will be to the lost, when we function as intended, furnished in abundance for every good work and charitable donation! Equipped to meet every need!

God wants you to be a vessel of His abundance, demonstrating His love, care, and concern to all who are in need. You are prosperous and philanthropic. You are compassionate and caring. You live in overflow and abundance. You are blessed to be a blessing.

Just as a pregnant woman must be well-nourished to meet the demands of her infant child who is dependent upon her, you are well-nourished financially to nourish others who rely upon you. It is false piety and damaging religious rhetoric to denounce prosperity and hold on to a poverty mindset as a position of perceived superior spirituality. James 1:27 (NLT) tells us, *"Pure and genuine religion in the sight of God the Father means **caring for orphans and widows in their distress** and refusing to let the world corrupt you."* We must move past the self-centeredness of the poverty mindset. We must move past the all-consuming quest to make it from paycheck to paycheck. We must also move past the greed of expanding and stockpiling our own personal wealth and fortune, as the world would define prosperity. Refuse to allow a worldly mindset to corrupt you. Abundance puts you in position to care for your family, enjoy your life, and **elevate your response to the needs of others** who are in distress. That is truly the Father's heart.

This is the second part of God's definition of financial wellness and wholeness. Write down your vision for helping others. How can you be a blessing to those who are in need? God has promised that you will be thoroughly equipped for every good work and charitable donation. What cause do you want to champion? What contribution will you give to the world?

Your Heavenly Father wants you to be financially well and whole. He does not want you subjected to the financial cancer of debt, lack, and insufficiency. God wants you to be able to:

- Provide for yourself and be self-sufficient (including being debt free)

- Provide for your family and extended family

- Plan for the future

- Prepare for the unexpected

- Provide a rich inheritance for your children and grandchildren

- Enjoy your life on the earth

- Build the Kingdom of God

- Share the gospel with the lost and hurting, and

- Give generously to others who are in distress.

Habakkuk 2:2 (NKJV) tells us, *"Write the vision and make it plain on tablets, That he may run who reads it."* Take time to write down your vision for financial wellness. What must change in your life for you to be financially whole? Write down the debts you are ready to eliminate. Make a list of your needs and desires. Write your vision for your family and extended family. Write your vision for leaving a legacy and an inheritance to future generations. Write your vision for being a blessing to others who are in need. What will you ask of the Lord? Expand your faith to place a demand on His riches in glory in Christ Jesus. Your Heavenly Father loves you and is ready to heal you financially as well as in every other area of your life. Stretch your mindset to go beyond the ordinary to the extraordinary.

Review 2 Corinthians 9:8 (AMP) once again and write down specifically what this promise means to you.

And God is able to make all grace (every favor and earthly blessing) come to you in abundance, so that you may always and under all circumstances and whatever the need be self-sufficient [possessing enough to require no aid or support and furnished in abundance for every good work and charitable donation].
2 Corinthians 9:8 (AMP)

Your Heavenly Father wants you well now! Get ready for your financial breakthrough!

6 | the cycle of blessing

J ust as the earth has natural cycles of seedtime, growth, and harvest, our Heavenly Father has put in place a supernatural cycle of blessing for His children. There is a divine design for how we are to be blessed, and then in turn, how we are to be a blessing to others. Let's look at this progression, which I will call God's cycle of blessing.

GOD'S STOREHOUSE: OPENING THE WINDOWS OF HEAVEN

Our Heavenly Father has an immeasurable storehouse of blessings in Heaven for His children. He has blessings stored in eternity, that at the appointed time, He sends to us in the continuum of time. God's blessings are too numerous to number. Your blessings have your name assigned to them. God's blessings include **spiritual riches** such as your eternal life, righteousness, joy, peace, favor, the presence of God, the protection of God, your authority over demonic forces, wisdom, knowledge, and understanding. God's blessings also include **natural riches** such as divine health and healing, a happy marriage, a blessed womb, healthy, obedient children, and lasting, loving relationships. God's blessings also include **material riches** such as freedom from debt and debt slavery, land, homes, businesses, inventions, property, promotions, raises, riches, new contracts, new territory, wealth, and abundance. They are yours.

God opens the windows of Heaven and sends spiritual, natural, and material blessings upon His children from His riches in glory in Christ Jesus. Everything we experience here on earth has a supernatural counterpart. The spiritual realm is the eternal realm. What we experience in the natural realm is actually temporary. Everything that is visible and touchable in the natural realm – in a manifested state – first started in the spiritual realm of eternal things. Just as God spoke the earth and all of its contents into existence, as recorded in the book of Genesis, every spiritual, natural, and material blessing in your life begins with the Heavenly Father and flows to you from His riches in glory in the heavenly realms.

James 1:17 (NKJV) tells us, *"Every good gift and every perfect gift is from above, and comes down from the Father of lights, with whom there is no variation or shadow of turning."*

Your blessings begin in the spiritual realm, travel to you, and are ultimately manifested in the natural, material realm. Faith is the ability to see what is in the spiritual realm that is stored up and on its way to you in the natural realm, but has not manifested to your natural senses yet. Hebrews 11:1 (NKJV) tells us, *"Now faith is the substance of things hoped for, the evidence of things not seen."*

Let's look more closely at Hebrews 11:1 in the Amplified Bible. *"Now **faith is** the assurance (the confirmation, **the title deed**) of the things [we] hope for, being **the proof** of things [we] do not see and the conviction of their reality* *[faith perceiving as real fact what is not revealed to the senses]."*

Our Heavenly Father tells us in His Word that He opens the windows of Heaven to pour out His blessings upon His children. In the pattern of the Holy Trinity (Father, Son, and Holy Spirit), you are created as a three-part being: you are a **spirit**, you live in a physical **body**, and you have a **soul** – your mind, emotions, and will. We are spiritual beings who live in physical bodies in a physical world, operating by natural senses. God's blessings are **both** spiritual and material. He sends spiritual blessings to meet our spiritual needs such as redemption, justification, eternal life, righteousness, peace, and joy. He sends material blessings to meet our natural needs during our time here on the earth such as money, homes, food, clothing, employment, businesses, raises, promotions, and increase.

God's blessings are complete. He will provide everything that you need spiritually and materially. Our Heavenly Father opens the windows of Heaven to abundantly supply what is needed by His children. This includes financial provision and material blessings.

We see God's storehouse in Deuteronomy 28:12 (NIV), which says, *"The Lord will open **the heavens, the storehouse of his bounty,** to send rain on your land in season and to bless all the work of your hands. You will lend to many nations but will borrow from none."*

God's blessings are material, and will come to you in abundance, so that you can live debt free, with no need to borrow, amply supplied for every good work, with enough overflow to lend generously to others.

God tells us in Malachi 3:10 (NKJV), *"Bring all the tithes into the storehouse, That there may be food in My house,*

And try Me now in this," Says the Lord of hosts, *"If I will not open for you the* **windows of heaven And pour out for you such blessing** *That there will not be room enough to receive it."*

We see this same picture of abundant supply and provision in the New Testament in Philippians 4:19 (AMP), where Paul tells us, *"And my God will liberally supply (fill to the full) your every need according to His riches in glory in Christ Jesus."*

God's storehouse of treasure in Heaven is depicted as His riches in glory in Christ Jesus. The heavens are God's storehouse of His bounty. He is amply supplied to meet your every need!

THE BELIEVER'S STOREHOUSE

Once the blessing has come down from Heaven, it comes into the storehouse of the believer, God's child. The blessings of God come under our personal stewardship. God will send the blessings to our homes, our land, and upon our work. Deuteronomy 28:8 (NKJV) tells us, *"The Lord will command the blessing on you* **in your storehouses and in all to which you set your hand,** *and He will bless you in* **the land** *which the Lord your God is giving you."*

God literally blessed the places where they stored their provision, which would be their barns and storage places for grain. He also sent the blessing upon their land. I like to think of our modern day storehouses as our homes, property, businesses, and bank accounts.

GOD'S EARTHLY STOREHOUSE:
THE CHURCH

Once the blessing has reached the believer, and is under the stewardship of the child of God, we have an immediate responsibility to sow back into the Lord's house. God has an earthly storehouse, which in Bible times, was the temple, and now is the church. This is His Command Center on the earth. God commands us to bring the first ten percent of our income, the tithe, to the local, earthly storehouse of the Lord which is His church.

Let's look back at Malachi 3 to see this step in God's cycle of blessing. The Lord tells us in Malachi 3:10 (NKJV), ***"Bring all the tithes into the storehouse, That there may be food in My house***, *And try Me now in this," Says the Lord of hosts, "If I will not open for you the windows of heaven And pour out for you such blessing That there will not be room enough to receive it."*

The tithe, or tenth, is the first ten percent of our income which is holy and belongs to the Lord (Leviticus 27:30). It is our first responsibility of stewardship to bring the firstfruits of our increase back to the Lord in His earthly storehouse, the church. The tithe is used to provide for the needs of those who have devoted their lives to serve the Kingdom of God. It covers all of the needs of the local church, provides food for the workers of the gospel, and provision for those who are in need. God is actively meeting the needs of the poor and less fortunate directly from His earthly storehouse, His Command Center on the earth, the church.

Tithing is an act of reverence and obedience to the Lord, and places us in proper spiritual alignment, cooperating with His cycle of blessing. We honor God when we return the firstfruits of our increase to the Lord. God's blessings immediately begin to flow in greater measure.

The first blessing of tithing is **increase**. Our Heavenly Father increases the flow of blessings to those who honor Him by promptly bringing the tithe to His earthly storehouse to keep the cycle of blessing moving forward.

God tells us in Malachi 3:10 (NKJV), *"Bring all the tithes into the storehouse, That there may be food in My house,* ***And try Me now in this,"*** *Says the Lord of hosts,* ***"If I will not open for you the windows of heaven And pour out for you such blessing That there will not be room enough to receive it."***

You see material blessing coming in such measure that there is tremendous overflow – so much that there is not room enough to receive all that God has for you! Your Heavenly Father challenges you to test Him – try Him in this – and watch Him deliver on His Word! He has given you His Word on it. You can stand on this promise!

The second blessing is **protection**. When we promptly tithe, God promises to rebuke the Devourer for our sakes. The enemy will come to steal and destroy your provision but God Himself will step in and protect it.

Let's review our definition of the Devourer that we covered earlier. The **Devourer** can be defined as: 1) a devouring pestilence, as to an overwhelming swarm of locusts, that cuts short, spreads, swarms over, devours, produces barrenness, wastes, and consumes until complete devastation is accomplished, and 2) a devouring, deadly, malignant disease, as to **cancer,** that expands locally by invasion and systematically by metastasis; is evil in nature, influence, or effect; injurious; passionately and relentlessly showing or arising from an intense, often vicious ill will, spite, or hatred; and aggressively desiring to see another suffer to an extent that is fixed and unreasonable; marked by an aggressive intent to commit an unlawful act or cause harm without legal justification or excuse; tending to produce death or deterioration; tending to infiltrate, metastasize, and terminate fatally.

You **do not** have to face down this formidable enemy alone – when you obey and honor God with the tithe, God Himself will step in and rebuke the Devourer for you! You have the victory! Praise the Lord!

Malachi 3:11 (NKJV) assures us, *"And I will rebuke the devourer for your sakes, So that he will not destroy the fruit of your ground, Nor shall the vine fail to bear fruit for you in the field,' Says the Lord of hosts."*

The third promise of tithing is that our blessing will be **visible and evident** to others, as a tangible evidence of the presence of God in our lives, bringing glory and honor to Him. Malachi 3:12 (NKJV) states, *"And **all nations will call you blessed**, For you will be a delightful land,' Says the Lord of hosts."*

The presence and blessing of God will be evident on your life as a testimony to the unbeliever. You should not be arrogant, but you should never feel ashamed, self-conscious, or sensitive to criticism because you are blessed by God. You are a child of the Most High God! It should be evident the Lord is with you! Your holistic blessings – spiritual, natural, and material – are a powerful testimony to the goodness of God in your life.

In Proverbs 3, we see the same promise of increase, abundance, and overflow when we cooperate with God's cycle of blessing by honoring Him with the firstfruits of our increase. Our personal storehouses for our provision – depicted here as barns and vats – will be filled to the full and will overflow with the increase from the Lord.

Proverbs 3:9-10 (NKJV) instructs us, *"Honor the Lord with your possessions, And with **the firstfruits of all your increase**; So your **barns will be filled with plenty**, And your **vats will overflow** with new wine."*

To break the cycle of blessing at this point is considered a very serious offense to the Lord. He is entrusting you with His full blessings, and He considers it an act of robbery against Him personally to not return the tithe or the tenth to the storehouse of the Lord for His work on the earth.

Malachi 3:8 (NKJV) tells us how serious it is to stay in alignment with God's cycle of blessing: *"Will a man rob God? **Yet you have robbed Me!** But you say, 'In what way have we robbed You?' In tithes and offerings."*

The tithe is sacred, and the Lord trusts us and entrusts us with the solemn responsibility to fund His earthly storehouse by immediately bringing in the tithe. To not do so is equivalent to robbing God!

Everything else that is given to you is yours to use to provide for your family, prepare for the future, put aside an inheritance, accomplish your purpose, enjoy your life, expand your territory, and generously help those who are in need. You will have more than enough for your life, such that you can be a generous blessing to others.

Once we have returned the tithe to the Lord through His local earthly storehouse, the church, we also have the exciting opportunity to determine in our own hearts an amount to give to the Lord in the form of an offering. This is free-will giving from your heart as an act of worship and thanksgiving to the Lord. Your offerings are your opportunity to cheerfully show your love for God and His blessings.

Review 2 Corinthians 9:7 (NLT) which says, *"You must each decide in your heart how much to give. And don't give reluctantly or in response to pressure. 'For God loves a person who gives cheerfully.'"*

Your free-will giving is also the seed you are planting for future increase. The Word promises you that if you sow sparingly, you will reap sparingly, but if you understand the cycle of blessing and you sow bountifully, you will reap bountifully!

We see this principle in 2 Corinthians 9:6 (AMP), which tells us, *"[Remember] this: he who sows sparingly and grudgingly will also reap sparingly and grudgingly, and he who sows generously [that blessings may come to someone] will also reap generously and with blessings."*

As you give, your Heavenly Father gives back so much more. You are demonstrating your trustworthiness to co-labor with the Lord to build the Kingdom. You become a conduit of blessing, a vessel through which God blesses His people, reaches the lost, and expands the Kingdom. The more you understand the cycle of blessing, the greater the blessing that will flow to you and through you. If you operate as a tiny tube of blessing, only a small trickle of God's increase will flow to you. As you learn to trust God and participate in the cycle of blessing in greater measure, the greater the blessing that will flow to you. When you become a large pipeline of generosity, and a huge conduit of blessing to and for God's people, you can expect a great overflow of the Lord's increase, abundance, and prosperity to flow to you. You can expect an abundance of God's spiritual, natural, and material blessings. My prayer is that I can expand my capacity to be a greater giver, and therefore a greater conduit for God's provision, blessing, and expansion of the Kingdom. That is my prayer for you as well.

We see this principle in Proverbs 11:24-26 (NKJV), which tells us, *"**There is one who scatters, yet increases more;** And there is one who withholds more than is right, But it leads to poverty. **The generous soul will be made rich**, And he who waters will also be watered himself. The people will curse him who withholds grain, But blessing will be on the head of him who sells it."*

God increases and abundantly blesses the **generous**. When you understand God's cycle of blessing, you will have no challenges in giving generously! As you give, your Heavenly Father simply replenishes you and expands your territory, causing the flow of blessing from His heavenly storehouse to your personal storehouse to increase in great measure!

The Message Bible puts it this way, in Proverbs 11:25 (MSG): *"The one who blesses others is abundantly blessed; those who help others are helped."*

GOD'S EARTHLY STOREHOUSE: SEEKING TO SAVE THE LOST

The church, in turn, is commissioned to use the tithes and offerings to care for the full-time ministers of the gospel, care for the physical needs of the house of the Lord (His sanctuary), and provide for the poor and others who are in need. The tithes and offerings must be used to build the Kingdom of God and share the good news of the gospel around the world. The tithes and offerings are used to send forth messengers of the gospel to share and demonstrate the love of God and Jesus Christ, empowered by the Holy Spirit. The ultimate objective is that **all people** around the world have the blessed opportunity to hear the good news of the gospel, come into the saving knowledge of the Lord Jesus Christ, and be reconciled back to God the Father who loves them!

Romans 10:14-16 (NLT) asks us, *"But how can they call on him to save them unless they believe in him? And how can they believe in him if they have never heard about him? And how can they hear about him unless someone tells them? And how will anyone go and tell them without being sent? That is why the Scriptures say, 'How beautiful are the feet of messengers who bring good news!'"*

BRINGING IN THE HARVEST

The cycle of blessing is complete when the seed of our giving comes to full harvest. What is the harvest? It is **souls**! It is the souls of those that are saved, redeemed, and reconciled back to God! God's blessings that are poured out from the windows of Heaven, His riches in glory, return to Him in full, glorious measure in the precious souls of those who were lost that are now found! What an exciting honor it is to participate in this wonderful cycle of salvation. You are blessed to provide for your family, help others, and ultimately to bring the blessing of salvation to others for all eternity.

The Lord waits on each of us patiently and lovingly, desiring the full harvest of souls to come in. He wants everyone to come into the saving knowledge of Jesus Christ. 2 Peter 3:9 (AMP) encourages us, *"The Lord does not delay and is not tardy or slow about what He promises, according to some people's conception of slowness, but **He is long-suffering (extraordinarily patient) toward you, not desiring that any should perish, but that all should turn to repentance.**"*

Jesus implored us to ask the Lord of the harvest to send workers into the harvest field. That is exactly what you are doing when you return the tithe and sow your offerings into God's earthly storehouse, the church. You are sending laborers into the harvest! Matthew 9:35-38 (NIV) shares this principle: *"Jesus went through all the towns and villages, teaching in their synagogues, proclaiming the good news of the kingdom and healing every disease and sickness. When he saw the crowds, he had compassion on them, because they were harassed and helpless, like sheep without a shepherd. Then he said to his disciples, **'The harvest is plentiful but the workers are few. Ask the Lord of the harvest, therefore, to send out workers into his harvest field.'"***

At this point in the cycle of blessing, God's provision is returning to Him in a magnificent harvest of souls saved. You are part of that amazing, eternal work. What an honor! God's Word will not return to Him void, and His material blessings also complete a full cycle of supernatural work in the earth when we participate in the cycle of blessing.

TREASURE IN HEAVEN

We see the completion of the cycle of blessing when souls are returned to the Father for all eternity. This is what Jesus was referring to when He encouraged the disciples to lay up treasure in Heaven. What is the treasure that we are to lay up in Heaven? The redeemed! The saved! The lost who are now found! God blesses our lives with His great treasure – spiritual blessings, natural blessings, and material blessings – so that we can co-labor with Him and store up eternal treasure: lives changed and transformed, and **souls saved** for all eternity.

In Matthew 6:19-21 (AMP), Jesus encourages us to complete the cycle of blessing and store up eternal treasure in Heaven: *"Do not gather and heap up and store up for yourselves treasures on earth, where moth and rust and worm consume and destroy, and where thieves break through and steal.* ***But gather and heap up and store for yourselves treasures in heaven****, where neither moth nor rust nor worm consume and destroy, and where thieves do not break through and steal; For where your treasure is, there will your heart be also."*

THE BLESSED LIFE

Our Heavenly Father wants us to enjoy our life on the earth. We are His children! If we are not consumed by money and greedy for gain, if we steward our blessings properly, if we honor God with the firstfruits of all our increase through tithes and offerings, if we understand that we are blessed to be a blessing, if we embrace the awesome privilege we have to participate in God's cycle of blessing through the Kingdom of God so that the good news of the gospel can reach everyone, and if we concentrate on storing up eternal treasure in Heaven, then we can most certainly and without fear of judgment enjoy a rich, rewarding life of overflow and abundance with God's blessing. Our Heavenly Father will go far beyond just meeting our daily needs. He takes pleasure in prospering us and lavishing us with His love and blessings, both spiritually and materially. We are His children!

1 Timothy 6:17 (NIV) tell us, *"Command those who are rich in this present world not to be arrogant nor to put their hope in wealth, which is so uncertain, but to **put their hope in***

God, who richly provides us with everything for our enjoyment."

Proverbs 10:22 (AMP) also encourages us that, *"**The blessing of the Lord—it makes [truly] rich,** and He adds no sorrow with it [neither does toiling increase it]."*

Psalm 35:27 (AMP) proclaims, *"Let those who favor my righteous cause and have pleasure in my uprightness shout for joy and be glad and say continually, Let the Lord be magnified, **Who takes pleasure in the prosperity of His servant.**"*

Let no mistake be made, your Heavenly Father has given you all things for your enjoyment and satisfaction in this life. When you do His will, and cooperate with God's cycle of blessing, you can be assured God wants you to be well cared for and abundantly blessed. God's blessings are spiritual, natural, and material and you are blessed to enjoy all three. Your Heavenly Father wants to meet all your needs and go far beyond that to overflow so that you may fully enjoy your life. Your eternal life starts now, in this time!

Let's review God's intended cycle of blessing.

The Cycle of Blessing – Figure 1

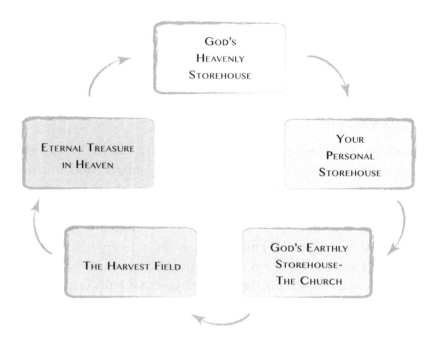

This cycle of blessing repeats again and again. Notice the movement and flow – God's resources are constantly moving through acts of giving and generosity. The more you give, the more God causes blessings to come to you in abundance through the hands of men. Luke 6:38 (NIV) tells us, *"Give, and it will be given to you. A good measure, pressed down, shaken together and running over, will be poured into your lap. For with the measure you use, it will be measured to you."*

The Cycle of Blessing – Figure 2

LOCATION	ACTION	MOVES TO	RESULT
God's Heavenly Storehouse	God opens the windows of Heaven; pours out blessings from His riches in glory	Your Personal Storehouse	Blessing and favor upon God's children
Your Personal Storehouse	Return the tithe (first tenth) Give offerings (free will generosity)	God's Earthly Storehouse -The Church	Honors God Increases blessing Devourer rebuked Provision protected Visible favor
God's Earthly Storehouse – The Church	Provide for ministers Care for God's House Send forth laborers into the harvest Share the gospel Care for the poor	The Harvest Field of the World The Lost The Hurting The Poor The Oppressed	Kingdom of God expanded The good news of Jesus preached everywhere
Harvest Field of the World	Many are saved and reconciled to God	God's Heavenly Storehouse	Harvest of Souls returns to the Lord in God's Heavenly Storehouse
God's Heavenly Storehouse	The souls of the redeemed are accepted into the Kingdom of God	God's presence for all eternity	You store up eternal treasure in Heaven

You sow bountifully, and therefore you reap bountifully. The more you participate in the building of the Kingdom of God, the greater the conduit you become for God's cycle of blessing. The more you give, the more that is given to you. God's blessings and abundance increase upon your life because you are demonstrating good stewardship, and God can trust you with greater and greater resources. You become a larger and larger conduit of blessing. You are a vessel of honor and increase. It is not difficult to release your finances into the Kingdom of God and to help others in need, because you know they will be multiplied and ultimately given back to you again in greater measure. You understand what it means to be blessed to be a blessing. You are storing up precious treasure in Heaven. You are faithful over little, knowing God will make you ruler over much. The more generous you are, the more opportunities that you will have to be generous. God promises to pour out such blessings upon you that you do not have room enough to receive them all!

You can enjoy God's goodness, favor, and blessings upon your life without guilt or condemnation because 1) you are God's child, 2) you are obedient to the Word of the Lord, 3) you are co-laboring with your Heavenly Father in the expansion of His Kingdom, 4) you are generous and kind to those who are in need, and 5) you understand your inheritance in the Lord. Your heart is pure and reverent toward God as you honor Him with the firstfruits of all your increase. You seek first the Kingdom of God and everything else shall be added to you as well (Matthew 6:33)!

RICHES IN GLORY

What are some of the blessings that will come to you from your Heavenly Father, that are now stored up for you in His riches in glory in Christ Jesus?

SPIRITUAL BLESSINGS
Eternal Life (through personal faith in Christ)
Presence of God
Unconditional Love
Justification and Redemption
Peace
Joy
Righteousness
Infilling of the Holy Spirit
Forgiveness of Sin
Fruit of the Spirit
Adoption
Inheritance
Name Written in the Book of Life
Authority over Demonic Spirits & Principalities
Endurance, Perseverance, and Tenacity
Steadfastness
Strength and Courage
Wisdom
Knowledge and Understanding
Discernment
Protection
The Devourer Rebuked
Hope
Faith
Purpose
Rest
"Well done, my good and faithful servant!"

NATURAL/MATERIAL BLESSINGS
Blessed Life on earth now in this time
Health and Divine Healing
Long Life Span
Youthfulness
Abundance and Overflow
Fulfillment of the Covenant with Patriarchs
Blessing of Abraham
Wealth and Prosperity
Expanded Territory
Ownership
Land
Houses
Businesses
All Needs Met
Debt Free
Ability to Give Generously
Multiple Streams of Income
Blessed Work
Rewarding Work
Promotions, Bonuses, and Raises
Loving Spouse
Blessed Womb
Unified Family
Healthy Children
Loving Relationships
Legacy – Ability to Leave Inheritances
Wealth Transfer

The cycle of blessing is God's plan to continually bless His children and bring in the harvest of the lost so that they, too, may enjoy eternal life with their Heavenly Father.

THE COUNTER-ATTACK

The enemy despises you and the Lord's plan to bless you. He is constantly at work to interrupt the flow of this cycle of blessing. The short-term objective is to disrupt your personal life by blocking and stealing your blessings. However, the long-term, big picture objective is to rob you of your relationship with God, and to block others from coming into a personal, eternal relationship with their Heavenly Father who loves them through Jesus Christ. Remember that the final result of God's cycle of blessing is the harvest of **souls** for eternity. That is the true treasure of Heaven!

The enemy has a counter-strategy to God's cycle of blessing. Let's look at the enemy's cycle of stealing, and break down the scheme he has devised to stop your financial breakthrough and the rich harvest the Lord intends for you.

7 | the cycle of stealing

T he thief does not come except to steal, and to kill, and to destroy. I have come that they may have life, and that they may have it more abundantly. *John 10:10 (NKJV)*

When you observe all of the immoral, illegal, unethical, and oppressive systems and institutions worldwide, have you ever wondered HOW Satan is able to finance and sustain such depravity all over the earth?

Think about it. The devil creates nothing. He came to the earth with nothing. In Luke 10:18-19 (NKJV), Jesus said, *"I saw Satan fall like lightning from heaven. Behold, I give you the authority to trample on serpents and scorpions, and over all the power of the enemy, and nothing shall by any means hurt you."*

God cast out Lucifer and the minor mutiny of fallen angels suddenly, without warning. Lucifer did not bring anything other than what is built into his being with him to the earth. So how is he funding his immoral and illegal enterprises on the earth? He does it by stealing and controlling the blessings intended for the children of God. He intercepts, steals, and snatches the blessings that are destined for you.

Remember Satan's intentions with the Trifold Attack. The enemy's first motivation is to **STEAL**. This attack is designed to steal your material blessings to ensure you do not have the finances necessary to meet your daily needs, provide for your family, fulfill your mission assignment on the earth, leave an inheritance for your children and grandchildren, and fund the work of the Kingdom of God to win souls. The strategy is to bring destruction to your life by taking away your basic needs, and to oppress you in a system of indebtedness that is a form of slavery. The stress of financial oppression opens the door to the Spirit of Infirmity, so that sickness and disease gain entry. The money and blessings he steals from you are used to fund his criminal and immoral enterprises. The enemy hopes to wear you down through discouragement and disillusionment so you will give up on your commitment to serve the Lord, and ultimately curse God.

SATAN'S STOCKPILE: THE STRONGMAN'S HOUSE

Satan opposes God's cycle of blessing by stealing and stockpiling the blessings of the children of God to fund his own illegal and immoral schemes and enterprises. God's blessings are intended to move from the storehouse of His bounty in Heaven, to the believer's personal storehouse, to God's earthly storehouse (the church), to the harvest field of the lost, and ultimately back to the Father in a rich harvest of souls saved. Satan's strategy is to disrupt the cycle of blessing and simply hoard what was taken for his own perverted purposes. There is no movement or blessing; he is simply stealing and stockpiling for his own selfish motives. Stealing and stockpiling, stealing and stockpiling. He is taking your blessings out of commission so they do not accomplish God's purpose in your life. He hates you and does not want you to enjoy any of the blessings of the Lord that are intended for you. He wants to stop the cycle of salvation to cause as many people as possible to suffer needlessly for eternity, forever separated from God.

After stealing from you, Satan stores up his booty in his version of a storehouse, which I will call Satan's stockpile. Isaiah 45:3 (NKJV) refers to this stockpile as *"treasures of darkness"* and *"hidden riches in secret places."* What are these treasures in darkness and hidden riches in secret places? They are the spiritual, natural, and material blessings stolen from the children of God, up to and including the souls of the unsaved.

If you were to visit Satan's stockpile in the spiritual realm, you would find a myriad of blessings he has stolen from you and your family over the years of your lifetime. You would find things like your dreams, your vision, and your creative ideas. You would find peace, joy, happiness, and loving relationships. Locked away you would uncover hope, faith, forgiveness, belief, trust, and encouragement. You would find buried treasures of virtue, integrity, honesty, righteousness, and obedience. You would uncover your health, strength, energy, and vitality.

Behind a door marked "DETOUR" you would find years of your life, your potential, and aborted purpose. You would discover promotions, raises, bonuses, job offers, and business concepts. You would locate lost contracts and broken business deals. You would find your hard-earned savings and investments. You would discover ample provision, abundant wealth, riches, and inheritances. All these things are rightfully yours. They belong to you. They are your blessings, your favor from God, and your inheritance as an heir of God and co-heir with Christ. Behind the last door marked "DESTROY" you would catch a gut-wrenching glimpse of the multitude of lost souls: the deceived, the discouraged, and the disillusioned.

Satan understands this is precious treasure and therefore his stockpile is heavily guarded. Matthew 12:29 refers to this guard as a Strongman. But even so, he is no match for our God! We see this in Matthew 12:29 (NLT), which tells us, *"For who is powerful enough to enter the house of a strong man like Satan and plunder his goods? Only someone even stronger—someone who could tie him up and then plunder his house."* We have the ability and the authority, in the mighty name of Jesus, to bind the Strongman and plunder his goods, which are ours in the first place! We are not to take on the Strongman in our human strength, but the weapons of our warfare are not carnal, but mighty in God for the pulling down of strongholds (2 Corinthians 10:4). We must use our spiritual weapons to bind the Strongman and plunder his goods, which are our stolen blessings! It is time to take back what rightfully belongs to you!

God has empowered you to:

1) **STOP** Satan's stealing and bring an immediate end to the home invasion already in progress,

2) **TAKE BACK** everything that has already been stolen that is rightfully yours, and

3) **ENFORCE** scriptural punishments for the act of the illegal trespass. Satan not only must return what was stolen, but he owes you damages for perpetrating the crime of stealing from you. It is illegal activity. He owes you a sevenfold payback on everything he has stolen from you. This is a scriptural

punishment you can enforce on all past wrongs (Proverbs 6:30-31).

God goes before you and has already secured the victory. Your role, once again, is to enforce it. Isaiah 45:2-3 (NKJV) tells us, *"I will go before you And make the crooked places straight; I will break in pieces the gates of bronze And cut the bars of iron. I will give you the treasures of darkness And hidden riches of secret places, That you may know that I, the Lord, Who calls you by your name, Am the God of Israel."*

Let's break down each of these three phases in detail to understand how the enemy steals from you, how you can stop it, and how you can reclaim what is rightfully yours, including the sevenfold restitution that is due to you. How does the enemy steal your blessings in the first place?

TEN WAYS
THE DEVIL STEALS YOUR BLESSINGS

The devil funds his criminal enterprises with the blessings of God's people. This started in the Garden of Eden with the deception of Eve, which led to the temptation and disobedience of Adam. Through this trickery, he stole their property and legal dominion over the Garden of Eden and all the earth, he introduced the sickness of sin to kill the body, and he attempted to destroy them eternally by fracturing their perfect relationship with God the Father (the Trifold Attack). We see this damage continue with Cain and Abel and throughout the Old Testament. Although sin was successfully introduced and passed to all mankind through the seed of Adam, God did not cut us off or cast us away. He immediately began to implement His redemptive plan to save us through His Son!

The devil uses ten primary schemes to steal your blessings.

Deception – he lies and deceives, just as he did from the beginning in the Garden of Eden. He wants you to be confused regarding God's promises, His commandments, and your birthright as a child of God (Genesis 3:1-13, John 8:44).

Disobedience – he seduces you to disobey the Word of God, to disqualify you from the blessings of obedience in the scripture (Ephesians 2:1-2, Ephesians 5:6).

Detainment – he attempts to intercept and oppose the answers to prayer and blessings that are en route to you in the spiritual realm (Daniel 10:1-14).

Delay – he places obstacles in your path to stall you and slow you down, and to impede the actions of others that are connected to your blessings and purpose (Genesis 39-40, Proverbs 13:12).

Distraction – he interferes with your mental focus and concentration to keep you from completing the tasks related to your mission assignment and divine purpose. He seduces you to procrastinate and put off what you should be completing today. He knows that God will bless the work of your hands, so distraction comes to keep you from completing that work in a timely manner, if you complete it at all. The enemy attempts to disrupt the timing of God's blessings by keeping you out of place and off schedule (Matthew 25:1-13, Luke 9:61-62).

Detours – he sets traps and schemes to get you off track from your purpose. These are longer-term distractions that can take you completely off course from your purpose and the main road to God's plan for your life. Detours often come in the form of people sent across your path to take you off course and negate your anointing in the Lord (Judges 16, 2 Samuel 11).

Diversions – he takes the blessings that are meant for you and diverts the actions of men so the blessings do not reach you. The blessings from your employment are often stolen in this manner. Raises, promotions, bonuses, and other blessings are diverted and given to others, or delayed (Genesis 31:5-7, James 5:4).

Devours – he devours your provision and supply as quickly as possible once it reaches you. He eats up your provision through debt and interest-bearing loans, increasing your cost of living, and causing accidents, illness, unexpected bills, and unnecessary fees. (Refer to Chapter 2, Figure 4 - The Trifold Attack, "Manifestations of Poverty and Lack" and Malachi 3.) He attempts to quickly devour your spiritual blessings by 1) snatching away the Word that is sown into your heart before you understand it, 2) bringing trouble or persecution because of the Word to cause you to fall away, or 3) choking out the Word with the worries of this life and the deceitfulness of riches (Matthew 13:18-22).

Discouragement – he causes you to focus on difficult circumstances or negativity in your life so you will stop pursuing the plans and purposes of God. This may begin with justifiable sorrow or sadness (Romans 9:2). Left unchecked and allowed to grow, this escalates to disappointment, discouragement, and ultimately despair (Proverbs 15:13).

Despair – he intensifies discouragement to the point that you feel completely disillusioned with life so you will give up. Galatians 6:9 (NIV) tells us, "*Let us not become weary in doing good, for at the proper time we will reap a harvest if we do not give up.*" The enemy wants to discourage you and create such disappointment that you will fall into the dregs of despair. In a state of hopelessness, you will give up on God and on your life. He hopes you will die in this state (Isaiah 61:3, Psalm 69:20).

Which of these tactics is the enemy attempting to use against you? Are you lacking knowledge of the Word of God, so that the enemy can easily twist the Word, trick you, and take your blessings? Do you battle distractions? Do detours frequently take you off course? Are you prone to feeling discouragement or even despair?

Two major components of financial breakthrough are to 1) understand the spiritual forces that are constantly working against you, and 2) use your power and authority in the name of Jesus to break down these spiritual barriers and combat them.

You must recognize the ten strategies the enemy uses against you. You can arrest the demonic forces in the act of stealing. What you bind on earth (declare as forbidden) will be bound in heaven (Matthew 18:18). Bind the enemy and cancel all assignments and manifestations set in motion against you. Look at your actions and determine how you may be cooperating with the enemy's plan of attack. Take action to submit to God and resist the devil. He must flee from you (James 4:7)!

If you are easily deceived, commit to renewing your mind with the Word of the Lord (you are doing that right now)! If you are distracted, take back your focus and move forward with purpose. If you have fallen for a detour, eliminate the toxic relationships and time-wasting projects sent as counterfeit decoys to get you off course from God's plan for your life.

If you are discouraged by a setback, or if it seems your dreams have been stolen, shake off that spirit of heaviness and put on your garment of praise! Your dream may have been delayed, but it has not been denied. You have to shake it off and start again, immediately. Don't waste another day being discouraged by what did not work out in the past. Every day that you wallow in the past is another day the enemy can successfully steal from you. Today is the day that you must say, "STOP!" By praising, praying, obeying the Word of God, tithing, giving, planning, producing, and making wise financial decisions, you can defeat the schemes of the evil one set in motion to steal your provision and promises from the Lord.

TAKING BACK WHAT HAS BEEN STOLEN

Your first act of warfare is to stop the process of stealing that is currently underway. You must become aware of what is occurring and stop the enemy's schemes of deception, distraction, disobedience, and discouragement that are operating in your life. Second, you must begin the process of taking back what is rightfully yours that the enemy has stolen in the past. In the name of Jesus, you have the authority to demand that the enemy return what he has stolen and make restitution to you. It is illegal activity. You can place a demand on past wrongs. You can bind the Strongman and spoil his goods.

When I began to get the revelation of this concept, I realized that we are often too passive and accepting of the enemy's violations. We cannot have the attitude, *"Oh well, what's done is done. There is nothing I can do."* No! Begin to declare now that what has been done will be undone, reversed, replaced, and restored in the name of Jesus. The enemy is under your feet. He must bow to the name of Jesus. You cannot be passive. You must be purposeful in your pursuit of the blessings of God. Matthew 11:12 (NIV) tells us, *"From the days of John the Baptist until now, the kingdom of* *heaven has been **forcefully advancing**, and **forceful men** lay hold of it.*" You must be forceful and powerful in your commitment to defend what is yours, lay hold of the blessings of God, and advance the Kingdom. Breakthrough is violent. You must vehemently reject limiting beliefs in your own mindset, and violently resist the demonic forces opposing you in the spiritual realm. You are not physically violent; you are spiritually armed and dangerous ... armed with the Word of God and dangerous to the enemy!

Matthew 11:12 (AMP) shows us this critical attitude: *"And from the days of John the Baptist until the present time, the kingdom of heaven has endured violent assault, and **violent men seize it by force [as a precious prize**—a share in the heavenly kingdom is sought with most ardent zeal and intense exertion].*" Does that describe your attitude? Are you seizing the Kingdom of God as a precious prize worth fighting for? You will encounter resistance en route to your breakthrough. Passivity will make you an easy victim, easy prey for the evil one. Recognize your authority as a child of God and enforce it in the name of Jesus.

In addition to developing a warring attitude, it is important to ensure you are not focusing on the people that the enemy may have used to steal from you. Many times, people are unknowing pawns in the spiritual chess game the enemy is attempting to execute against you. It is important that you do not hold unforgiveness or bitterness in your heart toward people. Ephesians 6:12 (NLT) tells us, *"**For we are not fighting against flesh-and-blood enemies**, but against evil rulers and authorities of the unseen world, against mighty powers in this dark world, and against evil spirits in the heavenly places.*"

You are dealing with the actions of people, but you are combating the spiritual wickedness that is motivating their actions. When the Holy Spirit began to illuminate to me the financial provision that the enemy had stolen from me, He showed me a series of promotions I had clearly earned throughout my corporate career that had been delayed or denied. The enemy had executed this tactic, a combination of satanic delay and diversion, numerous times over the course of my career. The same tactic was used again and again from company to company. Different people were involved. I never saw the interrelationship of these events until I stepped back and looked at it in the spiritual realm, guided by the Holy Spirit. I was an excellent employee and an outstanding performer, always earning numerous awards and recognition for my leadership, management, and results. The mishandling of my promotions never made sense to me, but I hadn't seen the satanic scheme that was at work from a spiritual perspective. I just accepted each individual occurrence with disappointment and a resilient attitude. I would bounce back, press forward, and work harder.

I am thankful that with perseverance, my career was very successful; however, in retrospect, I realize I could have accomplished exponentially more, given significantly more to the Kingdom, and blessed many more people had I not incurred these setbacks. The enemy had stolen from me again and again using a variation of the same attack. In one instance, he used the same person multiple times, four years in a row! I finally had had enough and took action in the natural realm. However, I harbored deep unforgiveness and bitterness toward the person involved. Every time the person crossed my mind, I would feel that anger rise up in my heart. The Holy Spirit showed me I needed to forgive the individual and focus on the enemy behind the scheme. I needed to go after the enemy and take back what was rightfully mine. Restitution was due to me for those trespasses. I needed to shift my focus.

I immediately prayed for the person, and I felt a huge weight lifted! Now I was in the proper posture (submission to God) and position (delegated authority in Christ) to fight the real fight, resist the devil, and demand restitution from the evil one who was behind the thievery for decades. I was overwhelmed with praise. I began to rejoice and praise God! What was meant for evil would now be turned around for my good (Genesis 50:20)! I was set up for divine promotion and increase! I was set up for multiplied blessings! All things work together for good for those who love the Lord and all called according to His purpose (Romans 8:28). My focus was now purposeful, not personal. With the right target in sight, I could take back what the enemy had stolen and enforce the punishment due for the trespass.

Is there a situation in your life where you must shift your focus from flesh and blood to the thief at work in the spiritual realm? Have you been passed over for promotion? Is your manager at work harsh and oppressive, withholding your fair wages, raises, and bonuses? Have you experienced an unfair contract or unscrupulous business deal? Has your business been impacted by a dishonest partner? Are you focusing on the person, and not the problem of spiritual wickedness? Do you need to forgive someone, and let go of a situation from the past that is still bothering you? Recognize that the individual is being used as a weapon formed against you. They are the vehicle through which the fiery dart is being launched. Forgive them, pray for them, and shift your focus to the spiritual realm where the real enemy is at work, and your total victory is complete. Praise God that what was meant for evil is about to be turned for your good! No weapon formed against you will prosper. The individuals involved cannot permanently harm you; all they accomplished was to set you up for a multiplied, compounded, comprehensive blessing of restoration!

ENFORCING SCRIPTURAL PUNISHMENTS

When the enemy trespasses on your life as a believer, do you realize that you not only have the authority in Christ to stop the trespass, but you can also enforce scriptural punishments for the unlawful act? That's true! You can stop the trespass, bind the Strongman, spoil his goods, take back what is rightfully yours, and demand and enforce restitution from the thief.

2 Corinthians 10:3-6 (NKJV) tells us, *"For though we walk in the flesh, we do not war according to the flesh. For the weapons of our warfare are not carnal but mighty in God for pulling down strongholds, casting down arguments and every high thing that exalts itself against the knowledge of God, bringing every thought into captivity to the obedience of Christ, **and being ready to punish all disobedience when your obedience is fulfilled.**"*

When you live in obedience to the Word of God by faith, you have the authority in Christ to punish disobedience. You can enforce punishments outlined in the scripture. With respect to stealing, let's examine the punishment that is contained in the Word of God.

Proverbs 6:30-31 (AMP) tells us, *"Men do not despise a thief if he steals to satisfy himself when he is hungry; **But if he is found out, he must restore seven times [what he stole]; he must give the whole substance of his house [if necessary—to meet his fine].**"*

In the instance of a thief who steals to satisfy hunger, we can have compassion and not despise him for his motive. *Yet, even in such cases where thievery would be understandable,* the thief is **still** required to repay seven times what he stole. Restitution is set at a sevenfold payback.

When we think of the enemy, he is not stealing to satisfy hunger or any other remotely justifiable reason. He is stealing from you because he hates you. He hates that you worship God. He hates that the Holy Spirit dwells on the very throne of your heart. He hates that you honor God. He wants to stop the plan of God from moving forward in your life. He is stealing simply to hoard and stockpile the blessings of the children of God to use them for decadence, depravity, and to ultimately destroy your life. You should have a sensation of holy anger toward the evil one at all times. You should have a relentless motivation to enforce justice. Your role is to command the thief to pay back to you all that is owed.

THE SEVENFOLD PAYBACK

God's system of restoration always leaves you in a position where you are better off than you were when you encountered trouble. Your Heavenly Father goes beyond making you whole. He ensures that your restoration includes a multiplied blessing. He multiplies back to you what has been lost.

Our court system uses a similar process. To pay back what is rightfully yours would be considered **compensatory damages**. You are fairly compensated for what has been taken from you. In addition, **punitive damages** are assessed for the wrong-doing – the crime that was committed against you.

The enemy cannot simply stop stealing from you and leave it at that. He cannot simply return to you your stolen goods. He has crossed the bloodline of protection that you have in the Lord Jesus Christ. This is an egregious violation in the spiritual realm. The **punitive damages** owed to you for this infraction equal the sevenfold return. You are owed seven times that which has been taken from you. It is a scriptural punishment – a spiritual fine – that you have every right to enforce on the enemy for crossing the bloodline and attempting to steal from you.

As believers we must stop giving in and giving up when the enemy steals from us! It is unacceptable. We must know the promises of God and enforce our authority. The devil does not get a free pass to wreak havoc in your life. When you bind the thief, the Devourer, and cancel all of his manifestations of stealing he must, by the authority of the name of Jesus, and enforced by the blood of Jesus:

- **Stop** stealing from you

- **Return** what he has stolen from you, and

- **Pay back** seven times what he has stolen from you.

Your restitution is not complete until all three of these actions have been completed.

I believe this is what is meant in Deuteronomy 28:7 (NKJV), which tells us, *"The Lord will cause your enemies who rise against you to be defeated before your face;* ***they shall come out against you one way and flee before you seven ways.****"* The enemy may come against you with one scheme, but he must repay seven times that which was stolen. Seven will return what was stolen from you, and then flee before your face.

Now that you know you have a right to impose the scriptural punishment of Proverbs 6:30-31, it is time to begin enforcing it. Use the following process to take back what has been stolen from you.

Identify what has been stolen. Take a moment to think back over your life, and consider all that the enemy has successful stolen from you in the past. Allow the Holy Spirit to remind you and bring back to your remembrance the attacks of the thief on your life. Take time to reflect on every spiritual, natural, and material blessing the enemy has disrupted and taken from you and your family. Write them down.

Make a list of everything you remember. Look at the patterns – the repeated offenses – where the enemy has used a particular scheme successfully, so he has used it again and again. Look at the impact on your personal life, your family, and your resources.

Forgive the people involved. Next, make a list of the people who were involved in each scenario. Take time to forgive them, pray for them, and release the issue in your heart. Make sure you are not harboring any unforgiveness or bitterness.

Repent of disobedience. Confess and repent of any actions where you were disobedient to the Word of God (1 John 1:9). Change your actions to submit to the Word of God. You may punish disobedience when your obedience is fulfilled (2 Corinthians 10:3-6).

Rebuke the Devourer. Stop the stealing already in progress. Return the tithe to the Lord and give your offerings, knowing God will rebuke the Devourer for your sake. His divine protection is over your provision (Malachi 3). Bind the work of the Devourer and cancel all manifestations (schemes) set in motion against you (Matthew 18:18). In the name and authority of Jesus, command the enemy to cease and desist. Extinguish every fiery dart (manifestation) set in motion against you (Ephesians 6:16).

Bind the Strongman. To take back what is yours, bind the Strongman to spoil his goods. The enemy hoards and guards your stolen blessings. He steals and stockpiles. His treasures of darkness are your blessings! It is your provision from the

Lord. You have the authority in the name of Jesus to take back what is rightfully yours (Matthew 12:29).

Enforce Scriptural Punishments. Demand the sevenfold payback which includes your compensatory and punitive damages for everything the thief has stolen from you over your lifetime. Stealing from you is a trespass against the blood of Jesus. Command the enemy to release your restitution. The sevenfold payback is a punishment you can enforce now in this time through prayer and spiritual warfare (Proverbs 6:30-31).

Stand your ground. Do not stop. Having done all the crisis demands, stand firmly in your place. Continue to pray and stand your ground against the attacks of the evil one. Don't tolerate the trespass! The stealing must stop, your blessings must be released, and the sevenfold payback must be paid.

Be strengthened by the Word of the Lord in Ephesians 6:11-13 (AMP) which encourages us, *"Put on God's whole armor [the armor of a heavy-armed soldier which God supplies], that you may be able successfully to **stand up against [all] the strategies and the deceits of the devil.***

For we are not wrestling with flesh and blood [contending only with physical opponents], but against the despotisms, against the powers, against [the master spirits who are] the world rulers of this present darkness, against the spirit forces of wickedness in the heavenly (supernatural) sphere.

*Therefore put on God's complete armor, that you may be able to resist and stand your ground on the evil day [of danger], and, **having done all [the crisis demands], to stand [firmly in your place]."***

Amen! Be encouraged! You have the victory!

8 | the warnings of wealth

I n addition to being on guard for the schemes that the
devil uses to steal your blessings, you must also be on
guard for the workings of the enemy within: the sin nature.
Your flesh nature is inclined to operate by destructive, selfish,
and sinful motives. Although wealth and riches are intended
to be powerful, useful blessings from the Lord, if your spirit
man is not in control, and if your mind is not renewed, wealth
and riches can bring out the very worst in your sin nature.

Think about the use of fire in your home. Fire is neutral. It is
neither good nor evil. In the stove, furnace, or fireplace, it
brings heat, warmth, comfort, hot meals, hot water, and more.
Yet, outside of these controlled environments, without
proper containment and supervision, fire will quickly
burn down your house.

Money, like fire, in and of itself is neutral; it is neither good
nor evil. It is an inanimate object. It is a circulating medium
of exchange, a measure of value, and a means of payment
for goods and services. Money is the currency we use to
establish value and facilitate transactions in our society.
In the hands of a mature believer with self-control and godly
motives, wealth is a tremendous blessing that can transform

the lives of millions. In the hands of an immature believer, lacking knowledge of the purpose and priorities of wealth, and driven by greed, selfishness, and carnal desires, wealth can quickly turn into a weapon of mass destruction. It will burn down your house.

Consider your car. Your automobile is neither good nor evil. It is neutral. In the hands of a responsible driver, it is a powerful vehicle to transport you from one place to another, and a valuable blessing and time-saver that greatly simplifies your life. Yet, in the hands of a reckless, irresponsible, or drunk driver, the same vehicle quickly turns into a deadly weapon, destroying the lives of all in its path. The car is neutral; the driver determines if it is a blessing or a curse. That is why it is required that you learn how to safely operate your vehicle, and obey the rules of the road. Before getting behind the wheel, you must pass a written exam to test your knowledge of the law, and a road test with a State Trooper who will assess your driving skills.

As a parent, you would never give the keys to your vehicle to your children if they cannot drive safely. They would injure or potentially kill themselves and others. You love your children entirely too much to do that! Your Heavenly Father is much the same way! He is so loving and gracious toward you that He will not bless you with His wealth beyond your capacity for good stewardship. Often, believers pray for blessings they are not ready to properly handle. God loves you too much to injure you. He will not grant you godly wealth, riches, abundance, and material blessings beyond your ability to manage them properly. In the same way that your vehicle becomes a weapon in the hands of a reckless driver, wealth becomes a weapon and a means of total destruction in the hands of a reckless, immature steward.

Many, intoxicated with the love of money, are unfit to drive the vehicle of prosperity. Others are joy-riders, blowing through their money as fast as they earn it. Others are speeders, loading up on lottery tickets, the latest get-rich-quick schemes, and not-so-legal side hustles. Wealth gained in haste, illegally, or with wrong motives will bring you to ruin.

God will not give you a blessing you are not ready to manage. You need to get your driver's license first. You must pass your driver's test. Your skills, attitude, and aptitude will be tested repeatedly. You must prove yourself to be reliable, faithful, diligent, and trustworthy. When you are faithful and trustworthy over little, He will make you ruler over much (Matthew 25:21).

Now please note, there is a big difference between **godly wealth**, abundance, and overflow and **worldly wealth** and riches. You can most certainly ignore the development process and pursue worldly wealth on your own, just as you can steal a car, drive without a license, drive with a suspended license, or drive without insurance. Many people do. You can "get on your grind," toil, overwork, and strive in your own strength; you can take a shortcut (which is the devil's crafty counterfeit for the favor of God); or you can be ruthless, manipulative, back-stabbing, callous, cold, and calculating to climb the corporate ladder, whatever the cost (*"It's just business."*). You can be selfish, stockpile, heap, and hoard your wealth; you can take advantage of others, withhold, discriminate, and oppress; you can sell out, compromise your morals, and profitably pander to the world's voracious appetite for sensuality and scandal; and you can flash the cash, squander, show off, and show out. You can do any of these things, and the world will love you. But it will cost you. Big time.

Worldly wealth always, and I repeat, ALWAYS, comes at a price. At the end of the day, there is a toll and you will have to pay up. You may become very rich by societal standards, but you will lose your peace of mind, your spouse, your children, your family, your health, your life, or your salvation in the process. Read today's newspaper and look at all of the loss of life over money – murders and mayhem with money at the root. Look at the celebrity pages and soberly consider the latest drug overdose or suicide of the super-wealthy. Consider those in your very own circle of friends and family who would gladly turn back the clock, and take a completely different course of action, if only they could get their spouse, their family, or their health back in the process. Even lottery winners lament the toll the hasty riches took from their lives. If you prosper the worldly way and lose everything of eternal value to you, what have you gained?

Matthew 16:26 (NLT) warns us, *"And what do you benefit if you **gain the whole world but lose your own soul?** Is anything worth more than your soul?"* The worldly way to wealth always comes at great personal cost. It will take its toll on you. It is a price that is far too high to pay and it is completely unnecessary.

On the contrary, Proverbs 10:22 (AMP) encourages us, *"The blessing of the Lord—it makes [truly] rich, and **He adds no sorrow with it [neither does toiling increase it].** As a child of God, if you follow the plan and purpose of God for your life, and cooperate with the cycle of blessing, His divine favor is upon you! One touch of God's favor on your life can do what years of toil and struggle could never do. The blessings of obedience, the favor of God, and the power of God will prosper you far beyond your wildest dreams – exceedingly, abundantly above all you could dare ask, think, or imagine (Ephesians 3:20)!

Godly riches are holistic. Your blessings are spiritual, natural, and material. You are financially wealthy and generous with righteousness, perfect peace, and joy in your heart. Your family is whole and abundantly blessed. You are encircled with loving, lasting relationships. You are stronger, healthier, and more vital than ever. You are enjoying and loving your life. You are not striving and struggling to hold it together. You are a blessing and a beacon of hope to others. Each day presents another exciting opportunity to be a blessing and generously help others. Money serves you — you are not serving money. Godly success looks and feels completely different than worldly gain.

However, to prosper in this manner, you have to get your driver's license. You have to pass your driver's test. God will not entrust you with the magnitude of the financial blessings He has in store for you until you can handle it. That is why 3 John 2 (NKJV) encourages us, *"Beloved, I pray that you may **prosper in all things** and be in health, **just as your soul prospers**."* You have to renew your mind. As you renew your money mindset to the Word of God, and subdue the cravings and carnal nature of the flesh, God's favor on your life will abound. You are serving God, not an ulterior motive for selfish gain. You are now in God's cycle of blessing. He takes great pleasure in prospering you! Psalm 35:27 (NKJV) tells us, *"Let them shout for joy and be glad, Who favor my righteous cause; And let them say continually, 'Let the Lord be magnified, **Who has pleasure in the prosperity of His servant.**'"*

To gain godly riches and abundance, we must heed the scriptural warnings of wealth and prepare properly. There are many warnings in the scripture that address the problematic results of being greedy for gain, and mishandling wealth. These warnings are not an indictment against money, wealth, or material blessings! Money is neutral. It is neither good nor evil. Wealth does not *change* your nature; it simply *exposes* your nature. If you are carnally minded, selfish, and greedy, that will be apparent in how you handle your money. If you are spiritually minded, generous, and responsible, that will be apparent in how you handle the abundant blessings of wealth that will come under your stewardship.

The warnings of wealth in the scripture address the aspects of the sin nature that will be exposed, and that will control your actions when you attain wealth, riches, and material gain. Wealth simply magnifies who you already are. If you have not subdued your sin nature, the drives of the flesh will take over when the potential for financial gain manifests itself.

James 4:2-3 (NIV) warns us, *"You do not have because you do not ask God. When you ask, you do not receive, because you ask with wrong motives, that you may spend what you get on your pleasures."*

If you are spiritually minded, and operate in the fruit of the spirit which includes self-control, God can trust you with great riches. You are cooperating with His cycle of blessing. You are blessed to be a blessing. There is no limit to the magnitude of blessing that can be entrusted to you when you keep God first and the cycle of blessing moving forward.

THE EIGHT WARNINGS OF WEALTH

There are eight warnings of wealth in the scripture. Each exposes a different drive in the sin nature that we must subdue within ourselves to inherit and properly steward the abundant blessings of the Lord.

The Eight Warnings of Wealth – Figure 1

WARNING	DRIVE OF THE SIN NATURE	SCRIPTURE REFERENCE
Idolatry	Serving Money	Matthew 6:24 (NIV)
		Matthew 16:26 (NLT)
		Luke 12:21 (NLT)
		Psalm 49:5-9 (NIV)
Greed	Love of Money	Ecclesiastes 5:10 (AMP), (MSG)
		Habakkuk 2:5 (NLT)
		Luke 12:15 (NLT)
		1 Timothy 6:6-10 (NIV)
		2 Timothy 3:2 (AMP)
Pride and Arrogance	Boasting of Money	Psalm 49:5-9 (NIV)
		Jeremiah 9:23-24 (AMP)
		Ezekiel 28:4-7 (NIV)
		1 Timothy 6:17-19 (NKJV)
		2 Timothy 3:2 (AMP)
Self-Sufficiency	Confidence in Money; Confidence in Personal Ability	Deuteronomy 8:17-18 (NIV)
		Proverbs 18:11 (MSG)
		1 Timothy 6:17-19 (NKJV)
		Ezekiel 28:4-7 (NIV)
		Zephaniah 3:1-2 (AMP)
Toiling	Overworking for Money	Psalm 127:1-2 (NIV)
		Proverbs 10:22 (AMP)
		Proverbs 23:4-5 (NLT)
		Mark 4:18-19 (NIV)
Squandering	Wasting Money; Wild Living	Proverbs 21:20 (NLT)
		Proverbs 29:3 (NIV)
		Luke 15:11-14 (NLT)
Hoarding	Stockpiling; Withholding Money	Ecclesiastes 5:13-15 (NLT)
		Psalm 39:6 (NIV)
		Psalm 73:12 (NIV)
		Proverbs 11:24 (NKJV)

WARNING	DRIVE OF THE SIN NATURE	SCRIPTURE REFERENCE
Oppression	Dominating Others Who Lack Money; Cruelty, Abuse, and Repression	Leviticus 19:13 (AMP)
		Psalm 62:10 (NLT)
		Proverbs 14:31 (NIV)
		Habakkuk 2:9 (NLT)
		James 5:1-4 (MSG), (NLT)

2 Timothy 3:1-5 (AMP) describes all of these drives of the sin nature working together in totality: *"But understand this, that in the last days will come (set in) perilous times of great stress and trouble [hard to deal with and hard to bear].*

*For people will be **lovers of self and [utterly] self-centered, lovers of money and aroused by an inordinate [greedy] desire for wealth, proud and arrogant and contemptuous boasters**. They will be **abusive** (blasphemous, scoffing), **disobedient** to parents, **ungrateful**, unholy and profane.*

*[They will be] without natural [human] affection (**callous and inhuman**), **relentless** (admitting of no truce or appeasement); [they will be] slanderers (false accusers, troublemakers), intemperate and **loose in morals and conduct, uncontrolled** and fierce, haters of good.*

*[They will be] **treacherous** [betrayers], rash, [and] **inflated with self-conceit. [They will be] lovers of sensual pleasures and vain amusements** more than and rather than lovers of God.*

*For [although] they hold a form of piety (true religion), they deny and reject and are strangers to the power of it [**their***

*conduct belies the genuineness of their profession].
Avoid [all] such people [turn away from them]."*

These aspects of the sin nature are in all of us. They are the works of the flesh. Your job is to take dominion over these drives, and subdue them by the Word of God. Unchecked, these strong drives of the sin nature will destroy your life. Let's take a closer look at each one.

IDOLATRY – SERVING MONEY

Idolatry is defined as the worship of a physical object as a god, or excessive devotion to a person or thing. If money becomes a more important pursuit and a greater love than your relationship with God, then money has now become an idol. Instead of serving God, you are now serving money. It has usurped the place of worship in your heart. Mammon literally means "the treasure a person trusts in." Matthew 6:24 (AMP) tells us, *"No one can serve two masters; for either he will hate the one and love the other, or he will stand by and be devoted to the one and despise and be against the other. You cannot serve God and mammon (deceitful riches, money, possessions, or whatever is trusted in)."* We must guard against allowing the sin nature to gravitate toward serving money. Your job, your business, or your investments can all become idols, if you trust them as your source instead of trusting God as your Source for everything. We must seek first the Kingdom of God and His righteousness, and everything else will be added (Matthew 6:33).

*No one can serve two masters. Either you will hate the one and love the other, or you will be devoted to the one and despise the other. **You cannot serve both God and money.** Matthew 6:24 (NIV)*

*And what do you benefit if you **gain the whole world but lose your own soul**? Is anything worth more than your soul?*
Matthew 16:26 (NLT)

*Yes, a person is a **fool to store up earthly wealth** but not have a rich relationship with God.*
Luke 12:21 (NLT)

*Why should I fear when evil days come, when wicked deceivers surround me — those who **trust in their wealth and boast of their great riches**? **No one can redeem the life of another** or give to God a ransom for them — the ransom for a life is costly, no payment is ever enough — so that they should live on forever and not see decay.*
Psalm 49:5-9 (NIV)

GREED – THE LOVE OF MONEY

Greed is an intense, excessive, and selfish desire to have more of something, especially money. Greed is a ravenous hunger for more that can never be satisfied. No matter how much you have, it is never enough. 1 Timothy 6:10 must be one of the most misquoted scriptures of all time. Money is *not* the root of all evil. You need money to manage your life! Money is neutral – neither good nor evil. Greed – *the love of money* – is a root of all kinds of evil. Greed is one of the strongest and most destructive appetites of the sin nature. Review the following scriptures that address the warning of wealth related to greed.

The one who loves money is never satisfied *with money, Nor the one who loves wealth with big profits. More smoke.*
Ecclesiastes 5:10 (MSG)

*Wealth is treacherous, and **the arrogant are never at rest**. They open their mouths as wide as the grave, and like death, **they are never satisfied**. In their greed they have gathered up many nations and swallowed many peoples.*
Habakkuk 2:5 (NLT)

*Then he said, "Beware! **Guard against every kind of greed**. Life is not measured by how much you own."*
Luke 12:15 (NLT)

*But godliness with contentment is great gain. For we brought nothing into the world, and we can take nothing out of it. But if we have food and clothing, we will be content with that. Those who want to get rich fall into temptation and a trap and into many foolish and harmful desires that plunge people into ruin and destruction. For **the love of money is a root of all kinds of evil**. Some people, **eager for money**, have wandered from the faith and pierced themselves with many griefs.*
1 Timothy 6:6-10 (NIV)

*For people will be lovers of self and [utterly] self-centered, **lovers of money and aroused by an inordinate [greedy] desire for wealth, proud and arrogant** and contemptuous boasters. They will be abusive (blasphemous, scoffing), disobedient to parents, ungrateful, unholy and profane.*
2 Timothy 3:2 (AMP)

PRIDE AND ARROGANCE – BOASTING OF MONEY

Pride and arrogance lead to boasting about money. Once a person has prospered, the sin nature wants to take all of the credit and glory for the accomplishments. Pride means that you feel that you are better or more important than others because of your wealth. Arrogance is defined as an insulting way of thinking or behaving that comes from believing that you are better, smarter, or more important than other people. If your wealth causes you to feel pride and arrogance, or the desire to boast or brag about your riches, your sin nature is in control. We can do nothing without the Lord giving us the very breath we breathe. We must be mindful to give our Heavenly Father all the honor and glory for our accomplishments, and maintain an attitude of humility.

Thus says the Lord: Let not the wise and skillful person glory and boast in his wisdom and skill; let not the mighty and powerful person glory and boast in his strength and power; **let not the person who is rich** *[in physical gratification and earthly wealth]* **glory and boast in his [temporal satisfactions and earthly] riches***; But let him who glories glory in this: that he understands and knows Me [personally and practically, directly discerning and recognizing My character], that I am the Lord, Who practices loving-kindness, judgment, and righteousness in the earth, for in these things I delight, says the Lord.* **Jeremiah 9:23-24 (AMP)**

By your wisdom and understanding you have gained wealth for yourself and amassed gold and silver in your treasuries. By your great skill in trading you have increased your wealth, and **because of your wealth your heart has grown proud***. Therefore this is what the Sovereign Lord says: "Because you think you are wise, as wise as a god, I am going to bring foreigners against you, the most ruthless of nations; they will draw their swords against your beauty and wisdom and pierce your shining splendor."* **Ezekiel 28:4-7 (NIV)**

*Why should I fear when evil days come, when wicked deceivers surround me — those who **trust in their wealth** and **boast of their great riches**? No one can redeem the life of another or give to God a ransom for them — the ransom for a life is costly, no payment is ever enough — so that they should live on forever and not see decay.* **Psalm 49:5-9 (NIV)**

Self-Sufficiency — Confidence in Money

Self-sufficiency sets in if we begin to believe we have produced wealth and riches on our own, apart from God. Our flesh nature wants to take credit and operate independently from a complete reliance on the Lord. The flesh has a false sense of autonomy and capability. Whatever you produce, remember that God gave you the gifts, talents, skills, abilities, power, and intellect to produce it. Confidence in money comes when we begin to feel a sense of safety, security, and protection due to our wealth instead of from God. Your financial condition can change in an instant. Be sure that you are confident in the Lord God Almighty who is your Strong Tower.

*You may say to yourself, "**My power and the strength of my hands have produced this wealth for me.**" But remember the Lord your God, for it is he who gives you the ability to produce wealth, and so confirms his covenant, which he swore to your ancestors, as it is today.* **Deuteronomy 8:17-18 (NIV)**

*Woe to her that is rebellious and polluted, the oppressing city [Jerusalem]! She did not listen to and heed the voice [of God]; she accepted no correction or instruction; **she trusted not in the Lord** [nor leaned on or was confident*

*in Him, **but was confident in her own wealth**]; she drew not near to her God [but to the god of Baal or Molech].*
Zephaniah 3:1-2 (AMP)

*The rich think their wealth protects them; **they imagine themselves safe** behind it.*
Proverbs 18:11 (MSG)

*Command those who are rich in this present age not to be haughty, **nor to trust in uncertain riches but in the living God**, who gives us richly all things to enjoy. Let them do good, that they be rich in good works, ready to give, willing to share, storing up for themselves a good foundation for the time to come, that they may lay hold on eternal life.*
1 Timothy 6:17-19 (NKJV)

TOILING — OVERWORKING FOR MONEY

Toiling means to work very hard for a long time; to move slowly with a lot of effort. To toil is to plod, struggle, and strive. Toiling is long, strenuous, fatiguing labor. We are no longer under the curse of toiling (Genesis 3:17-19). When we are working in our human strength, often with great resistance, we can feel the sensation of toiling. God has not called you to toil! Do not confuse toiling with perseverance, diligence, or determination. Toiling is slow, arduous work that does not have the blessing of the Lord upon it. It is grueling. It is drudgery.

You may be working on a job or in a career that is not aligned with your purpose; therefore, you are not anointed to do it. You may be pushing ahead of the Lord's timing on a project or in a business. You may be operating out of greed. If you are working outside of the plans and purposes of God, it can often become toiling.

Unfortunately, much of corporate America has adopted toiling as the standard work ethic. It is expected of you to overwork, sacrifice your health, and sacrifice your family to get ahead. You must push back against this spirit of the age. When you work hard, using your highest gifts and talents, with diligence, excellence, and the anointing of the Lord, you will see progress, productivity, and profit.

Unless the Lord builds the house, the builders labor in vain. Unless the Lord watches over the city, the guards stand watch in vain. **In vain you rise early and stay up late, toiling for food to eat**— *for he grants sleep to those he loves.* ***Psalm 127:1-2 (NIV)***

*The blessing of the Lord—it makes [truly] rich, and He adds no sorrow with it [**neither does toiling increase it**].* ***Proverbs 10:22 (Amplified)***

Don't wear yourself out trying to get rich*. Be wise enough to know when to quit. In the blink of an eye wealth disappears, for it will sprout wings and fly away like an eagle.* ***Proverbs 23:4-5 (NLT)***

Still others, like seed sown among thorns, hear the word; but **the worries of this life, the deceitfulness of wealth and the desires for other things** *come in and choke the word, making it unfruitful.* ***Mark 4:18-19 (NIV)***

SQUANDERING —
WASTING MONEY AND WILD LIVING

To squander means to spend extravagantly or foolishly. You are wasting money or over-consuming. There is tremendous pressure in our society to squander and use your money for things that are unnecessary or beyond your budget. Through the media, you are bombarded with the commercialism of every holiday, and the constant advertisement of the latest "must-have" mania. The television, music, and film industries often depict the wild life as exciting, adventurous, and fulfilling, pandering to the base instincts within us. The flesh nature has a strong appetite for wild, unrestricted living. Many are drawn to the party life.

We must exercise good judgment and self-control to combat the desires to waste money and live wildly. God gives us wisdom, knowledge, and the fruit of the Spirit which includes self-control to subdue this drive. Mentally play the movie to the very end – there is always a downside that comes after the fun is done. The enemy preys upon this carnal mindset to entrap you in all forms of evil that are difficult to get out of once you are caught.

*The wise have wealth and luxury, but **fools spend whatever they get**.*
Proverbs 21:20 (NLT)

*A man who loves wisdom brings joy to his father, but **a companion of prostitutes squanders his wealth**.*
Proverbs 29:3 (NIV)

*To illustrate the point further, Jesus told them this story: "A man had two sons. The younger son told his father, 'I want my share of your estate now before you die.' So his father agreed to divide his wealth between his sons. A few days later this younger son packed all his belongings and moved to a distant land, and **there he wasted all his money in wild living**. About the time his money ran out, a great famine swept over the land, and he began to starve."*
Luke 15:11-14 (NLT)

Hoarding –
Stockpiling or Withholding Money

To hoard is to store up a large amount of treasure, and keep it hidden only for oneself. Hoarding goes beyond planning, saving, and investing. Hoarding is withholding more than what is right. The root of hoarding is selfishness and greed. Hoarding is detrimental to you; it actually leads to poverty! Withholding through selfishness removes you from God's cycle of blessing. It is the exact opposite of the nature of God, which is to give. Hoarding robs you of an eternal perspective, and focuses on only the span of your lifetime. Your ability to leave a legacy and store up eternal treasure in Heaven is canceled out by the fleshly drive to hoard. Hoarding also stems from a spirit of fear. If you are trusting God as your Source, and you are confident in the Lord's ability to care for you, there is no reason to hoard. You will be blessed in greater measure when you resist the sin nature's drive to stockpile riches and wealth.

There is another serious problem I have seen under the sun. **Hoarding riches harms the saver.** *Money is put into risky investments that turn sour, and everything is lost. In the end, there is nothing left to pass on to one's children. We all come to the end of our lives as naked and empty-handed as on the day we were born.* **We can't take our riches with us.** *Ecclesiastes 5:13-15 (NLT)*

This is what the wicked are like — always free of care, they go on **amassing wealth.** *Psalm 73:12 (NIV)*

Surely everyone goes around like a mere phantom; in vain they rush about, **heaping up wealth** *without knowing whose it will finally be.* *Psalm 39:6 (NIV)*

*There is one who scatters, yet increases more; And there is **one who withholds** more than is right, But it leads to poverty.*
Proverbs 11:24 (NKJV)

OPPRESSION –
HURTING OTHERS WHO LACK MONEY

To oppress means to treat a person or group of people in an unfair way; to crush or burden by abuse of power or authority. As we gain wealth, we are not to use it to oppress or injure others. Those who are in roles of authority such as political leaders, business owners, managers, and corporate heads must be especially vigilant to treat citizens, workers, and employees with fairness, equity, and kindness. We are not to withhold wages, pay unfair wages, discriminate, overwork, or otherwise abuse those who are in a position of submission to our authority. We are admonished to be kind and generous to the poor. The Lord of the Sabaoth (Lord of Heaven's Armies) will personally defend and avenge the oppressed!

*You shall not defraud or **oppress your neighbor** or rob him; **the wages of a hired servant shall not remain with you all night** until morning.*
Leviticus 19:13 (AMP)

*What sorrow awaits you who build big houses with **money gained dishonestly**! You believe your wealth will buy security, putting your family's nest beyond the reach of danger.*
Habakkuk 2:9 (NLT)

*Don't make your living **by extortion** or put your hope in stealing. And if your wealth increases, don't make it the center of your life.*
Psalm 62:10 (NLT)

*He who **oppresses the poor** shows contempt for their Maker, but whoever is kind to the needy honors God.*
Proverbs 14:31 (NIV)

*Look here, you rich people: Weep and groan with anguish because of all the terrible troubles ahead of you. Your wealth is rotting away, and your fine clothes are moth-eaten rags. Your gold and silver have become worthless. The very wealth you were counting on will eat away your flesh like fire. **This treasure you have accumulated will stand as evidence against you** on the day of judgment. For listen! **Hear the cries of the field workers whom you have cheated of their pay. The wages you held back** cry out against you. The cries of those who harvest your fields have reached the ears of the Lord of Heaven's Armies.*
James 5:1-4 (NLT)

COUNTERING THE DRIVES OF THE SIN NATURE

When we subdue the desires of the sin nature, we are in position to handle the blessing of wealth responsibly and effectively. Wealth, riches, abundance, and overflow are blessings of the Lord. Our Heavenly Father desires to bless us abundantly, but He will not release the blessing prematurely, if we are not prepared to manage it properly. Your blessings have your name on them. The Lord will release them to you when you have passed the tests to be licensed to drive the vehicle of prosperity with generosity and self-control.

There are specific actions you can take to subdue the sin nature and keep it under control. Giving is the most important action you can take to free yourself of the desires of the sin nature! Generosity is the antidote for greed and selfishness. Giving takes the focus off of you and allows you to be a blessing to others.

Subduing the Sin Nature – Figure 2

DRIVE OF THE SIN NATURE	SUBDUING ACTION	SCRIPTURE REFERENCE
Idolatry *Serving Money*	Tithing Giving Firstfruits	Leviticus 27:30 (NKJV) Malachi 3:8-12 (AMP) Proverbs 3:9-10 (NKJV) Luke 11:42 (NIV)
Greed *Love of Money*	Giving	Luke 6:38 (NKJV) 2 Corinthians 9:6 (AMP) Psalm 41:1-3 (NLT)
Pride and Arrogance *Boasting of Money*	Humility Anonymity	Proverbs 22:4 (NLT) Matthew 6:1-4 (AMP)
Self-Sufficiency *Confidence in Money; Confidence in Personal Ability*	Trusting God as Your Source	Psalm 34:8-10 (NLT) Deuteronomy 8:18 (NIV) Jeremiah 17:7 (AMP)
Toiling *Overworking for Money*	Trusting God Planning Your Time Not Worrying	Proverbs 21:5 (NLT) Matthew 6:25-34 (NIV) Numbers 14:7-8 (AMP)
Squandering *Wasting Money; Wild Living*	Stewarding Multiplying Investing	Matthew 25:14-29 (NKJV) Luke 16:10-12 (NIV) Luke 12:42-44 (NLT)

Drive of the Sin Nature	Subduing Action	Scripture Reference
Hoarding *Stockpiling; Withholding Money*	Helping Others; Giving Stewarding	Psalm 41:1-3 (NLT) Proverbs 11:24-26 (NKJV)
Oppression *Dominating Others Who Lack Money; Cruelty, Abuse, and Repression*	Freeing; Emancipating Fairness Honesty and Integrity	Ezekiel 18:5, 7, 8, 9 (NIV) Psalm 112:5 (NLT) Luke 14:12 (MSG)

Review the eight warnings of wealth, and reflect on your own life. In which areas do you need to counteract the drive of the sin nature?

- Idolatry — *Serving Money*

- Greed — *The Love of Money*

- Pride and Arrogance — *Boasting of Money*

- Self-Sufficiency — *Confidence in Money, Personal Ability*

- Toiling — *Overworking for Money*

- Squandering — *Wasting Money; Wild Living*

- Hoarding — *Stockpiling; Withholding Money,* and

- Oppression — *Dominating Others Who Lack Money.*

As you battle for breakthrough in your own finances, it is important to keep the sin nature in check. When you do, you will open the door for the Lord to bless you with His abundance, increase, and overflow. In the next chapter, we will take a closer look at the bountiful blessings of wealth.

9 | the blessings of wealth

And God is able to make all grace (every favor and earthly blessing) come to you in abundance, so that you may always and under all circumstances and whatever the need be self-sufficient [possessing enough to require no aid or support and furnished in abundance for every good work and charitable donation].
2 Corinthians 9:8 (AMP)

As you mature as a believer, subdue the drives of the sin nature, participate in God's cycle of blessing, and shut down the enemy's cycle of stealing, you will be positioned to see the tremendous outpouring of the Lord's blessings on your life. You are positioned for increase, abundance, and overflow. You are positioned for wealth, riches, and prosperity. The Lord promises to pour out such blessing that you will not have room enough to receive it (Malachi 3:10)! As you stay in the flow of God's cycle of blessing, there are *blessings compounded upon blessings* on the way to you. You cannot help but to be blessed! This compounding effect is described in scripture. Deuteronomy 28:2 (NKJV) states, *"And all these blessings shall come upon you and overtake you, because you obey the voice of the Lord your God..."*

Proverbs 10:6 (NLT) proclaims, *"The godly are showered with blessings."* Proverbs 13:21 (The Living Bible) tells us, *"Curses chase sinners, while blessings chase the righteous!"* The blessings of God will chase you down!

God's blessings are multiplied, compounded, and overflowing. John 1:16-17 (AMP) tells us, *"For out of His fullness (abundance) we have all received [all had a share and we were all supplied with] one grace after another and spiritual blessing upon spiritual blessing and even favor upon favor and gift [heaped] upon gift. For while the Law was given through Moses, grace (unearned, undeserved favor and spiritual blessing) and truth came through Jesus Christ."*

I want you to stop and thank your Heavenly Father right now for this powerful blessing! Lift your hands and pray this prayer out loud. "Father, I thank You that I am Your child. I will obey and honor Your Word. You alone have blessed me with one grace after another, spiritual blessing upon spiritual blessing, favor upon favor, and gift heaped upon gift through Jesus Christ my Lord! I recognize it is unearned and undeserved. It is through faith in Jesus Christ. I believe it and I receive it now in the mighty name of Jesus! Amen and thank God!"

How does the Lord make all grace (every favor and earthly blessing) come to you in abundance? There are twelve different blessings of wealth outlined in the scripture. Your Heavenly Father uses twelve different avenues to get His blessings to you. Let's look at the twelve ways that the Lord sends His blessings. The blessings of wealth come from:

- Obedience
- Favor
- Tithing
- Giving
- Diligence
- Stewardship
- Production
- Multiplication
- Birthright
- Bloodline
- Enduring in Trial
- Sacrifice.

The Twelve Blessings of Wealth – Figure 1

BLESSING	DESCRIPTION	SCRIPTURE REFERENCE
Obedience	Willingly obeying the commands of the Lord	Deuteronomy 28:1-14 (NKJV, AMP)
		Deuteronomy 5:33 (NLT)
		Deuteronomy 15:4-6 (NIV)
		Psalm 112:1-3 (NIV)
		Psalm 128:1-2 (NIV)
		Isaiah 1:19 (NKJV)
Favor	Unmerited, unearned blessing; special acts of grace, special generosity, or special approval	Psalm 5:12 (NIV)
		Psalm 106:4-5 (NLT)
		Proverbs 12:2 (NKJV)
		John 1:16-17 (AMP)
		2 Corinthians 8:9 (AMP)
		2 Corinthians 9:8 (AMP)
Tithing	Returning the tithe to the Lord, the first ten percent of your income	Malachi 3:10-12 (AMP)
		Proverbs 3:9-10 (NKJV)
Giving	Free-will giving beyond returning the tithe	Luke 6:38 (NIV)
		2 Corinthians 9:6-8 (AMP)
		Proverbs 11:24-26 (NKJV, NLT)
Diligence	Industriousness; hard work; constant earnest effort	Proverbs 10:4 (NIV)
		Proverbs 12:24 (NKJV)
		Proverbs 12:27 (AMP)
		Proverbs 13:4 (AMP)
		Proverbs 14:23 (NIV)
		Proverbs 22:29 (AMP)
Stewardship	Faithful oversight of present blessings	Luke 12:42-44 (NLT)
		Luke 16:10-12 (NIV)
		Matthew 25:29 (NLT)
Production	Applying the Word by faith; fruitfulness	Mark 4:20 (AMP)

BLESSING	DESCRIPTION	SCRIPTURE REFERENCE
Multiplication	Multiplying gifts and talents	Matthew 25:14-29 (NKJV)
Birthright	Adoption into the family of God; sonship Jesus is the firstborn Son	Romans 8:14-17 (NIV) Galatians 4:1-7 (NIV) Ephesians 3:5-6 (AMP, NLT)
Bloodline	Lineage of faith through Abraham, as Abraham's seed; The blessing of Abraham is upon all who are in Christ	Genesis 13:2 (NIV) Genesis 24:34-35 (NLT) Genesis 26:12-14 (NKJV) Genesis 30:43 (NLT) Romans 10:12 (AMP) Galatians 3:13-14 (NKJV) Galatians 3:26-29 (NIV)
Enduring in Trial	Enduring through trial, difficulty, and trouble	Job 42:10 (NIV) Psalm 34:17 (NKJV) Psalm 34:19 (NKJV) Isaiah 61:6-9 (AMP)
Sacrifice	Giving up; sacrificing for the Kingdom of God and the gospel of Jesus Christ	1 Kings 17:7-16 (NIV) Mark 10:17-30 (NIV) Mark 10:29-30 (AMP)

Let's take a closer look at each of the blessings of wealth.

OBEDIENCE

Your obedience to the scripture releases many of the blessings of God. When you set your heart to live according to God's Word and not by worldly standards, you become eligible for many of the conditional blessings in the Word of God. To be obedient means to be submissive to the restraint or command of authority; to be willing to obey. It also means to be submissive to another's will; dutifully complying with the commands or instructions of those in authority.

Our obedience to the scripture is an act of worship; we obey out of *love*, not out of *law*. Jesus tells us in John 14:15 (AMP), *"If you [really] love Me, you will keep (obey) My commands."* The most important aspect of our obedience is our heart attitude. We obey the Word of the Lord not because we *"have to"* but because we *"get to."* If you find yourself looking for loopholes and loose interpretations of scripture to get out of obeying the Word of the Lord, check your heart condition. Isaiah 1:19 (NKJV) tells us, *"If you are willing and obedient, You shall eat the good of the land."*

The blessings of obedience are extensive in scripture, including abundance, prosperity, and long life! Meditate on the following power promises of obedience.

__Stay on the path__ that the Lord your God has commanded you to follow. Then __you will live long and prosperous lives__ in the land you are about to enter and occupy.
__*Deuteronomy 5:33 (NLT)*__

And you shall return and obey the voice of the Lord and do all His commandments which I command you today. And the Lord your God will make you __abundantly prosperous__ in every work of your hand, in the fruit of your body, of your cattle, of your land, for good; for the Lord will again delight in prospering you, as He took delight in your fathers.
__*Deuteronomy 30:8-9 (AMP)*__

Praise the Lord! How joyful are those who fear the Lord and __delight in obeying his commands__. Their __children will be successful__ everywhere; an entire generation of godly people will be blessed. __They themselves will be wealthy__, and their good deeds will last forever.
__*Psalm 112:1-3 (NLT)*__

*Blessed are all who fear the Lord, who **walk in obedience** to him. You will eat the fruit of your labor; **blessings and prosperity** will be yours.*
Psalm 128:1-2 (NIV)

He who covers his transgressions will not prosper, but whoever confesses and forsakes his sins will obtain mercy.
Proverbs 28:13 (AMP)

If you are willing and obedient, You shall eat the good of the land.
Isaiah 1:19 (NKJV)

*Now it shall come to pass, if you **diligently obey** the voice of the Lord your God, to observe carefully all His commandments which I command you today, that the Lord your God will set you high above all nations of the earth. And all these blessings shall come upon you and overtake you, because you obey the voice of the Lord your God:*

Blessed shall you be in the city, and blessed shall you be in the country.

Blessed shall be the fruit of your body, the produce of your ground and the increase of your herds, the increase of your cattle and the offspring of your flocks.

Blessed shall be your basket and your kneading bowl.

Blessed shall you be when you come in, and blessed shall you be when you go out.

The Lord will cause your enemies who rise against you to be defeated before your face; they shall come out against you one way and flee before you seven ways.

The Lord will command the blessing on you in your storehouses and in all to which you set your hand, and He will bless you in the land which the Lord your God is giving you.

The Lord will establish you as a holy people to Himself, just as He has sworn to you, if you keep the commandments of the Lord your God and walk in His ways. Then all peoples of the earth shall see that you are called by the name of the Lord, and they shall be afraid of you. And the Lord will grant you plenty of goods, in the fruit of your body, in the increase of your livestock, and in the produce of your ground, in the land of which the Lord swore to your fathers to give you. The Lord will open to you His good treasure, the heavens, to give the rain to your land in its season, and to bless all the work of your hand. You shall lend to many nations, but you shall not borrow. And the Lord will make you the head and not the tail; you shall be above only, and not be beneath, if you heed the commandments of the Lord your God, which I command you today, and are careful to observe them. So you shall not turn aside from any of the words which I command you this day, to the right or the left, to go after other gods to serve them.
Deuteronomy 28:1-14 (NKJV)

FAVOR

The second blessing of wealth is favor. Favor is defined as special acts of grace, special generosity, or special approval. To favor means to show delight in, and to extend acceptance toward. When you experience the Lord's favor, you gain His approval, acceptance, special benefits, and abundant blessings. Favor is the divine blessing upon the righteous. The Lord shows His delight and good pleasure in you. There is a close association among favor, grace, and mercy. They are unmerited and unearned.

King David describes the vast shields used by the ancient warriors that were as extensive as a man's whole person, and

152

would surround him entirely. The Lord's favor over your life operates in the same way. Psalm 5:12 (NIV) states, *"Surely, Lord, you bless the righteous; you surround them with your favor as with a shield."* God's favor surrounds you! Through acts of divine favor, the Lord will accelerate and multiply blessings upon your life. He will advance, promote, and elevate you. By divine favor, your Heavenly Father will bless you in ways that are unexpected, unparalleled, and unprecedented.

Remember me, Lord, when you show favor to your people; come near and rescue me. Let me share in the prosperity of your chosen ones. Let me rejoice in the joy of your people; let me praise you with those who are your heritage.
Psalm 106:4-5 (NLT)

A good man obtains favor from the Lord, But a man of wicked intentions He will condemn.
Proverbs 12:2 (NKJV)

For out of His fullness (abundance) we have all received [all had a share and we were all supplied with] one grace after another and spiritual blessing upon spiritual blessing and even favor upon favor and gift [heaped] upon gift. For while the Law was given through Moses, grace (unearned, undeserved favor and spiritual blessing) and truth came through Jesus Christ.
John 1:16-17 (AMP)

For you are becoming progressively acquainted with and recognizing more strongly and clearly the grace of our Lord Jesus Christ (His kindness, His gracious generosity, His undeserved favor and spiritual blessing), [in] that though He was [so very] rich, yet for your sakes He became [so very] poor, in order that by His poverty you might become enriched (abundantly supplied).
2 Corinthians 8:9 (AMP)

TITHING

The first ten percent of your income belongs to the Lord and is holy (Leviticus 27:30). As we have seen extensively in previous chapters, when you honor the Lord with the firstfruits of all your increase, He will bless you with even greater increase, protect you from the devastation of the Devourer, and cause your prosperity to be so vast that it is visible and evident to others. Returning the tithe to the Lord's earthly storehouse is a key component of cooperating with the Lord's cycle of blessing on your life. He promises to pour out blessings you do not have room enough to receive!

Bring all the tithes (the whole tenth of your income) into the storehouse, that there may be food in My house, and prove Me now by it, says the Lord of hosts, if I will not open the windows of heaven for you and pour you out a blessing, that there shall not be room enough to receive it. And I will rebuke the devourer [insects and plagues] for your sakes and he shall not destroy the fruits of your ground, neither shall your vine drop its fruit before the time in the field, says the Lord of hosts. And all nations shall call you happy and blessed, for you shall be a land of delight, says the Lord of hosts.
Malachi 3:10-12 (AMP)

Honor the Lord with your possessions, And with the firstfruits of all your increase; So your barns will be filled with plenty, And your vats will overflow with new wine.
Proverbs 3:9-10 (NKJV)

Jesus said to them, Pay to Caesar the things that are Caesar's and to God the things that are God's. And they stood marveling and greatly amazed at Him.
Mark 12:17 (AMP)

GIVING

Your Heavenly Father will multiply blessings upon your giving! As you give, a greater measure of blessing and abundance is entrusted to you. Your giving is an act of worship and your free-will choice. Give cheerfully! When you sow generously, you will also reap a generous harvest of blessing. The seed you have sown over your lifetime compounds into a continuous cycle of harvest. You will continually come into new harvests from previous seeds sown! As you continue to sow, new harvests are in your future. As you become a greater conduit of blessing to others, the Lord will enlarge your territory. Generosity is a master key to God's blessings of wealth and prosperity. Give and it shall be given!

Give freely and become more wealthy; be stingy and lose everything. The generous will prosper; those who refresh others will themselves be refreshed. People curse those who hoard their grain, but they bless the one who sells in time of need.
Proverbs 11:24-26 (NLT)

Give, and it will be given to you. A good measure, pressed down, shaken together and running over, will be poured into your lap. For with the measure you use, it will be measured to you.
Luke 6:38 (NIV)

[Remember] this: he who sows sparingly and grudgingly will also reap sparingly and grudgingly, and he who sows generously [that blessings may come to someone] will also reap generously and with blessings. Let each one [give] as he has made up his own mind and purposed in his heart, not reluctantly or sorrowfully or under compulsion, for God loves (He takes pleasure in, prizes above other things, and

155

is unwilling to abandon or to do without) a cheerful (joyous, "prompt to do it") giver [whose heart is in his giving]. And God is able to make all grace (every favor and earthly blessing) come to you in abundance, so that you may always and under all circumstances and whatever the need be self-sufficient [possessing enough to require no aid or support and furnished in abundance for every good work and charitable donation].
2 Corinthians 9:6-8 (AMP)

DILIGENCE

The Lord blesses the diligent! When you are industrious and hard-working, your Heavenly Father will abundantly bless the work of your hands. Throughout the book of Proverbs, King Solomon reminds us that idleness, laziness, and slothfulness will lead to abject poverty, but hard work, perseverance, diligence, and determination will lead to prosperity, wealth, and riches. Proverbs 21:25 (NLT) warns us, *"Despite their desires, the lazy will come to ruin, for their hands refuse to work."* Desire is not enough! Most everyone wants to prosper and succeed, but very few will put in the consistent effort required with excellence and endurance. God promises to bless the work of your hands; give Him something great to bless! Put the work in. Promotion comes from the Lord. Believe by faith that your Heavenly Father will extensively bless you on your job and in your businesses.

Lazy hands make for poverty, but diligent hands bring wealth.
Proverbs 10:4 (NIV)

The hand of the diligent will rule, But the lazy man will be put to forced labor.
Proverbs 12:24 (NKJV)

The slothful man does not catch his game or roast it once he kills it, but the diligent man gets precious possessions.
Proverbs 12:27 (AMP)

The appetite of the sluggard craves and gets nothing, but the appetite of the diligent is abundantly supplied.
Proverbs 13:4 (AMP)

All hard work brings a profit, but mere talk leads only to poverty.
Proverbs 14:23 (NIV)

A lazy person's way is blocked with briers, but the path of the upright is an open highway.
Proverbs 15:19 (NLT)

Do you see a man diligent and skillful in his business? He will stand before kings; he will not stand before obscure men.
Proverbs 22:29 (AMP)

STEWARDSHIP

The sixth blessing of wealth is on your stewardship. How you manage what you have right now is directly related to how the Lord will bless you with greater wealth in the future. Faithful oversight of your present resources determines your trustworthiness with greater riches. When you budget, manage, multiply, and utilize your current resources effectively, you are demonstrating your competence and capacity for promotion. Responsible stewardship shows you are ready to handle the greater riches!

And the Lord replied, "A faithful, sensible servant is one to whom the master can give the responsibility of managing his other household servants and feeding them. If the master returns and finds that the servant has done a good job, there

will be a reward. I tell you the truth, the master will put that servant in charge of all he owns.
Luke 12:42-44 (NLT)

Whoever can be trusted with very little can also be trusted with much, and whoever is dishonest with very little will also be dishonest with much. So if you have not been trustworthy in handling worldly wealth, who will trust you with true riches? And if you have not been trustworthy with someone else's property, who will give you property of your own?
Luke 16:10-12 (NIV)

To those who use well what they are given, even more will be given, and they will have an abundance. But from those who do nothing, even what little they have will be taken away.
Matthew 25:29 (NLT)

PRODUCTION

The seventh blessing of wealth is on your production from the Word of God. The Lord blesses us as we hear the Word, receive it by faith, apply it, and produce fruit. When you are actively putting the Word of God into action, your Heavenly Father sends a multiplied blessing on your fruitfulness and productivity! Believe God for a thirty, sixty, and even a hundredfold return on the Word that you put into practice. Ask the Lord to multiply your productivity so that you bear much fruit.

And those sown on the good (well-adapted) soil are the ones who hear the Word and receive and accept and welcome it and bear fruit—some thirty times as much as was sown, some sixty times as much, and some [even] a hundred times as much.
Mark 4:20 (AMP)

MULTIPLICATION

The Lord has given each of us unique gifts, talents, and resources that we are responsible to use over the course of our lifetime to complete our mission assignment. Your Heavenly Father expects you to use and multiply all of the talents you have been given. When you use your talents to produce increase, the Lord will reward your faithfulness and will bless you with even more! When you are faithful over a few things, God will make you ruler over much! However, if you sit on your gifts and talents, and essentially bury them in the ground, the Lord calls that laziness and wickedness! Even the resources you have will be taken away and given to someone else who will put them to good use.

Do not fall into the trap of comparing your gifts and talents to others. Some are called to be five-talent people, some are two-talent people, and some are one-talent people. The issue is not how much you are given in comparison to others. We cannot become arrogant over the quantity, quality, or nature of our gifts. God gives gifts to each of us according to our own ability to manage and multiply them. To whom much is given, much is required (Luke 12:48). The key is to multiply your talents, whatever you have been given, by creatively putting them to work. We are to multiply, invest, and increase what we have been given. The Lord will bless your increase and continually give you more resources according to your willingness to employ and multiply what you already have.

"For the kingdom of heaven is like a man traveling to a far country, who called his own servants and delivered his goods to them. And to one he gave five talents, to another two, and to another one, to each according to his own ability; and immediately he went on a journey. Then he who had received the five talents went and traded with them, and made another

159

five talents. And likewise he who had received two gained two more also. But he who had received one went and dug in the ground, and hid his lord's money. After a long time the lord of those servants came and settled accounts with them.

"So he who had received five talents came and brought five other talents, saying, 'Lord, you delivered to me five talents; look, I have gained five more talents besides them.' His lord said to him, 'Well done, good and faithful servant; you were faithful over a few things, I will make you ruler over many things. Enter into the joy of your lord.' He also who had received two talents came and said, 'Lord, you delivered to me two talents; look, I have gained two more talents besides them.' His lord said to him, 'Well done, good and faithful servant; you have been faithful over a few things, I will make you ruler over many things. Enter into the joy of your lord.'

"Then he who had received the one talent came and said, 'Lord, I knew you to be a hard man, reaping where you have not sown, and gathering where you have not scattered seed. And I was afraid, and went and hid your talent in the ground. Look, there you have what is yours.'

"But his lord answered and said to him, 'You wicked and lazy servant, you knew that I reap where I have not sown, and gather where I have not scattered seed. So you ought to have deposited my money with the bankers, and at my coming I would have received back my own with interest. Therefore take the talent from him, and give it to him who has ten talents.

'For to everyone who has, more will be given, and he will have abundance; but from him who does not have, even what he has will be taken away.'"
Matthew 25:14-29 (NKJV)

BIRTHRIGHT

The ninth blessing of wealth is through birthright. Your Heavenly Father sends His blessing of wealth to you simply because you are His child and it is your inheritance. You have been adopted into the family of God, and you have the rights of an heir! The word birthright denotes the special privileges and advantages belonging to the firstborn son among the Jews. He became the priest of the family. The firstborn son also had allotted to him a double portion of the paternal inheritance. Jesus Christ is the firstborn Son of the Father, and by faith you are in Christ. Romans 8:29 (NKJV) tells us, *"For whom He foreknew, He also predestined to be conformed to the image of His Son, that He might be the firstborn among many brethren."*

Huiothesia, the Greek word for *adoption to sonship*, as it is used in Romans 8:15, is a term referring to the full legal standing of an adopted male heir in Roman culture. By adoption to sonship, you have the full legal standing of an heir of God. You are an heir of God and co-heir with Christ!

Romans 8:17 (AMP) tells us, *"And if we are [His] children, then we are [His] heirs also:* **heirs of God and fellow heirs with Christ [sharing His inheritance with Him];** *only we must share His suffering if we are to share His glory."* Your Heavenly Father has special blessings for your life that He bestows through inheritance, because you are adopted to sonship.

For those who are led by the Spirit of God are the children of God. The Spirit you received does not make you slaves, so that you live in fear again; rather, the Spirit you received brought about your adoption to sonship. And by him we cry, "Abba, Father." The Spirit himself testifies with our spirit that we are

God's children. Now if we are children, then we are heirs—heirs of God and co-heirs with Christ, if indeed we share in his sufferings in order that we may also share in his glory.
Romans 8:14-17 (NIV)

What I am saying is that as long as an heir is underage, he is no different from a slave, although he owns the whole estate. The heir is subject to guardians and trustees until the time set by his father. So also, when we were underage, we were in slavery under the elemental spiritual forces of the world. But when the set time had fully come, God sent his Son, born of a woman, born under the law, to redeem those under the law, that we might receive adoption to sonship. Because you are his sons, God sent the Spirit of his Son into our hearts, the Spirit who calls out, "Abba, Father." So you are no longer a slave, but God's child; and since you are his child, God has made you also an heir.
Galatians 4:1-7 (NIV)

God did not reveal it to previous generations, but now by his Spirit he has revealed it to his holy apostles and prophets. And this is God's plan: Both Gentiles and Jews who believe the Good News share equally in the riches inherited by God's children. Both are part of the same body, and both enjoy the promise of blessings because they belong to Christ Jesus.
Ephesians 3:5-6 (NLT)

BLOODLINE

The tenth blessing of wealth is through our spiritual bloodline as Abraham's seed. We are adopted into the family of God as sons, and we are placed into a specific family lineage through Abraham, the father of our faith. You are a recipient of the blessing of Abraham. The patriarchal blessings pronounced over Abraham and his seed apply to you through Christ. You are of the family lineage of Abraham, Isaac, and Jacob. This is an extraordinarily powerful promise, and I want you to grasp the fullness of it. Galatians 3:29 (NLT) tells us, *"And now that you belong to Christ, you are the true children of Abraham. You are his heirs, and **God's promise to Abraham belongs to you**."*

The covenant promises and blessings upon Abraham require a comprehensive and exhaustive study of the scriptures which we cannot delve into in its fullness in this particular volume. I wish that we could! I will offer just a few scriptural key points to give you a very high level view of this blessing of wealth.

God demonstrated His covenant with Abraham in the lives of Abraham, Isaac, Jacob and their descendants with blessings of:

- **property** ownership
- **paternity** (blessed family lineage)
- **posterity** (blessed future generations)
- **possessions** (material abundance)
- **provision** (abundant silver and gold)
- the future **promise** (promised land of abundance, flowing with milk and honey), and most importantly,
- His everlasting **presence** with them, to be their God.

Their covenant with God was evident in the blessings of the Lord that were upon their lives. These same blessings that were upon Abraham, Isaac, and Jacob are ours as well, through the Lord Jesus Christ.

You will see these blessings and covenant promises in the following scriptures. In Genesis 13, Abraham (then Abram) was promised both land (property ownership) and blessed posterity. Genesis 13:14-16 (NIV) tells us, *"The Lord said to Abram after Lot had parted from him, 'Look around from where you are, to the north and south, to the east and west. All the land that you see I will give to you and your offspring forever. I will make your offspring like the dust of the earth, so that if anyone could count the dust, then your offspring could be counted. Go, walk through the length and breadth of the land, for I am giving it to you.'"*

In Genesis 17:3-8 (NIV), we see the Lord form a covenant with Abraham, again sealed with land, a blessed lineage, and an everlasting relationship with Abraham's descendants: *"Abram fell facedown, and God said to him, 'As for me, this is my covenant with you: You will be the father of many nations. No longer will you be called Abram; your name will be Abraham, for I have made you a father of many nations. I will make you very fruitful; I will make nations of you, and kings will come from you. I will establish my covenant as an everlasting covenant between me and you and your descendants after you for the generations to come, to be your God and the God of your descendants after you. The whole land of Canaan, where you now reside as a foreigner, I will give as an everlasting possession to you and your descendants after you; and I will be their God.'"*

In Genesis 22:15-18 (NIV), when Abraham was about to sacrifice his son Isaac in obedience to the Lord, we see the following blessing: *"The angel of the LORD called to Abraham from heaven a second time and said, 'I swear by myself, declares the LORD, that because you have done this and have not withheld your son, your only son, I will surely bless you and make your descendants as numerous as the stars in the sky and as the sand on the seashore. Your descendants will take possession of the cities of their enemies, and through your offspring all nations on earth will be blessed, because you have obeyed me.'"*

In Genesis 22:18 (AMP), we see that we are included in this blessing, because the offspring described is Christ, and we are in Christ: *"And in your Seed [Christ] shall all the nations of the earth be blessed and [by Him] bless themselves, because you have heard and obeyed My voice."* We receive the blessing of Abraham through Christ.

In the following scriptures, I want you to see that in addition to our rich spiritual heritage and bloodline, the blessings of Abraham include wealth, riches, and abundant prosperity. That is part of our heritage as a child of God. We see the Lord bless His children repeatedly with wealth. That same blessing is ours today. We must understand our birthright in Christ and our bloodline through Abraham. You are Abraham's seed and therefore, an heir to the promise, including the promise of wealth.

Now Abram was extremely rich in livestock and in silver and in gold.
Genesis 13:2 (NIV)

"I am Abraham's servant," he explained. "And the Lord has greatly blessed my master; he has become a wealthy man. The Lord has given him flocks of sheep and goats, herds of cattle, a fortune in silver and gold, and many male and female servants and camels and donkeys."
Genesis 24:34-35 (NLT)

Then Isaac sowed in that land, and reaped in the same year a hundredfold; and the Lord blessed him. The man began to prosper, and continued prospering until he became very prosperous; for he had possessions of flocks and possessions of herds and a great number of servants. So the Philistines

165

envied him.
Genesis 26:12-14 (NKJV)

As a result, Jacob became very wealthy, with large flocks of sheep and goats, female and male servants, and many camels and donkeys.
Genesis 30:43 (NLT)

[No one] for there is no distinction between Jew and Greek. The same Lord is Lord over all [of us] and He generously bestows His riches upon all who call upon Him [in faith].
Romans 10:12 (AMP)

Christ has redeemed us from the curse of the law, having become a curse for us (for it is written, "Cursed is everyone who hangs on a tree"), that the blessing of Abraham might come upon the Gentiles in Christ Jesus, that we might receive the promise of the Spirit through faith.
Galatians 3:13-14 (NKJV)

So in Christ Jesus you are all children of God through faith, for all of you who were baptized into Christ have clothed yourselves with Christ. There is neither Jew nor Gentile, neither slave nor free, nor is there male and female, for you are all one in Christ Jesus. If you belong to Christ, then you are Abraham's seed, and heirs according to the promise.
Galatians 3:26-29 (NIV)

ENDURING IN TRIAL

One of the most comforting blessings of wealth that is promised in scripture is the blessing of restoration. The blessing of restoration describes what we shall receive from the Lord for enduring in trial. Jesus said in John 16:33 (NIV), *"I have told you these things, so that in me you may have peace. In this world you will have trouble. But take heart! I have overcome the world."* You will have trials, tribulations, and trouble, but Jesus has already overcome them all! Your task is to endure and stay in faith in the midst of trouble. You must remain confident the Lord will deliver you in trial. Your Heavenly Father will bring complete restoration!

When the Lord restores, He always will put you in a better position than where you were before the trouble occurred. You will come out better than before! Romans 8:28 (NLT) encourages us, *"And we know that God causes everything to work together for the good of those who love God and are called according to his purpose for them."* God sees the end from the beginning. He is not limited by the linear nature of time, as we are. Our Heavenly Father sees how everything will ultimately fit together, in alignment with His divine purpose and plan. He will cause your trials and troubles to work on your behalf and ultimately benefit you in His divine order.

Joseph understood this principle when he reconciled with his brothers and saved his family. After he endured the abuse of his brothers, the false accusations of Potiphar's wife, and being forgotten in prison, he rose to become second-in-command to Pharoah, in charge of all of Egypt (Genesis 41:39-44). In Genesis 50:20 (NLT), Joseph consoles his brothers saying, *"You intended to harm me, but God intended it all for good. He brought me to this position so I could save the lives of many people."*

In scripture, the Lord restores to us double what we have lost in the midst of trial. Even in difficulty and hardship, you shall be blessed. The Lord restored to Job twice as much as he had before (Job 42:10). We see the promise of the double portion in Isaiah 61:7 which states, *"Instead of your shame you will receive **a double portion**, and instead of disgrace you will rejoice in your inheritance. And so you* *will inherit a double portion in your land, and everlasting joy will be yours."*

When you go through troubling times, remember this power promise and declare that all things are working together for your good. You shall receive a double portion as your blessing of restoration from the Lord.

After Job had prayed for his friends, the LORD restored his fortunes and gave him twice as much as he had before.
Job 42:10 (NIV)

The righteous cry out, and the Lord hears, And delivers them out of all their troubles.
Psalm 34:17 (NKJV)

Many are the afflictions of the righteous, But the Lord delivers him out of them all.
Psalm 34:19 (NKJV)

*But you shall be called the priests of the Lord; people will speak of you as the ministers of our God. You shall eat the wealth of the nations, and the glory [once that of your captors] shall be yours. Instead of your [former] shame **you shall have a twofold recompense***; *instead of dishonor and reproach [your people] shall rejoice in their portion. Therefore in their land **they shall possess double** [what they had forfeited]; everlasting joy shall be theirs. For I the Lord love justice; I hate robbery and wrong with violence or a burnt offering. And I will faithfully give them their recompense in truth, and I will make an everlasting covenant or league with them. And their offspring shall be known among the nations and their descendants among the peoples. All who see them [in their prosperity] will recognize and acknowledge that they are the people whom the Lord has blessed.*
Isaiah 61:6-9 (AMP)

SACRIFICE

The twelfth and final blessing of wealth is the Lord's blessing upon your sacrifice. We have already discussed the blessing of wealth upon your *giving*. This is a different blessing on what you *give up* for the sake of advancing the Kingdom of God and the gospel of Jesus Christ. The Lord has reserved a special blessing for sacrificial giving.

In 1 Kings 17 we are told the account of Elijah and the poor widow. 1 Kings 17:7-16 (NIV) tells us, *"Some time later the brook dried up because there had been no rain in the land. Then the word of the Lord came to him: 'Go at once to Zarephath in the region of Sidon and stay there.* **I have directed a widow there to supply you with food.***' So he went to Zarephath. When he came to the town gate, a widow was there gathering sticks. He called to her and asked, 'Would you bring me a little water in a jar so I may have a drink?' As she was going to get it, he called, 'And bring me, please, a piece of bread.'*

*'As surely as the Lord your God lives,' she replied, '***I don't have any bread***—only a handful of flour in a jar and a little olive oil in a jug. I am gathering a few sticks to take home and make a meal for myself and my son, that we may eat it—and die.'*

Elijah said to her, 'Don't be afraid. Go home and do as you have said. But first make a small loaf of bread for me from what you have and bring it to me, and then make something for yourself and your son. For this is what the Lord, the God of Israel, says: 'The jar of flour will not be used up and the jug of oil will not run dry until the day the Lord sends rain on the land.'"

She went away and did as Elijah had told her. **So there was food every day for Elijah and for the woman and her family.** *For* **the jar of flour was not used up** *and* **the jug of oil did not run dry,** *in keeping with the word of the Lord spoken by Elijah."*

The poor widow was facing dire circumstances: she had just enough flour and oil for a final meal for her and her son in the midst of a drought. Despair had already set in – she was preparing to die. Yet, because the widow obeyed the word of the Lord given through the prophet Elijah, and gave sacrificially to feed Elijah out of the very little she had, in keeping with God the Father's instruction to her, she was abundantly blessed with supernatural supply for the duration of the drought. In the natural circumstance, she did not have enough to sustain her own family, but with the blessing of the Lord on her *sacrificial giving,* she was abundantly supplied with more than enough to care for her family and Elijah's needs as well! She trusted the word of the Lord, not the circumstances.

Sacrificial giving does not make sense to the natural mind. It is contrary to rational reasoning and common logic. There are times when **the Lord will direct you** to do something contrary to human wisdom, and it will unlock a supernatural miracle of provision in your life. **God the Father** had directed the woman to give sacrificially of her remaining resources to care for Elijah. The prophet confirmed this word in his instruction to the widow, and she obeyed. The Lord's directive was not meant to take something *from her*; He was using her sacrificial giving to get a blessing *to her.* God supernaturally provided for her throughout the drought. The Lord blessed her sacrificial giving with supernatural supply.

In contrast, in Mark Chapter 10, we see the account of the rich young ruler who came to Jesus with an important question. Let's read this account in Mark 10:17-26 (NIV).

As Jesus started on his way, a man ran up to him and fell on his knees before him. "Good teacher," he asked, "what must I do to inherit eternal life?"

"Why do you call me good?" Jesus answered. "No one is good—except God alone. You know the commandments: 'You shall not murder, you shall not commit adultery, you shall not steal, you shall not give false testimony, you shall not defraud, honor your father and mother.'"

"Teacher," he declared, "all these I have kept since I was a boy."

Jesus looked at him and loved him. "One thing you lack," he said. "Go, sell everything you have and give to the poor, and you will have treasure in heaven. Then come, follow me."

At this the man's face fell. He went away sad, because he had great wealth.

Jesus looked around and said to his disciples, "How hard it is for the rich to enter the kingdom of God!"

The disciples were amazed at his words. But Jesus said again, "Children, how hard it is to enter the kingdom of God! It is easier for a camel to go through the eye of a needle than for someone who is rich to enter the kingdom of God."

The disciples were even more amazed, and said to each other, "Who then can be saved?"

Jesus said to the rich man, one thing you lack. I believe the one thing he lacked was the ability to *completely trust God* with everything in His life. He did not pass the trust test. He thought he had fulfilled all of the commandments in his own estimation. Jesus was testing his heart condition. Would he put the Lord before money? The scripture says Jesus loved him. Would he respond to that love? Jesus was offering an even higher level of life. Jesus was inviting the man to even greater riches. He told him: 1) go sell everything you have, 2) give to the poor and you will have treasure in Heaven (participate in God's cycle of blessing), and then, 3) come follow Me. If the rich man had discerned who was speaking to him, he would have understood this was an invitation to a higher life! The riches he had in his possession amounted to very little in comparison to Who was before him, the Lord Jesus Christ, and all that He was offering to him, including true riches beyond the young man's imagination! *"Sell what you have, give to the poor, then come follow Me."* Jesus was essentially saying (I paraphrase), "Trust Me, not your riches. Take the higher life. I will give you so much more than you could ever *give up* to follow Me."

I believe Jesus was inviting him to give sacrificially as a trust test, to see his heart condition, so that He could bring him into an *even greater* quality of life – eternal life in Christ through faith. Let go of what you have to follow Me, and I will give you so much more! Jesus was not asking him to become poor. He was inviting him to a higher life. He was inviting him to experience the true riches!

However, the young man went away sad, because he had great wealth. He chose to trust in his wealth and not in the Lord. He forfeited the true riches. Jesus then commented on how hard it is to pass the trust test. Jesus observed that it is difficult for the rich to not allow money to be an idol, taking the place of God on the throne of the heart (see Chapter 8, The Warnings of Wealth).

The disciples were stunned and asked, *"Who then can be saved?"* Let's continue with the account. Jesus answers with a powerful blessing of wealth for those who give sacrificially. Let's pick up with Mark 10:27-31 (NIV).

Jesus looked at them and said, "With man this is impossible, but not with God; all things are possible with God."

Then Peter spoke up, "We have left everything to follow you!"

*"Truly I tell you," Jesus replied, "no one who has left home or brothers or sisters or mother or father or children or fields for me and the gospel will fail to receive **a hundred times as much in this present age**: homes, brothers, sisters, mothers, children and fields — along with persecutions — **and in the age to come eternal life**. But many who are first will be last, and the last first."*

Let's examine the response Jesus gave to Peter. Peter said to Jesus, *"We have given up everything to follow you."* Peter expressed the sacrificial nature of their commitment to follow Christ, and Jesus acknowledged that commitment by pronouncing the blessing that is upon sacrificial giving. I paraphrase: "No one who has sacrificed for Me and for the sake of the gospel will fail to receive **a hundred times as much in this present age** – and in the age to come, eternal life."

Jesus pronounced a hundredfold return of natural and material blessings on sacrificial giving now in this time, and the spiritual blessing of eternal life in the age to come.

Notice that the poor widow with Elijah and the rich young ruler with Jesus faced the same test of *trust*. They were both asked to trust the word of the Lord. They were both asked to give sacrificially. They both had supernatural blessings to come. The poor widow needed a supernatural supply of food.

The rich man stood to gain his eternal salvation, the stunning opportunity to walk with the Lord Jesus on the earth, and at least a hundredfold return on what he would have given up sacrificially. Yet, his misplaced trust in his wealth caused him to forfeit his blessings.

The hundredfold return on sacrificial giving for the sake of the gospel is yours today. What you give up for the sake of the gospel, to care for the needs of others, and to advance the Kingdom of God will be given back to you a hundred times over in this life. This blessing includes spiritual, natural, and material blessings. Jesus included relationships, houses, lands, and in the age to come, eternal life. Jesus sees your sacrifice. He sees your trust. He sees your faith. Jesus is the same yesterday, today, and forever. The hundredfold return He pronounced as a blessing on what you *give up* sacrificially is yours. You can believe God now for the hundredfold return on what you have given for the sake of the gospel. Let's review it again.

So Jesus answered and said, "Assuredly, I say to you, there is no one who has left house or brothers or sisters or father or mother or wife or children or lands, for My sake and the gospel's, who shall not receive **a hundredfold now in this time**—*houses and brothers and sisters and mothers and children and lands, with persecutions—and in the age to come, eternal life.*
Mark 10:29-30 (AMP)

SUMMARY – THE BLESSINGS OF WEALTH

In summary, let's review one more time the twelve blessings of wealth, all of which are the rich reward of our blessed life in Christ by faith.

The blessings of wealth are:

- Obedience – *These Blessings Shall Come Upon You and Overtake You*

- Favor – *Special Generosity: Unearned, Unparalleled, Unprecedented*

- Tithing – *Opening the Windows of Heaven*

- Giving – *A Bountiful Harvest*

- Diligence – *Diligent Hands Bring Wealth*

- Stewardship – *Faithful Over Little, Ruler Over Much*

- Production – *Thirty, Sixty, and a Hundredfold Return*

- Multiplication – *More Will Be Given*

- Birthright – *Heirs of God and Joint Heirs with Christ*

- Bloodline – *The Blessing of Abraham*

- Enduring in Trial – *The Double Portion*

- Sacrifice – *The Hundredfold Return.*

God's blessings are multiplied, compounded, and overflowing! Begin to thank God right now for His abundant blessings upon your life! Remember John 1:16-17 (AMP): *"For out of His fullness (abundance) we have all received [all had a share and we were all supplied with] one grace after another and spiritual blessing upon spiritual blessing and even favor upon favor and gift [heaped] upon gift. For while the Law was given through Moses, grace (unearned, undeserved favor and spiritual blessing) and truth came through Jesus Christ."*

10 || wealth strategies in the word

> T hus says the Lord, your Redeemer, the Holy One of
> Israel: I am the Lord your God, Who teaches you to
> profit, Who leads you in the way that you should go.
> **Isaiah 48:17 (AMP)**

The Lord promises to send blessing upon blessing, favor
upon favor, and gift heaped upon gift! In order to receive
the blessings of wealth, you must put yourself in the proper
position. Your Heavenly Father not only promises to bless
you, He also teaches you how to profit. In addition to the
twelve blessings of wealth in the Word of God, your Heavenly
Father has outlined specific strategies for wealth creation in
His Word. The key to *receiving* the blessings of wealth is to
implement the wealth generation strategies in the Word of
God. The Lord will teach you specifically the way in which
you should go.

If you have a single source of income through your job,
you may wonder how the Lord can possibly get all of those
compounded, multiplied blessings to you. It may be difficult

to envision. That is why it is so important to renew your mind first and foremost. You have to radically renew your money mindset to be properly positioned for prosperity. In Isaiah 55:8-9 (NLT) the Lord tells us, *"'My thoughts are nothing like your thoughts,' says the Lord. 'And my ways are far beyond anything you could imagine. For just as the heavens are higher than the earth, so my ways are higher than your ways and my thoughts higher than your thoughts.'"*

The Lord promises in Isaiah 48:17 that He will teach you to profit. The Hebrew word for "teach" is *"lamad"* which means to diligently, expertly, and skillfully teach and instruct. The word "profit" is the Hebrew word *"yawal"* which means to gain profit or to be profitable. Your Heavenly Father not only promises to send compounded, multiplied blessings to you in twelve different ways, He will also diligently, expertly, and skillfully teach you how to gain profit and continue to be profitable! The success strategies you need to prosper abundantly are found in the Word of God!

As you renew your mind and embrace the wealth creation strategies in the Word of God, you will be challenged to let go of conventional thinking. Romans 12:2 (NLT) instructs us, *"Don't copy the behavior and customs of this world, but let God transform you into a new person by changing the way you think. Then you will learn to know God's will for you, which is good and pleasing and perfect."*

By faith, release group thinking and embrace Kingdom thinking. Proverbs 3:5-6 (NKJV) tells us, *"Trust in the Lord with all your heart, And lean not on your own understanding; In all your ways acknowledge Him, And He shall direct your paths."*

There are ten primary wealth generation strategies in the Word of God. Before we break down the ten strategies, let's discuss some core concepts that are vitally important to understanding God's methods of breakthrough.

Understanding Poverty and Lack

Remember, the first aspect of the Trifold Attack is Poverty and Lack. Poverty is defined as the state of being poor; the state of one who lacks a usual or socially acceptable amount of money or material possessions — scarcity. To be poor means to have little money or few possessions; poverty is not having enough money for the basic things that people need to live properly.

You may not be in poverty, but you still may suffer from LACK. To experience **lack** means **to not have, to not have enough, or to stand in need of**. To experience lack means you do not have enough *in any area*. Your daily needs may be met, but you may still be lacking – not having enough to afford a higher level of living, or pursue your mission and purpose in the Lord.

Your needs for your home, car, clothes, and food may be met, but you may not have the additional funds to enjoy your life. This is part of God's blessing of abundance for you. You may be lacking the additional finances necessary to step forward with your purpose or the dream for your life. Your daily needs are met, but your mission is hindered. You are unable to start your business, start your ministry, start a family, pay for your education, take a vacation, help your family members, or give to a cause you care about. This is also LACK.

Lack has the power to delay the plans that the Lord has for you from moving forward. God will not give you a mission assignment and then withhold the resources necessary to complete it. If He has given you the purpose, He will also send you the provision. The enemy cannot *stop* your purpose, but he can *stall* your purpose by hindering the necessary provision and resources from arriving, and by stealing them when they have arrived, leaving you in the condition of lack.

The presence of **debt** indicates the presence of lack. Debt is an amount of money that you owe to a person, bank, or company. It is the state of owing money to someone or something. If you owe money in any area, that means you are experiencing a lack in that area. Your Heavenly Father promises that you shall not lack (Psalm 23:1).

Debt indicates the presence of lack.

If a person carries a debt, such as a mortgage, car note, student loan, credit card balance, business loan, medical bill, etc., it indicates they did not have enough money at the point in time of purchase to cover the specific need in that area, without negatively impacting other areas of their life (e.g., their savings). The person is lacking sufficient resources to pay for their home, car, education, medical treatment, or other needs in full. They are borrowing against their earning power in the future, because they lack the full resources to cover the need today. Borrowing means you do not have enough at the present time to meet the need, and in biblical terminology, that is LACK.

In our world's system, to borrow against our future earning power is commonplace and an accepted way of thinking. We do not think of it as lacking when we borrow against our future. Our borrowing power is actually viewed as a measure of how well we are doing in the world's economy. God's covenant blessing is greater than the world's system. God's thoughts are not our thoughts and His ways are not our ways. His thoughts are higher than our thoughts and His ways our higher. God wants you to be free of the encumbrance of debt. God wants you to be thoroughly equipped for every good work with enough extra to be in *overflow*.

In our world's system, as long as you have enough money to cover all of your monthly payments, barring any unforeseen circumstances such as an interruption to your income or earning power, you are considered to be doing well. However, your Heavenly Father has a higher level of life for you. Your Heavenly Father wants you to be free of any payments that leverage your future, or put you at risk, where an unforeseen circumstance can dramatically change the condition of your life.

Borrowing against your future earning power means, by definition, you do not have enough at the *moment of purchase* to pay in full. When you go to the bank or credit union to finance your home or vehicle, you are borrowing money from the bank to complete your purchase with a promise to pay back what you borrowed (principal) at a fee (interest). The longer it takes you to pay back the principal, the more of a fee you pay. Interest is the penalty you pay for lack. God's promise to you is that you shall not lack for anything! God's promises do not come with a penalty. This is LACK.

Interest is the penalty you pay for lack.

God's economy is a cash economy – He operates from a perspective of overflow and abundance. You have more than enough to meet every need. You do not need to leverage tomorrow for today's needs. He does not want you enslaved to anyone through debt.

As I was studying for this work, I heard the Father say to me, not out loud but as an impression in my spirit, **"I do not have to borrow to bless you."** The Lord is saying, "I do not need to have you borrow money, putting you under the world's system of debt, giving the Devourer access to you, to get My blessing to you." I felt the Lord saying to me in my spirit, "I do not have to borrow from Bank of America, JP Morgan Chase, Wells Fargo, or anyone else to bless you. Everything in and upon the earth is Mine. I can bless you directly through sufficient provision for your needs to be fully met with overflow, without putting you into debt. I do not need to put you into a position of servitude to someone else to get a blessing to you from Me."

I had to stop and consider this! This was a major paradigm shift. With small purchases, we easily understand the concept, but for houses, cars, land, education, properties, buildings, businesses, and larger ticket items, this is a challenging concept that requires a radical mindset shift. The Lord would say:

- *The earth is the Lord's, and everything in it, the world, and all who live in it.*
  Psalm 24:1 (NIV)

- *For every beast of the forest is Mine, And the cattle on a thousand hills.*
  Psalm 50:10 (NKJV)

- *The rich rules over the poor, and the borrower becomes the lender's slave.*
  Proverbs 22:7 (NASB)

- *You will lend to many nations but will borrow from none.*
  Deuteronomy 28:12 (NIV)

181

- *Let no debt remain outstanding, except the continuing debt to love one another.*
  Romans 13:8 (NIV).

God can put you into position to purchase your next vehicle in cash without a car payment. You can complete your education without being saddled with student loan debt at graduation. Your Heavenly Father can greatly accelerate your ability to pay off an existing loan or mortgage, so that you can pay it ahead of schedule, and eliminate the penalty of interest on the debt. God can and will bless you such that you can purchase a home with cash, without a 30-year or 15-year mortgage. Cash transactions occur every day, but this practice is not taught to us as the norm. We are indoctrinated into a dependence on debt.

There is no condemnation for where we are now (Romans 8:1)! All of us can expand our mindset in this area (Romans 12:2)! If you believe these blessings are possible in your life, then you will see them come to pass. According to your faith, be it unto you (Matthew 9:29). God is challenging us to come up higher to His level of thinking and His ways of doing things.

I do not believe there is anything inherently wrong with financing major purchases, but it is clearly not God's highest level of blessing. Debt is not a sin, but it is a weight (Hebrews 12:1). Pray and ask the Holy Spirit for His guidance. All scriptural references to debt are in a negative light – we are instructed to avoid it. What if we can challenge our thinking and expand our faith to believe:

- God can and will increase our income and improve our stewardship such that we can greatly accelerate the payoff of major purchases such as cars, homes, land, home improvements, educational needs, etc.,

182

so that we quickly come out from under the system of debt.

- God can and will meet our needs for major purchases without debt. He is able to bless us so that we can maintain a cash position and pay in full with funds remaining.

- God will help us renew our minds and redefine the need to borrow as a form of lack, and deal with it as such through our covenant promises as believers and heirs of God. Lack is a challenge to be eliminated, not tolerated.

Your Heavenly Father does not want you to experience lack in any area of your life. God's children stand in need of nothing! With the Lord God Almighty as your Heavenly Father, you can take complete dominion over debt and lack. Your Heavenly Father is Jehovah Jireh, *The Lord Who Sees and Provides*. He is El Shaddai, which literally means, *The Almighty, All-Sufficient, Multi-Breasted One Who Nourishes, Supplies, and Satisfies*. Hallelujah! As a mother's milk provides total nutrition for her newborn child who is completely dependent upon her, God's blessings are likewise full and complete. He blesses abundantly, comprehensively, with all manner of blessings. With God as your Heavenly Father, there is no reason to not have, to not have enough, or to stand in need of anything in your life.

When you honor the Lord, He will put you in the polar opposite condition to lack, which is *overflow*. God will cause you to be abundantly supplied, with more than enough for every good work. Psalm 34:10 (NLT) states, *"Those who trust in the Lord will lack no good thing."* Change your faith confession today. In every circumstance in your life, begin to declare the Word of God in Psalm 23:1 (AMP): *"The Lord is*

my Shepherd, to feed, guide, and shield me, I shall not lack."
Renew your mind regarding the necessity of debt. Declare
on a daily basis that you are debt free. Do not allow lack to
exist in your life unchallenged and unchecked. Do not accept
it as a normal condition. Speak to it. Take dominion over it.
Declare over your life now, "I shall not lack!"

Now that we have a better understanding of debt and lack, let's
begin our study of the wealth strategies in the Word of God.

WEALTH STRATEGIES IN THE WORD

There are ten wealth generation strategies in the Word of
God that will produce abundance and overflow. The ten
strategies are:

1. Get out and stay out of debt.

2. Use multiplication for income growth.

3. Get positioned for promotion.

4. Own your own business.

5. Create multiple streams of income.

6. Diversify your income sources.

7. Own land, homes, and property.

8. Use your highest level gifting to create wealth.

9. Use leverage, not time.

10. Maximize teamwork.

The Ten Wealth Strategies in the Word – Figure 1

WEALTH STRATEGY	SCRIPTURE REFERENCES
Get out and stay out of debt.	Deuteronomy 15:4-6 (NIV), (AMP)
	Deuteronomy 28:12 (NIV), (NKJV)
	Leviticus 25:35-38 (NLT)
	Psalm 37:21 (NIV)
	Psalm 112:5 (NLT)
	Proverbs 6:1-5 (AMP), (NLT)
	Proverbs 22:26-27 (NIV)
	Proverbs 11:15 (NLT)
	Proverbs 22:7 (NIV) (NASB)
	Ezekiel 18:5, 7, 8, 9 (NIV)
	Romans 13:8 (NIV)
Use multiplication for income growth.	Genesis 26:12-14 (NKJV)
	Matthew 25:14-30 (NIV)
	Mark 4:20 (AMP)
Get positioned for promotion.	Genesis 39:2-5 (NIV)
	Genesis 39:22-23 (NIV)
	Genesis 41:38-41 (NIV)
	Psalm 75:6-7 (AMP)
	Proverbs 22:29 (AMP)
	Daniel 2:46-49 (NIV)
	Daniel 6:1-4 (NIV)
	Matthew 5:16 (NKJV)
	Luke 12:42-44 (NLT)

WEALTH STRATEGY	SCRIPTURE REFERENCES
Own your own business.	Genesis 13:2, 5-6 (NIV)
	Genesis 30:25-30 (NLT)
	Genesis 31:4-7 (NIV)
	Exodus 5:6-9 (NIV)
	Deuteronomy 28:12 (NIV)
	Proverbs 6:6-8 (NIV)
	Proverbs 31:16, 18, 24 (NIV)
	Matthew 20:6-7 (NIV)
	Luke 5:4-7 (NLT)
	John 21:4-6 (NLT)
	1 Thessalonians 4:11-12 (NIV)
Create multiple streams of income.	Deuteronomy 28:4 (NKJV)
	Deuteronomy 30:9 (AMP)
	Ecclesiastes 11:2, 6 (NIV)
	Proverbs 31:16, 18, 24 (NIV)
Diversify your income sources.	Genesis 13:2 (AMP)
	Genesis 24:34-35 (NLT)
	Ecclesiastes 11:2, 6 (NIV)
	Proverbs 31:16, 18, 24 (NIV)
Buy land, homes, property, and income-generating assets.	Genesis 33:19 (NLT)
	Deuteronomy 8:10-14, 18 (NIV)
	Deuteronomy 28:8 (NKJV)
	1 Chronicles 4:10 (AMP)
	Proverbs 19:14 (NKJV)
	Proverbs 24:3-4 (NIV)
	Proverbs 31:16 (NIV)
	Isaiah 54:2-3 (NKJV)
	Psalm 68:6 (AMP)
	Matthew 7:24 (NLT)

Wealth Strategy	Scripture References
Use your highest level gifting to create wealth.	Exodus 35:10 (NLT)
	Exodus 35:30-35 (NLT)
	1 Kings 10:23 (NIV)
	1 Kings 5:5-6 (NIV)
	1 Chronicles 15:22 (NIV)
	Proverbs 31:19, 22, 24 (NIV)
	Jeremiah 1:5 (NKJV)
	Matthew 25:14-30 (NIV)
	1 Peter 4:10 (AMP)
Use leverage, not time.	Proverbs 31:16 (NIV)
	Mark 12:1-2 (NIV)
	Matthew 20:1-2 (NIV)
Maximize teamwork.	Genesis 11:6 (NLT)
	1 Kings 5:5-6 (NIV)
	Ecclesiastes 4:8 (NKJV)
	Ecclesiastes 4:9-10 (NIV)
	Ecclesiastes 4:12 (NLT)
	Leviticus 26:8 (NLT)
	Deuteronomy 32:30-31 (NIV)
	Matthew 18:19-20 (NKJV)

Let's take a closer look at each one.

GET OUT AND STAY OUT OF DEBT

The first wealth strategy in the Word of God is to get out and stay out of debt. Proverbs 22:7 (NIV) warns us, *"The rich rule over the poor, and the borrower is slave to the lender."* The Lord wants you to operate in freedom, not in a position of debt servitude or debt slavery to any person or institution. Debt opens the door to the Devourer, and gives him access to systematically eat away at your provision. God does not want you to be subjected to the financial cancer of debt. Remember, debt allows a portion of your provision to be consumed by interest, which is the penalty you pay on lack. In the case of a mortgage, the interest penalty is very significant (multiple times the initial value of your home) and front-loaded into the loan, greatly extending the payback period up to thirty years. Debt is the primary tool the Devourer uses to destroy your provision. We must attack it aggressively and eliminate it completely.

The biblical instructions regarding debt are clear and emphatic. Although we are indoctrinated into a debt mentality in our culture, to generate biblical wealth, we must raise our level of thinking to God's level. Colossians 3:2 (AMP) tells us, *"And set your minds and keep them set on what is above (the higher things), not on the things that are on the earth."* Set your mind on the higher things of debt-free living, abundance, and overflow to be equipped for every good work. There is no condemnation for those who are in Christ Jesus! Start from wherever you are now, and begin to make the changes the Lord prescribes to raise your standards to His standards. In scripture, the Lord instructs us to do four things.

Pay off the debt that you already have. Romans 13:8 (NIV) instructs us, *"Let no debt remain outstanding, except the continuing debt to love one another, for whoever loves others* *has fulfilled the law."* Designate a portion of your net income (income – expenses) to be used for debt reduction each month. Pay off your consumer debt, starting from the smallest bill to the largest. With each monthly mortgage installment, pay additional money on the principal of your loan, to reduce the balance that is subject to the penalty of interest. Use rapid debt reduction strategies to pay off all outstanding debt, including your mortgage, ahead of the planned payment schedule. Two simple debt reduction strategies will be provided in the Financial Wellness Action Plan.

Do not incur new debt. Believe God to open the storehouse of His bounty to bless the work of your hands and increase your income sources, such that you can pay off your existing debt and complete your future purchases and investments without debt. Deuteronomy 28:12 (NKJV) states, *"The Lord will open to you His good treasure, the heavens, to give the rain to your land in its season, and to bless all the work of your hand. You shall lend to many nations, but you shall not borrow."*

Do not become the guaranty for another person's debt. Do not co-sign for another person's debt. It puts you at risk. Proverbs 22:26-27 (NLT) instructs us, *"Don't agree to guarantee another person's debt or put up security for someone else. If you can't pay it, even your bed will be snatched from under you."*

Do not charge interest when lending to help another in need. When you are in position to lend to others in a difficult situation, do not charge them interest on the loan. Interest is the fee or penalty the world's system charges on lack – the need to borrow money. In the Lord's economy, when we are lending from a position of overflow, we are to lend without penalizing our brothers and sisters with interest. We are not to exploit the difficult circumstances of another for profit. Take special note of the Lord's thoughts on interest. We are not to pay it by borrowing, or charge it when lending! It is the world system's penalty on lack. Leviticus 25:35-38 (NLT) tells us, *"If one of your fellow Israelites falls into poverty and cannot support himself, support him as you would a foreigner or a temporary resident and allow him to live with you.* **Do not charge interest** *or make a profit at his expense. Instead, show your fear of God by letting him live with you as your relative. Remember,* **do not charge interest on money you lend him** *or make a profit on food you sell him. I am the Lord your God, who brought you out of the land of Egypt to give you the land of Canaan and to be your God."*

Meditate on the following scriptures to eliminate debt and interest-bearing loans.

But there will be no poor among you, for the Lord will surely bless you in the land which the Lord your God gives you for an inheritance to possess, If only you carefully listen to the voice of the Lord your God, to do watchfully all these commandments which I command you this day. When the Lord your God blesses you as He promised you, then you shall lend to many nations, but you shall not borrow; and you shall rule over many nations, but they shall not rule over you.
Deuteronomy 15:4-6 (NIV)

The Lord will open the heavens, the storehouse of his bounty, to send rain on your land in season and to bless all the work of your hands. You will lend to many nations but will borrow from none.
Deuteronomy 28:12 (NIV)

If one of your fellow Israelites falls into poverty and cannot support himself, support him as you would a foreigner

or a temporary resident and allow him to live with you. Do not charge interest or make a profit at his expense. Instead, show your fear of God by letting him live with you as your relative. Remember, do not charge interest on money you lend him or make a profit on food you sell him. I am the Lord your God, who brought you out of the land of Egypt to give you the land of Canaan and to be your God.
Leviticus 25:35-38 (NLT)

The wicked borrow and do not repay, but the righteous give generously.
Psalm 37:21 (NIV)

Good comes to those who lend money generously and conduct their business fairly.
Psalm 112:5 (NLT)

My child, if you have put up security for a friend's debt or agreed to guarantee the debt of a stranger — if you have trapped yourself by your agreement and are caught by what you said — follow my advice and save yourself, for you have placed yourself at your friend's mercy. Now swallow your pride; go and beg to have your name erased. Don't put it off; do it now! Don't rest until you do. Save yourself like a gazelle escaping from a hunter, like a bird fleeing from a net.
Proverbs 6:1-5 (NLT)

Don't agree to guarantee another person's debt or put up security for someone else. If you can't pay it, even your bed will be snatched from under you.
Proverbs 22:26-27 (NIV)

There's danger in putting up security for a stranger's debt; it's safer not to guarantee another person's debt.
Proverbs 11:15 (NLT)

191

The rich rule over the poor, and the borrower is slave to the lender.
Proverbs 22:7 (NIV)

Suppose there is a righteous man who does what is just and right. He does not oppress anyone, but returns what he took in pledge for a loan. He does not commit robbery but gives his food to the hungry and provides clothing for the naked. He does not lend to them at interest or take a profit from them. He withholds his hand from doing wrong and judges fairly between two parties. He follows my decrees and faithfully keeps my laws. That man is righteous; he will surely live, declares the Sovereign Lord.
Ezekiel 18:5, 7, 8, 9 (NIV)

Let no debt remain outstanding, except the continuing debt to love one another, for whoever loves others has fulfilled the law.
Romans 13:8 (NIV)

USE MULTIPLICATION FOR INCOME GROWTH

The second wealth strategy in the Word of God is to use multiplication for income growth. There are two equations you will want to focus on for wealth creation:

Income – Expenses = Net Income
(to invest/save/compound)

Assets – Liabilities = Net Worth (what you own)

Your **income** is the amount of money that you have coming into your household each month from your job, businesses, investments, properties, royalties, etc. Your **expenses** constitute the amount of money going out of your household each month to cover your needs, such as your mortgage or rent, utilities, food, car payments, insurance, etc. If you increase your income and decrease your expenses, you will have greater net income to invest, save, and compound. You will use your net income (income minus expenses) to invest in assets. An **asset** is something of value that you own that brings additional income into your household. For a working definition, I like the definition of assets offered by Robert Kiyosaki, best-selling author of the "Rich Dad, Poor Dad" series. He defines an asset as "something that puts money in your pocket, whether you work or not." An asset could be a business you own, rental property, or intellectual property to which you own the rights. An asset generates income. Your goal is to use your net income to invest in assets – those items that will bring more income into your household. Your **liabilities** are your debts and anything that is taking money out of your household.

Assuming you have set a budget and you are practicing good stewardship with your existing resources, from a wealth creation standpoint, you want to focus the majority of your attention on **increasing your income and your income sources** rather than on cutting expenses. You will see a far greater impact on your personal wealth by concentrating on generating greater income sources. You want to focus your attention on using your gifts and talents to 1) increase your income, 2) increase your income sources, and 3) invest in income-generating assets.

The good and faithful servants in Matthew 25:14-30 did not produce small, fractional income growth. They both doubled what they had been given. Renew your money mindset to think in terms of multiplied, compounded growth, not fractional growth. When the Lord brings a return on seed sown, it is multiplied growth – thirty, sixty, and even a hundredfold return (Mark 4:20). The Lord promises to bless the work of your hands. You must put your efforts into those endeavors that have the potential to produce multiplied returns. Put yourself in position for multiplied income growth. Once you have set up an effective budget, this is a far better use of your time, talent, and resources than focusing on cost-cutting measures. Use multiplication for income growth.

Meditate on the following scriptures on using multiplication for income growth.

Isaac planted crops in that land and the same year reaped a hundredfold, because the Lord blessed him. The man became rich, and his wealth continued to grow until he became very wealthy. He had so many flocks and herds and servants that the Philistines envied him.
Genesis 26:12-14 (NIV)

"So he who had received five talents came and brought five other talents, saying, 'Lord, you delivered to me five talents; look, I have gained five more talents besides them.' His lord said to him, 'Well done, good and faithful servant; you were faithful over a few things, I will make you ruler over many things. Enter into the joy of your lord.' He also who had received two talents came and said, 'Lord, you delivered to me two talents; look, I have gained two more talents besides them.' His lord said to him, 'Well done, good and faithful servant; you have been faithful over a few things, I will make you ruler over many things. Enter into the joy of your lord.'"
Matthew 25:20-23 (NKJV)

And those sown on the good (well-adapted) soil are the ones who hear the Word and receive and accept and welcome it and bear fruit—some thirty times as much as was sown, some sixty times as much, and some [even] a hundred times as much.
Mark 4:20 (AMP)

GET POSITIONED FOR PROMOTION

The third wealth strategy in the Word of God is to get positioned for promotion. Maximize your earning potential from your current employment or business. Promotion comes from the Lord. Colossians 3:23-24 (AMP) instructs us, *"Whatever may be your task, work at it heartily (from the soul), as [something done] for the Lord and not for men, Knowing [with all certainty] that it is from the Lord [and not from men] that you will receive the inheritance which is your [real] reward. [The One Whom] you are actually serving [is] the Lord Christ (the Messiah)."* Whether you are working in a full-time job or in your own business, you want to position yourself so the Lord can promote you to the next level.

Position yourself for increase by being excellent in everything you do. Do not allow yourself to deliver a mediocre, average, or middle-of-the-pack performance. Matthew 5:16 (NKJV) tells us, *"Let your light so shine before men, that they may see your good works and glorify your Father in heaven."* Your task is to drastically differentiate yourself. Make every effort to go beyond the norm. Your work ethic, efficiency, effectiveness, productivity, and work quality should be stellar and should stand out. Go beyond the boundaries of your job description. Be the source of solutions to challenging problems on the job or in your business. Display an excellent attitude. Make yourself indispensable to your clientele.

Advance your education, take training courses, and obtain certifications that prepare you for the next level. Seek out stretch assignments and challenging projects that give you the opportunity to showcase your skills. Demonstrate your leadership and management capabilities regardless of your job title and position description. Seek out opportunities for promotion and apply for them.

When you position yourself for promotion, God can show His favor upon you and bring financial increase. Your Heavenly Father can accelerate raises, bonuses, and promotions. He can move you to a different department with greater advancement opportunity. He can open doors in other companies offering higher salaries and benefits. He can promote you to run your own business. He can elevate the quality and increase the quantity of your business clientele. No matter what position you are in, or how you are being treated by your manager, peers, or co-workers, make the decision to do your work as unto the Lord, excelling at everything you do.

Joseph was promoted despite being sold into slavery and wrongfully imprisoned. Despite his captivity, Daniel displayed an excellent spirit that caused him to be noticed, favored, and promoted. When you perform with excellence, you position yourself for favor, promotion, abundance, and increase.

Meditate on the following scriptures to get positioned for promotion.

The Lord was with Joseph so that he prospered, and he lived in the house of his Egyptian master. When his master saw that the Lord was with him and that the Lord gave him success in everything he did, Joseph found favor in his eyes and became his attendant. Potiphar put him in charge of his household, and he entrusted to his care everything he owned. From the time he put him in charge of his household and of all that he owned, the Lord blessed the household of the Egyptian because of Joseph. The blessing of the Lord was on everything Potiphar had, both in the house and in the field. **Genesis 39:2-5 (NIV)**

So the warden put Joseph in charge of all those held in the prison, and he was made responsible for all that was done there. The warden paid no attention to anything under

Joseph's care, because the Lord was with Joseph and gave him success in whatever he did.
Genesis 39:22-23 (NIV)

So Pharaoh asked them, "Can we find anyone like this man, one in whom is the spirit of God?" Then Pharaoh said to Joseph, "Since God has made all this known to you, there is no one so discerning and wise as you. You shall be in charge of my palace, and all my people are to submit to your orders. Only with respect to the throne will I be greater than you." So Pharaoh said to Joseph, "I hereby put you in charge of the whole land of Egypt."
Genesis 41:38-41 (NIV)

For not from the east nor from the west nor from the south come promotion and lifting up. But God is the Judge! He puts down one and lifts up another.
Psalm 75:6-7 (AMP)

Do you see a man diligent and skillful in his business? He will stand before kings; he will not stand before obscure men.
Proverbs 22:29 (AMP)

Then King Nebuchadnezzar fell prostrate before Daniel and paid him honor and ordered that an offering and incense be presented to him. The king said to Daniel, "Surely your God is the God of gods and the Lord of kings and a revealer of mysteries, for you were able to reveal this mystery." Then the king placed Daniel in a high position and lavished many gifts on him. He made him ruler over the entire province of Babylon and placed him in charge of all its wise men. Moreover, at Daniel's request the king appointed Shadrach, Meshach and Abednego administrators over the province of Babylon, while Daniel himself remained at the royal court.
Daniel 2:46-49 (NIV)

It pleased Darius to appoint 120 satraps to rule throughout the kingdom, with three administrators over them, one of whom was Daniel. The satraps were made accountable to them so that the king might not suffer loss. Now Daniel so distinguished himself among the administrators and the satraps by his exceptional qualities that the king planned to set him over the whole kingdom. At this, the administrators and the satraps tried to find grounds for charges against Daniel in his conduct of government affairs, but they were unable to do so. They could find no corruption in him, because he was trustworthy and neither corrupt nor negligent.
Daniel 6:1-4 (NIV)

Let your light so shine before men, that they may see your good works and glorify your Father in heaven.
Matthew 5:16 (NKJV)

And the Lord replied, "A faithful, sensible servant is one to whom the master can give the responsibility of managing his other household servants and feeding them. If the master returns and finds that the servant has done a good job, there will be a reward. I tell you the truth, the master will put that servant in charge of all he owns.
Luke 12:42-44 (NLT)

OWN YOUR OWN BUSINESS

The fourth wealth strategy in the Word of God is to own your own business. Ownership is a master key to creating multi-generational wealth. Business ownership is not for a select few, it is for everyone! The concept of long-term employment (that does not produce ownership) as we know it today is a product of the industrial age. It is not a biblical concept for wealth generation. Employment does not create generational wealth. Wealth in the Bible is directly related to ownership. In the Bible, we see a predominantly agricultural context, with an emphasis on farming and fishing. They owned land, produced crops, planted vineyards, and raised livestock. A family's wealth was often measured by their land ownership and the size of the herds and flocks they owned (Genesis 24:34-35). You will also see examples of skilled craftsmen, merchants, and sea traders, working in a multitude of different trades, importing and exporting a variety of goods. In the New Testament, we also see an emphasis on skilled fisherman. In all of these instances, they were business owners – they were in control of their own livelihood – what we would term "self-employed" in our day and age. A family established wealth through what they owned, passed down, and maintained generationally through the inheritance.

Those who worked for others were predominantly servants, slaves, and in one setting, contract laborers (Matthew 20:1-16). A person could end up in servitude to another as a result of a debt that could not be paid, or as a result of being conquered in war. A person could sell himself into servitude to pay off his debt.

Servitude was temporary. The servant would be freed during the year of Jubilee (Leviticus 25:39-41), or after six years of service (Exodus 21:2-4). The servant would be free and the remaining debt would be canceled in the seventh year. A servant could choose to stay in servitude for life (Exodus 21:6), but most would desire their freedom, so they could re-establish ownership of their own property and businesses for their own families. Those who worked for others on a short-term, free-will basis were apprentices, and would eventually leave to own their own enterprise and establish wealth for their own family. In all cases, whether servant or slave, their objective was freedom – to own and establish assets that could be passed down generationally in their own family lineage.

We see this principle in the account of Jacob, who served under Laban for fourteen years to marry Rachel (Genesis 29:15-30). After his service was completed, Jacob wanted his freedom from his difficult relationship with Laban, to establish his legacy for his own family (Genesis 30:25-29).

Overwhelmingly, God blessed His children directly through what they **owned** and **controlled**. He gave them land to own, and then He blessed the work of their hands (Deuteronomy 30:9 AMP). He blessed their crops, multiplied their flocks and herds, and increased the production of their vineyards and winepresses (Deuteronomy 28:4, 8, 11, 12; Proverbs 3:9-10).

Abram and Lot had to part ways because their flocks had become so numerous they could not continue to travel together (Genesis 13:2, 5-6). We see the principle of generational wealth with Abraham, Isaac, and Jacob who were all extraordinarily blessed in their fields and flocks. Isaac reaped a hundredfold return in one year (Genesis 26:12-14). Jacob became very wealthy with large flocks (Genesis 30:43). The Proverbs 31 woman prospered in four different businesses that she owned (Proverbs 31:16-25). In the New Testament, when Jesus called the disciples, He blessed Peter's fishing business, along with James and John, his partners, to the point that the nets were breaking and the boats were sinking under the load of fish (Luke 5:7)! Jesus repeated this blessing when He appeared to Peter and the disciples in John 21:4-8.

The same principle of wealth through ownership applies to us today and produces the same results. The Lord does not change (Malachi 3:6)! Today, God blesses His children abundantly through what we own and control. The most prosperous individuals in today's society are business owners and heirs of generational wealth produced through ownership. The Lord will abundantly bless the work of your hands (1 Thessalonians 4:11-12). The Lord will bless your ability to work independently and gather your harvest without a commander or overseer (Proverbs 6:6-8). When you open up a direct conduit for the Lord to bless you through what you own and control, you are positioning yourself for the Lord's greatest blessings of wealth, riches, abundance, and overflow.

If you are in a full-time job, with a single source of income, it is imperative that you open up another avenue of blessing that you control directly. Get a direct line to the windows of Heaven (Deuteronomy 28:12). Open up direct access to the twelve blessings of wealth. Keep your job and build a business. Long-term employment does not end in ownership. Eventually, you must leave your job. You do not own it. You will not establish generational wealth through your job, simply because you cannot own it, control it, gift it, or pass it down as an inheritance. You can and should work hard with diligence and excellence to maximize your earnings from your job, but for *wealth generation*, establish **ownership**. You must own your own business. Position for promotion on your job, and build a side business using your gifting, through which the Lord can bless you directly and abundantly for maximum profitability.

When you own your own business, you eliminate the process of waiting to be hired, promoted, or given a raise. Through your own diligence, discipline, and determination, you have a direct line of blessing from the Father (Matthew 20:6-7).

Long-term employment that ends in retirement, not ownership, is a product of the industrial age. It is not a biblical construct for *wealth creation*. Apprenticeship ends in ownership. You are working for someone else temporarily, on your way to your abundant blessing through ownership. See your job as a temporary apprenticeship, on your way to ownership! The closest parallel to employment without ownership in the Bible is the concept of the servant. The Lord frees servants so they can become heirs (Galatians 4:7). Heirs receive an inheritance. Heirs inherit ownership. You are no longer a servant, but an heir of God, and joint heir with Christ! Step into your inheritance. Wealth comes through ownership.

If you own a business, see your business as your conduit of direct blessing from the Lord. Work with diligence, and expand your enterprise. Stretch out your tent. Enlarge your territory!

Meditate on the following scriptures that demonstrate the wealth creation strategy of owning your own business. Wealth comes through ownership!

Soon after Rachel had given birth to Joseph, Jacob said to Laban, "Please release me so I can go home to my own country. Let me take my wives and children, for I have earned them by serving you, and let me be on my way. You certainly know how hard I have worked for you." "Please listen to me," Laban replied. "I have become wealthy, for the Lord has blessed me because of you. Tell me how much I owe you. Whatever it is, I'll pay it." Jacob replied, "You know how hard I've worked for you, and how your flocks and herds have grown under my care. You had little indeed before I came, but your wealth has increased enormously. The Lord has blessed you through everything I've done. But now, what about me? When can I start providing for my own family? **Genesis 30:25-30 (NLT)**

So Jacob sent word to Rachel and Leah to come out to the fields where his flocks were. He said to them, "I see that your father's attitude toward me is not what it was before, but the God of my father has been with me. You know that I've worked for your father with all my strength, yet your father has cheated me by changing my wages ten times. However, God has not allowed him to harm me..."

Genesis 31:4-7 (NIV)

The Lord will open the heavens, the storehouse of his bounty, to send rain on your land in season and to bless all the work of your hands. You will lend to many nations but will borrow from none.

Deuteronomy 28:12 (NIV)

Go to the ant, you sluggard; consider its ways and be wise! It has no commander, no overseer or ruler, yet it stores its provisions in summer and gathers its food at harvest.

Proverbs 6:6-8 (NIV)

She considers a field and buys it; out of her earnings she plants a vineyard. She sees that her trading is profitable, and her lamp does not go out at night. She makes linen garments and sells them, and supplies the merchants with sashes.

Proverbs 31:16, 18, 24 (NIV)

About five in the afternoon he went out and found still others standing around. He asked them, 'Why have you been standing here all day long doing nothing?' "'Because no one has hired us,' they answered. "He said to them, 'You also go and work in my vineyard.'

Matthew 20:6-7 (NIV)

When he had finished speaking, he said to Simon, "Now go out where it is deeper, and let down your nets to catch some fish." "Master," Simon replied, "we worked hard all last night and didn't catch a thing. But if you say so, I'll let the nets down again." And this time their nets were so full of fish they began to tear! A shout for help brought their

*partners in the other boat, and soon both boats were filled
with fish and on the verge of sinking.*
Luke 5:4-7 (NLT)

*At dawn Jesus was standing on the beach, but the disciples
couldn't see who he was. He called out, "Fellows, have you
caught any fish?" "No," they replied. Then he said, "Throw
out your net on the right-hand side of the boat, and you'll
get some!" So they did, and they couldn't haul in the net
because there were so many fish in it.*
John 21:4-6 (NLT)

*...make it your ambition to lead a quiet life: You should
mind your own business and work with your hands, just as
we told you, so that your daily life may win the respect of
outsiders and so that you will not be dependent on anybody.*
1 Thessalonians 4:11-12 (NIV)

CREATE MULTIPLE STREAMS OF INCOME

The fifth wealth strategy in the Word of God is to create
multiple streams of income. If you have a single income
stream from your job or business, you are at significant risk
if something should happen to disrupt your primary source
of income. Consider what could happen to you and your
family if you experienced a job layoff, or if your business
experienced a significant setback. The enemy is looking for
those who are vulnerable to attack. Having a single source
of income is a major vulnerability. If the enemy can disrupt
your income, your provision can drop to zero. Many people
have experienced this in the midst of an economic downturn,
natural disaster, major illness, or serious accident. Through
the wisdom of King Solomon, your Heavenly Father advises
you on how to protect yourself and eliminate the risk of a

catastrophic income loss. It is vital to have more than one income source coming into your household. Ecclesiastes 11:2, 6 (NIV) instructs us, *"**Invest in seven ventures, yes, in eight**; you do not know what disaster may come upon the land. Sow your seed in the morning, and at evening let your hands not be idle, for you do not know which will succeed, whether this or that, or whether both will do equally well."*

Your objective is to have multiple streams of income, not one! The biblical strategy of wealth creation is to have at least seven streams of income, and preferably eight. If you have eight income streams, and you experience a job layoff or business setback, you still have six or seven other income sources to protect you. If the enemy penetrates your lines of defense and disrupts one or more income paths, you still have multiple ways that the Lord is delivering provision to you.

In addition, not only are you protected from economic downturn, but you are also strategically positioned for increase. As you build and invest in multiple business ventures, you will not know at the outset which one will bring in the greatest revenue. One venture may prove to be the most profitable, or they may do equally well. You are strategically positioned for increase with multiple income streams through which the Lord can bring abundance and overflow. In the financial arena, having multiple streams of income is the master key to receiving multiplied, compounded blessings from the Lord: blessing upon blessing, favor upon favor, gift heaped upon gift!

How can you achieve this goal of multiple income streams? Start from where you are now, and immediately begin the process to add one additional income source. Over time, add additional streams of income until you have multiple conduits of blessing in place. You can utilize a combination of income sources including job income, business income, and income-generating assets such as real property, intellectual property, and investments such as stocks, bonds, and securities. If you have a single source of income through your job, begin by adding a side business. Next, you could begin adding investments, including property. If you own a business, you can create multiple income streams by adding new product lines, or expanding into new markets. You can invest in multiple businesses. You can add a business to your portfolio that has a multi-tiered compensation structure, so that you have multiple streams of income coming to you from within one business.

Your goal is to reach seven to eight streams of income. The key is to focus your attention on adding at least **one** additional income source now. As your competence and confidence in business ownership increase, you can add additional streams of income. The Proverbs 31 woman has four businesses listed in her description. Not only is she an entrepreneur, but she wisely has four different sources of business income. She uses the profits from the first business, real estate, to invest in the second, a vineyard (Proverbs 31:16, 18, 24).

Meditate on the following scriptures that demonstrate the wealth creation strategy of creating multiple streams of income.

Blessed shall be the fruit of your body, the produce of your ground and the increase of your herds, the increase of your cattle and the offspring of your flocks.
Deuteronomy 28:4 (NKJV)

And the Lord your God will make you abundantly prosperous in every work of your hand, in the fruit of your body, of your cattle, of your land, for good; for the Lord will again

delight in prospering you, as He took delight in your fathers,
Deuteronomy 30:9 (AMP)

Invest in seven ventures, yes, in eight; you do not know what disaster may come upon the land. Sow your seed in the morning, and at evening let your hands not be idle, for you do not know which will succeed, whether this or that, or whether both will do equally well.
Ecclesiastes 11:2, 6 (NIV)

She considers a field and buys it; out of her earnings she plants a vineyard. She sees that her trading is profitable, and her lamp does not go out at night. She makes linen garments and sells them, and supplies the merchants with sashes.
Proverbs 31:16, 18, 24 (NIV)

DIVERSIFY YOUR INCOME SOURCES

The sixth wealth strategy in the Word of God is to diversify your streams of income. This strategy is closely related to number five. In addition to adding multiple income sources, you want to ensure they are in different, unrelated industries for diversification. If one industry is affected by an economic downturn or disaster, your other, unrelated income sources remain unaffected. However, if all of your income sources are related, you can be severely impacted. For example, if all of your income sources are connected to the real estate industry, and we experience an economic downturn, you are not as protected as you would be if you had diversified into other industries such as energy, food production, manufacturing, technology, health and wellness, etc., unrelated to real estate.

The Bible tells us Abraham was extremely wealthy; he diversified his assets within his flocks and in precious metals.

He owned flocks of sheep, goats, cattle, camels, and donkeys, as well as silver and gold (Genesis 24:34-35 NLT).

In the example of the Proverbs 31 woman, she has invested in real estate, a vineyard, a clothing line, and a specialty line of sashes for merchant traders (Proverbs 31:16, 18, 24). Your businesses and other income sources should be diversified as well.

Review the following scriptures that demonstrate the wealth creation strategy of diversifying your income sources.

Now Abram was extremely rich in livestock and in silver and in gold.
Genesis 13:2 (AMP)

"I am Abraham's servant," he explained. "And the Lord has greatly blessed my master; he has become a wealthy man. The Lord has given him flocks of sheep and goats, herds of cattle, a fortune in silver and gold, and many male and female servants and camels and donkeys."
Genesis 24:34-35 (NLT)

Invest in seven ventures, yes, in eight; you do not know what disaster may come upon the land. Sow your seed in the morning, and at evening let your hands not be idle, for you do not know which will succeed, whether this or that, or whether both will do equally well.
Ecclesiastes 11:2, 6 (NIV)

She considers a field and buys it; out of her earnings she plants a vineyard. She sees that her trading is profitable, and her lamp does not go out at night. She makes linen garments and sells them, and supplies the merchants with sashes.
Proverbs 31:16, 18, 24 (NIV)

Own land, homes, and property

The seventh wealth strategy in the Word of God is to own land, homes, and property. The Lord sealed His covenant with Abraham and his descendants with land ownership (Genesis 17:3-8). We consistently see the Lord bless His children with land, homes, and fertile properties (Deuteronomy 6:10-12). Land and property ownership should be a priority in your wealth generation strategy. It is the foundation of wealth.

We have already discussed in detail the importance of business ownership for your income sources. You want to supplement your current employment with business ventures that you own, and eventually transition to an ownership model for all of your income sources.

As your income increases, you will have greater resources available to pay off debt and to invest in income-generating assets, such as land, homes, and rental properties. Remember

Income − Expenses = Net Income
(to save, invest, and compound).

Many people make the mistake of squandering their net income by overspending on consumer goods that do not produce any income. Instead of investing, they buy consumer goods and status symbols that depreciate in value. You certainly should enjoy your life, but make it a top priority to re-invest your net income into other income-generating assets for wealth generation. Make investments that appreciate in value and add to your generational wealth. Make it a priority to invest in land, homes, rental properties, and commercial properties.

Business ownership and property ownership are critical components of your wealth generation strategy. Meditate on the following scriptures that demonstrate the wealth creation strategy of owning land, homes, and property.

Jacob bought the plot of land where he camped from the family of Hamor, the father of Shechem, for 100 pieces of silver.
Genesis 33:19 (NLT)

When you have eaten and are satisfied, praise the Lord your God for the good land he has given you. Be careful that you do not forget the Lord your God, failing to observe his commands, his laws and his decrees that I am giving you this day. Otherwise, when you eat and are satisfied, when you build fine houses and settle down, and when your herds and flocks grow large and your silver and gold increase and all you have is multiplied, then your heart will become proud and you will forget the Lord your God, who brought you out of Egypt, out of the land of slavery... But remember the Lord your God, for it is he who gives you the ability to produce wealth, and so confirms his covenant, which he swore to your ancestors, as it is today.
Deuteronomy 8:10-14, 18 (NIV)

The Lord will command the blessing on you in your storehouses and in all to which you set your hand, and He will bless you in the land which the Lord your God is giving you.
Deuteronomy 28:8 (NKJV)

Jabez cried to the God of Israel, saying, Oh, that You would bless me and enlarge my border, and that Your hand might be with me, and You would keep me from evil so it might not hurt me! And God granted his request.
1 Chronicles 4:10 (AMP)

Houses and riches are an inheritance from fathers, But a prudent wife is from the Lord.
Proverbs 19:14 (NKJV)

By wisdom a house is built, and through understanding it is established; through knowledge its rooms are filled with rare and beautiful treasures.
Proverbs 24:3-4 (NIV)

She considers a field and buys it; From her profits she plants a vineyard.
Proverbs 31:16 (NKJV)

Enlarge the place of your tent, And let them stretch out the curtains of your dwellings; Do not spare; Lengthen your cords, And strengthen your stakes. For you shall expand to the right and to the left, And your descendants will inherit the nations, And make the desolate cities inhabited.
Isaiah 54:2-3 (NKJV)

God places the solitary in families and gives the desolate a home in which to dwell; He leads the prisoners out to prosperity; but the rebellious dwell in a parched land.
Psalm 68:6 (AMP)

"Anyone who listens to my teaching and follows it is wise, like a person who builds a house on solid rock..."
Matthew 7:24 (NLT)

USE YOUR HIGHEST LEVEL GIFTING

The eighth wealth strategy in the Word of God is to use your highest level gifting to create wealth. Your Heavenly Father has blessed you with innate gifts and talents that are your keys to wealth, abundance, and overflow. Your gifting is directly related to your mission assignment – why you are here on the earth at this specific point in time. Your natural gifts and talents hold the highest income potential for your life. When you use your gifting in the service of your mission assignment to help others, you will unlock your maximum personal earning potential. Your task is to identify your gifts and talents and then create income streams that effectively monetize what you are gifted to do.

Many people have not discovered their unique gifting, or they underestimate the potential of their gifts. They overlook their own special talents as unimportant. David's gifting with a slingshot does not seem particularly impressive until Goliath comes onto the scene. David's expert marksmanship with a slingshot and small, smooth stones was exactly what was needed to slay Goliath and win the battle for Israel (1 Samuel 17:40-51). This victory fueled David's ascension to the throne.

You have multiple gifts, talents, skills and abilities, but you have been blessed with one to three, and potentially five *high level gifts – extraordinary talents* that come easily and naturally to you. These are the gifts you will use to build your income streams. When we look at athletes, actors, musicians, and artists, it is easy to mistakenly believe they were singled out and blessed in a special manner that others were not. That is not true! All of us are created in the image and likeness of God. Our Heavenly Father has gifted every one of us with something unique and special that we can do that reflects a unique aspect of His divine essence. Our gifts are different, but we are all gifted. Professional athletes and celebrity artists have identified their highest level gifts. Their talents are displayed on a public stage. These gifts are obvious to the masses. Others in anonymity or obscurity are also gifted by God – their gifts may not be publicly displayed, but they are just as valuable to society and for wealth creation.

The Lord does not bless one and ignore another. The Lord has considered each of us individually and blessed us uniquely.

Jeremiah 1:5 (NKJV) tells us, *"Before I formed you in the womb I knew you; Before you were born I sanctified you; I ordained you a prophet to the nations."* The quantity and characteristics of the gifts are different in each person, bestowed by God the Father according to each one's ability, to equip each individual for their divine mission assignment.

Do not compare yourself to other people. Use what you have been given to the fullest! You have everything you need to fulfill your mission and purpose on the earth, and to produce wealth for you and your family. The professional athlete is not preferred by God over the teacher – Michael Jordan was not endowed more richly than Marva Collins – the athlete's gifts are just more visible on a public stage. The creative person, skilled in music, writing, or art, is not more or less valuable than the analytical person gifted in math, science, or technology. Every gift is needed in the service of humanity. Every gift has wealth potential assigned to it. The process of identifying, cultivating, using, and monetizing your highest level gifting is vital to unlocking your wealth potential.

King Solomon used his gifting of divine wisdom to serve and lead the people of Israel. Many traveled from distant nations to receive his instruction and hear his wise guidance. King Solomon became the wealthiest man in the world (1 Kings 10:23). What has the Lord given to you?

The Proverbs 31 woman used her gifting as a clothing designer and seamstress to generate wealth (Proverbs 31:19, 22, 24). Ask the Lord to reveal your divine mission assignment, and the specific gifts He has given you to fulfill it. Use your gifting to serve others, and you will unlock your personal wealth potential.

Take a complete inventory of your gifts, talents, skills and abilities, and identify your *highest level gifts*. What comes naturally and easily to you? What are you passionate about? The gifts and talents you have been given are the tools you will use to access your provision to fund your purpose. The Lord expects you to use and multiply your talents (Matthew 25:20-21). Do not allow your talents to stay dormant inside of you. If you bury your talent and do not use it, the Lord considers that to be wickedness and laziness (Matthew 25:24-29). Once you identify your highest level gifting, you will create income streams that allow you to use your gifts to serve others. Create a business that allows you to use your gifts. Open up a direct line of blessing from the Father using the gifting He has given you. You deserve to be highly compensated for your contributions to society to serve humanity. Your talents are precious natural resources inside of you, to be used to generate wealth for you and your family.

Meditate on the following scriptures regarding using your highest level gifts and talents for wealth creation.

Come, all of you who are gifted craftsmen. Construct everything that the Lord has commanded:
Exodus 35:10 (NLT)

Then Moses told the people of Israel, "The Lord has specifically chosen Bezalel son of Uri, grandson of Hur, of the tribe of Judah. The Lord has filled Bezalel with the Spirit of God, giving him great wisdom, ability, and expertise in all kinds of crafts. He is a master craftsman, expert in working with gold, silver, and bronze. He is skilled in engraving and mounting gemstones and in carving wood. He is a master at every craft. And the Lord has given both him and Oholiab son of Ahisamach, of the tribe of Dan, the ability to teach their skills to others. The Lord has given them special skills as engravers, designers, embroiderers in blue, purple, and scarlet thread on fine linen cloth,

and weavers. They excel as craftsmen and as designers."
Exodus 35:30-35 (NLT)

King Solomon was greater in riches and wisdom than all the other kings of the earth.
1 Kings 10:23 (NIV)

"I intend, therefore, to build a temple for the Name of the Lord my God, as the Lord told my father David, when he said, 'Your son whom I will put on the throne in your place will build the temple for my Name.' "So give orders that cedars of Lebanon be cut for me. My men will work with yours, and I will pay you for your men whatever wages you set. You know that we have no one so skilled in felling timber as the Sidonians."
1 Kings 5:5-6 (NIV)

Kenaniah the head Levite was in charge of the singing; that was his responsibility because he was skillful at it.
1 Chronicles 15:22 (NIV)

In her hand she holds the distaff and grasps the spindle with her fingers. She makes coverings for her bed; she is clothed in fine linen and purple. She makes linen garments and sells them, and supplies the merchants with sashes.
Proverbs 31:19, 22, 24 (NIV)

"Before I formed you in the womb I knew you; Before you were born I sanctified you; I ordained you a prophet to the nations."
Jeremiah 1:5 (NKJV)

For the kingdom of heaven is like a man traveling to a far country, who called his own servants and delivered his goods to them. And to one he gave five talents, to another two, and to another one, to each according to his own ability; and immediately he went on a journey. Then he who had

received the five talents went and traded with them, and made another five talents. And likewise he who had received two gained two more also...
Matthew 25:14-17 (NIV)

As each of you has received a gift (a particular spiritual talent, a gracious divine endowment), employ it for one another as [befits] good trustees of God's many-sided grace [faithful stewards of the extremely diverse powers and gifts granted to Christians by unmerited favor].
1 Peter 4:10 (AMP)

USE LEVERAGE, NOT TIME

The ninth wealth strategy in the Word of God is to use leverage, not time, to build your income sources. When your income is linked to the expenditure of time, there is a natural limitation on what you can earn. If you earn a wage per hour, there is a restriction on your wealth potential. You can only work a finite number of hours per day; the maximum would be 24 hours. However, if one or more of your income sources produce passive, residual income, meaning you continue to earn income if you do not work, you remove the restriction of time from your income potential.

You can use leverage instead of time by:

- Creating income sources where you are paid *multiple* times for work that you do *one* time

- Utilizing the manpower of other people so your income is not limited by the amount of hours you alone can work, and

- Investing in income-generating assets that work for you, such as real estate.

When there is a linear relationship between the number of hours you work and what you earn, you are using time – for example, you earn $25 per hour. Each hour you work, you are paid your specified wage of $25. That is a time-based income model.

When you create a sustaining income source that continues to pay you without working a specified number of hours, you are using leverage. For example, let's say that you invest 40 hours of your time to purchase a piece of real estate, and you lease the property to a tenant. Each month that the tenant pays rent, you have leveraged your initial investment of the time it took to secure and lease the property. If the tenant stays in the property for 12 months, you have established 12 months of passive income without working additional hours beyond the initial investment of 40 hours, to generate that income. Each month, you will receive the rent on the property without additional work. That is an example of leverage. You are paid *multiple* times for the work that you did *one* time.

If you are a musician and you are paid a fee to deliver a live performance on a specific date, you are using time. You are paid for the hours that you perform at the concert. If you record and distribute your music on a CD or through online distribution, you are using leverage. Each time your music project is sold, you are earning residual income from the initial investment of your time, creativity, and effort to record the project. You record the project one time, but you reap the benefit multiple times. You can reach potentially millions of people all over the world with your music using leverage, depending on the demand for your project. Month after month, year after year, you are still earning from your initial investment of time and energy into your music project. You can earn income while you are at rest, spending time with your family, or investing your time in something else.

217

Your income streams will most likely include a combination of time-based models and leveraged models that produce residual and passive income. The more that you can use leverage over time, the higher your income potential will be. Leveraged income is not limited by the number of hours you have available to devote to a project. Time-based income has a natural limitation, because there are a finite number of hours that you can work in each day. If you stop working, your income stops.

As you establish multiple and diversified income streams, be sure to include income sources that are leveraged, and are not dependent on a personal, daily time investment to maximize your wealth potential. In a leveraged model that produces passive income, even if you stop working, your income continues. Meditate on the following scriptures that demonstrate the wealth creation strategy of the power of leverage.

She considers a field and buys it; out of her earnings she plants a vineyard.
Proverbs 31:16 (NIV)

Jesus then began to speak to them in parables: "A man planted a vineyard. He put a wall around it, dug a pit for the winepress and built a watchtower. Then he rented the vineyard to some farmers and moved to another place. At harvest time he sent a servant to the tenants to collect from them some of the fruit of the vineyard.
Mark 12:1-2 (NIV)

For the kingdom of heaven is like a landowner who went out early in the morning to hire workers for his vineyard. He agreed to pay them a denarius for the day and sent them into his vineyard.
Matthew 20:1-2 (NIV)

MAXIMIZE TEAMWORK

The tenth wealth strategy in the Word of God is to maximize teamwork. The biblical model of wealth generation is based on collaboration, not competition. Teamwork is greatly valued over individual effort. In Ecclesiastes 4:7-8 (NKJV), King Solomon tells us, *"Then I returned, and I saw vanity under the sun: There is one alone, without companion: He has neither son nor brother. Yet there is no end to all his labors, Nor is his eye satisfied with riches. But he never asks, 'For whom do I toil and deprive myself of good?' This also is vanity and a grave misfortune."* The key to exponential wealth creation is to maximize teamwork. There are multiple benefits of working in a team-based business model.

First, when you work in a team-based business model, the wealth strategy of leverage is built in. Ecclesiastes 4:9 (MSG) tells us, *"It's better to have a partner than go it alone. Share the work, share the wealth."* You have a greater return for your labor working together with others than working independently. You are rewarded financially for the compounded, collective efforts of the team. Collaboration produces greater results than competition. You have a vested financial interest in the success of your partners, and your partners have a vested financial interest in your success. As you serve and help others to succeed, you will be richly blessed.

Second, as an added benefit, you have help available if you experience a setback. Ecclesiastes 4:9-10 (NLT) instructs us, *"Two people are better off than one, for they can help each other succeed. If one person falls, the other can reach out and help. But someone who falls alone is in real trouble."* If you have multiple sources of income and one is interrupted, you are protected because the trouble spot is not your sole source of income. Likewise, if you have multiple business partners and one of you experiences a setback, there are others to continue moving the business forward.

Third, you have protection against attack. The thief does not come except to steal, kill, and destroy (John 10:10). The enemy is roaming about like a roaring lion, seeking whom he may devour (1 Peter 5:8). Standing alone makes you much more vulnerable to attack, but in a team environment, you have great protection. You can defeat an attack more successfully. Ecclesiastes 4:12 (NLT) tells us, *"A person standing alone can be attacked and defeated, but two can stand back-to-back and conquer. Three are even better, for a triple-braided cord is not easily broken."*

Fourth, when you maximize teamwork, the compounding effect on your results is **exponential** not linear. Leviticus 26:8 (NLT) states, *"Five of you will chase a hundred, and a hundred of you will chase ten thousand! All your enemies will fall beneath your sword."* A compounding effect takes over, multiplying your results. Using a team model adds an exponential growth component to your wealth generation strategies.

I believe every person should have at least one team-based business in their portfolio of multiple income streams. A team-based business incorporates all of the benefits of business ownership, mitigates the downside of self-employment, and capitalizes on the enormous benefits of building wealth in a collaborative, cooperative environment that maximizes teamwork. A team-based business is highly leveraged, therefore it has an extremely high upside profit potential, benefiting from the exponential, compounding effect that teamwork has on wealth generation.

We live in a unique time in history, when business models have advanced dramatically. I believe the team-based, relationship marketing or network marketing business model is the strongest business model of our time for wealth generation, as it incorporates all of the biblical strategies of wealth creation, held together with a servant leadership framework. As a micro-franchise, a network marketing business is affordable and accessible to everyone, making business ownership practical and realistic for working people. With careful vetting and business selection, strong leadership, personal mentoring, and detailed training from skilled professionals who adhere to biblical principles, I believe a relationship marketing or network marketing micro-franchise can be an extraordinarily profitable addition to your wealth generation plan.

Meditate on the following scriptures on creating wealth by maximizing teamwork.

The Lord said, "If as one people speaking the same language they have begun to do this, then nothing they plan to do will be impossible for them."
Genesis 11:6 (NLT)

"I intend, therefore, to build a temple for the Name of the Lord my God, as the Lord told my father David, when he said, 'Your son whom I will put on the throne in your place will build the temple for my Name.' "So give orders that cedars of Lebanon be cut for me. My men will work with yours, and I will pay you for your men whatever wages you set. You know that we have no one so skilled in felling timber as the Sidonians."
1 Kings 5:5-6 (NIV)

There is one alone, without companion: He has neither son nor brother. Yet there is no end to all his labors, Nor is his eye satisfied with riches. But he never asks, "For whom do

I toil and deprive myself of good?" This also is vanity and a grave misfortune.
Ecclesiastes 4:8 (NKJV)

Two people are better off than one, for they can help each other succeed. If one person falls, the other can reach out and help. But someone who falls alone is in real trouble.
Ecclesiastes 4:9-10 (NLT)

A person standing alone can be attacked and defeated, but two can stand back-to-back and conquer. Three are even better, for a triple-braided cord is not easily broken.
Ecclesiastes 4:12 (NLT)

Five of you will chase a hundred, and a hundred of you will chase ten thousand! All your enemies will fall beneath your sword.
Leviticus 26:8 (NLT)

How could one man chase a thousand, or two put ten thousand to flight, unless their Rock had sold them, unless the Lord had given them up? For their rock is not like our Rock, as even our enemies concede.
Deuteronomy 32:30-31 (NIV)

"Again I say to you that if two of you agree on earth concerning anything that they ask, it will be done for them by My Father in heaven. For where two or three are gathered together in My name, I am there in the midst of them."
Matthew 18:19-20 (NKJV)

Summary –
WEALTH STRATEGIES IN THE WORD

In summary, let's review the ten powerful wealth generation strategies in the Word of God, which are your master keys to increase, prosperity, abundance, and overflow.

1. Get out and stay out of debt.

2. Use multiplication for income growth.

3. Get positioned for promotion.

4. Own your own business.

5. Create multiple streams of income.

6. Diversify your income sources.

7. Own land, homes, and property.

8. Use your highest level gifting to create wealth.

9. Use leverage, not time.

10. Maximize teamwork.

Your Heavenly Father not only promises to bless you, He also teaches you how to **profit** (Isaiah 48:17). Proverbs 14:23 (NIV) tells us, "*All hard work brings a **profit**, but mere talk leads only to poverty.*" You may say to yourself, "I *already* work hard, but I'm not prospering and I'm not wealthy." Notice that the Lord said he would teach you to **profit**. If you have a single income source through your job, you are earning an hourly wage or an annual salary. You do not make a **profit** on a job. You must own your own business to make a **profit**! Wealth comes through **ownership**. When you implement the ten powerful wealth generation strategies, you will eliminate any limitations on your provision, and you will experience blessing upon blessing, favor upon favor, and gift heaped upon gift! These are the keys to your financial breakthrough.

I would like for you to make this list personal and prophetic, by beginning to speak these wealth generation strategies as faith declarations over your life immediately. Faith comes by hearing, and hearing by the Word of God (Romans 10:17).

Read the following statements out loud on a daily basis.

1. I will get out and stay out of debt. I am debt free.

2. I will use multiplication for income growth. I receive a thirty, sixty, and a hundredfold return on my labor.

3. I am positioned for promotion. I have divine favor for raises, promotions, bonuses, new clients, and advancement opportunities.

4. I own my own business. I am a successful business owner.

5. I am creating multiple streams of income. I have seven, yes eight streams of income. I own multiple businesses and income-generating assets.

6. I am diversifying my income sources.

7. I own land, homes, real property, and intellectual property.

8. I use my highest level gifting to create wealth.

9. I will use leverage, not time, to create wealth and abundance.

10. I will maximize teamwork.

The Lord is abundantly blessing all of the work of my hands. In the name of Jesus, Amen.

11 | the prosperity diversion

And if a kingdom is divided and rebelling against itself, that kingdom cannot stand. And if a house is divided (split into factions and rebelling) against itself, that house will not be able to last.
Mark 3:24-25 (AMP)

The enemy is well aware of the Word of God. He knows that God wants you to be well and whole financially, not debilitated by the financial cancer of debt and lack. He knows that your Heavenly Father wants you to be *abundantly blessed* so that you can liberally provide for yourself and your family, prepare for the future, provide an inheritance for your children's children, be prepared for the unexpected, build the Kingdom of God, and give generously to the needs of others – thoroughly equipped for every good work. The enemy knows that the tithe is holy, and opens the windows of Heaven to you. He knows that when you tithe, God Himself will protect you from the devastation of the Devourer. He knows that giving is the key to subduing greed, and unlocking your prosperity.

He knows that the cycle of blessing brings increase to your life, builds the Kingdom of God, and produces a harvest of souls saved for eternity. He knows that if you have the abundant provision promised in the Word, you will successfully complete your mission assignment, expand your territory, and enforce the victory of the cross. He knows he owes you a sevenfold payback on everything he has stolen from you in your lifetime.

The enemy knows that the Lord has twelve different blessings of wealth in store for you. He knows your Heavenly Father is about to bless you with one grace after another, spiritual blessing upon spiritual blessing, favor upon favor, and gift heaped upon gift through Jesus Christ the Lord. He knows there is a hundredfold return on its way to you for everything you have sacrificed for the Kingdom. He knows that once you are debt free, you are no longer subject to the oppression of debt slavery. He knows you are an heir of God and joint heir with Jesus Christ. He knows you are Abraham's seed, and the blessing of Abraham is on your life. He knows you are destined to own land, houses, properties, multiple businesses, and much silver and gold. He knows.

The enemy desperately hopes that you still do not know. The last thing the devil wants you to do is learn the Word of God for yourself. He does not want you to master the principles of financial wellness from the Word, meditate in the Word day and night, and memorize the scriptures so that the Holy Spirit can bring them to your remembrance. He does not want you to pray the Word of God on a daily basis because if you do, he knows the Word will not return void. It will accomplish everything that God sent it forth to do in your life (Isaiah 55:11)! He wants the Body of Christ to stay in an ignorant, inactive state.

The devil has a cunning plan in work against the Body of Christ. If it were obvious that the devil himself and his demonic forces are opposing you financially, you would be more apt to resist his attack immediately. So, to continue the cycle of stealing and stockpiling uninterrupted, he craftily diverts the attention away from himself so you are distracted by something else entirely. He wants you to question God's blessings of prosperity for your life. "Does God *really* want you to prosper?" This is the same type of manipulative trickery he used on Adam and Eve (Genesis 3:1). I call this scheme the Prosperity Diversion.

The enemy knows that a house divided cannot stand (Mark 3:24-25). So the best way to render the church ineffective is to divide it *from the inside*. The Prosperity Diversion is a scheme to keep the church divided into factions. Some believe the scriptural promises of financial blessing and some do not. Using the Prosperity Diversion, he can keep the church busy with arguments, accusations, attacks, and in-fighting while he continues to steal, kill, and destroy the members of the family of God. The Prosperity Diversion provides good air cover – it is a major distraction to the Body, so the enemy can work under the radar and continue to devour your resources unchecked and unhindered.

Here is how the Prosperity Diversion works. The enemy:

- Deceives the family of God by twisting the scriptures regarding money

- Deceives you into believing God wants you to be poor, not whole and well financially

- Diverts attention away from himself by focusing the church on arguments, accusations, and in-fighting with one another

- Divides the church into factions which weakens the Army of the Lord

- Distracts the church by focusing on the prosperity of individuals, instead of financial wellness and healing from the cancer of debt and lack for the entire Body

- Devours the blessings of the righteous while they are distracted; steals, kills, and destroys; stockpiles the stolen resources for his own illegal and immoral purposes, and

- Diverts resources away from the Kingdom of God to prevent the gospel from being preached and the poor from being helped.

The Prosperity Diversion is a scheme the enemy uses to attack those who are prospering with right motives. He causes the Body of Christ to be stuck on an endless debate of whether or not God wants you to prosper, when the answer is clearly outlined in the scripture. While the members of the Body are debating, criticizing, and attacking their own brothers and sisters, the enemy, undetected, is free to steal, kill, and destroy without resistance! While many argue over someone's new car, the enemy is quietly advancing his financial cancer!

We must get our focus on defeating the Devourer and achieving financial wellness. If you are fulfilling your responsibilities and using good stewardship with your resources, the Lord delights in you enjoying your life (1 Timothy 6:17). We must focus on helping the millions of people suffering under the tyranny of debt and lack. We must get our focus on the real enemy, not tear at each other over what kind of houses we live in. These petty arguments distract the Army of the Lord from the real battlefield and give the enemy free reign to steal our resources. We are fighting over houses and cars instead of beating back the Devourer! This is the mission of the Prosperity Diversion. It is a distraction. Settle it in your heart right now the Lord desires for you to be blessed abundantly to the point of overflow, so you can meet every need. He has twelve different blessings of wealth and prosperity prepared for you.

As you battle for your financial breakthrough, you will surely encounter the effects of the Prosperity Diversion, so I want you to be aware of it so you can recognize and resist the attack. The enemy will use anyone he can to stop you. Not everyone around you will understand the changes in your attitude and actions. They will tell you all the reasons why God doesn't want you to prosper. Recognize that you do not wrestle against flesh and blood, but against principalities, powers, rulers of the darkness, and spiritual hosts of wickedness in heavenly places (Ephesians 6:12). Do not be seduced to participate in arguments (Proverbs 9:7-8, Titus 3:9-10). Pray for them.

Many people are deeply deceived regarding what the Bible says about money. That is why I want you to master, meditate, and memorize the Word of God for yourself. It is not enough to know two or three scriptures. I want you to be fully equipped with over 90 verses. You cannot be moved by another person's misinterpretation, misrepresentation, or misquotation of the Bible. Know it for yourself! Then you can be a lifeline to those still under the deception of the enemy.

It is important that you have a complete and balanced understanding of the Word of God. There are two extremes to the Prosperity Diversion. Some erroneously believe that money is the root of all evil and that poverty is a godly condition that equals spirituality. Careful study of the scriptures will show you this is clearly not true! We are called to be the solution to help the poor. The other extreme is the viewpoint that we can use the scriptures to ask for whatever we want and the Lord is obligated to give it to us, like a genie in a bottle. The drives of the sin nature are unchecked and out of control. There is no focus on giving, generosity, building the Kingdom, or helping others who are in need. Money has become an idol. This is a manipulation of scripture — prosperity for selfish gain. Both of these perspectives are perversions of the scripture and come from the evil one to keep you from knowing and living the balanced truth of God's Word.

Someone will say, "You shouldn't pray and ask the Lord to bless you financially. Money is the root of all evil. You cannot serve both God and money. Believing God for financial increase means you're greedy for gain." Prosperity Diversion. The *love of money* is a root of all kinds of evil (1 Timothy 6:10). They don't know that you understand the eight warnings of wealth. You've already studied, subdued the drives of your sin nature, and gotten your driver's license. You are ready to properly steward the blessings of wealth from the Lord without burning down your house.

Someone else will say, "It's easier for a camel to go through the eye of a needle than for a rich man to enter the Kingdom of Heaven. Jesus said to sell all you have and give it to the poor." Prosperity Diversion. They don't know the rest of the story. Wealth is a blessing from the Lord. *Trusting in wealth* stopped the rich young ruler. They do not understand the trust test or the blessing of the hundredfold return for sacrificial giving (Mark 10:29-30).

"It's not wise to pay off your house...you need the mortgage interest for a tax write-off." Debt slavery. No thank you. The borrower becomes the lender's slave (Proverbs 22:7).

"If God wants me to be rich then how come I lost my job? I'm just trying to make ends meet. Every time I get a little money in the bank, something happens. I stopped giving my money to that church...that preacher just wanted my money." Home invasion! Doors and windows are wide open to the cycle of stealing! The Devourer is in full force. They are outside of the covering of the cycle of blessing, ignorant of the cycle of stealing, and vulnerable to the devastation of the Devourer. Red alert! Now you can help!

You will hear the Prosperity Diversion all around you. Many people will point to examples of men and women who have abused the Word of the Lord for selfish gain and have suffered the consequences. Yes, there are some in business and ministry who have let selfish motives and the unchecked drives of the sin nature get the best of them. They have misused the scriptures to hoard wealth for themselves instead of giving generously and building the Kingdom. They did not heed the warnings of wealth. In each case, it burned down their house. I asked the Lord about this and I heard the Holy Spirit say to me in my spirit, *"The failings of men do not negate the promises of God. Teach the Word."*

The failings of men do not negate the promises of God.

You cannot allow the mistakes of others to affect your belief in the scripture and your blessings from the Lord. In your personal battle for breakthrough, you cannot allow the enemy to divert your attention from the scripture. Stay focused on the Word! We must elevate our personal experience to align with the Word of God. We must not attempt to fit the Word into the confines of our personal experience. God's thoughts are higher than our thoughts, and His ways are higher than our ways (Isaiah 55:8-9).

I am truly thankful to the Lord that I have had the privilege to serve in numerous churches with men and women of God with extraordinary honesty and integrity, a passion to help people in need, and a drive to reach the lost. I believe they are indicative of the vast majority of the Body of Christ. I am thankful for the numerous business owners and entrepreneurs who use their businesses as conduits of blessing and generosity to others. I am thankful they have been extraordinarily blessed of the Lord. I rejoice in their abundant prosperity as they build the Kingdom of God. They understand what it means to be blessed to be a blessing. Through these examples, both in business and ministry, I understand what a financial bridge to the Kingdom of God looks like. I trust the Heavenly Father to make the crooked places straight and the rough places plain (Isaiah 40:4). I have participated in the cycle of blessing and watched it work exactly as the Lord intended. I have seen and experienced the blessing of the Lord on the righteous.

Do not allow the enemy to misquote and manipulate the Word of God to keep you from your financial breakthrough. He has been using that tactic since the Garden of Eden. Be aware of the Prosperity Diversion. Do not entertain the attacks on other members of the Body of Christ. A house divided will not stand. Recognize the enemy is working behind the scenes.

Some people will undoubtedly criticize you or even persecute you for believing God for His blessings of wealth, riches, abundance, and overflow. Some will accuse you of being greedy for gain. Some will criticize you when your abundant blessings manifest from the Lord. Continue to pray fervently. Continue to sow bountifully. Continue to work diligently. Continue to give generously. You are entering your Promised Land. Resistance will come. Understand this is the enemy's last ditch effort to stop the blessings of God from flowing into your life in abundance. He knows you are about to enlarge your territory. You are expanding the Kingdom. You are leaving your legacy. You are helping others who are in need. You are storing up precious eternal treasure in Heaven. Pray, and press forward! You are destined for breakthrough!

PART II

THE WEAPONS
OF OUR WARFARE

12 | preparing for breakthrough

W hat exactly is a *breakthrough*? This is a common term that we hear thrown around a lot. I want to explain what it really is, so you have the right concept in your mind. Sometimes when we pray, we say, "Lord, I seriously need a breakthrough!" What we *really* mean is, "I need a RESCUE! I need a miracle! I need divine intervention! Lord, get me out of this situation!"

I like to watch old war movies, and in every movie, there is always a tense scene where you see a few stranded soldiers, trapped deeply behind enemy lines. They are lying in the grass or in a foxhole, doing their best to take cover and remain undetected by the enemy. The enemy forces are encroaching slowly but surely...it is inevitable that the hidden position of the stranded soldiers will be uncovered, and they will be taken captive, injured, or killed. Just when it seems that all hope is lost, you begin to hear the faint whir of military helicopters approaching from a distance. In just the nick of time, reinforcements arrive! The Special Forces rescue unit comes and you see the powerful warriors dropping down out of the sky. Some engage in direct combat with the enemy, while others on rope ladders drop from the helicopters. In dramatic fashion, the stranded or injured soldiers are quickly lifted up and out of the war zone. What a rescue!

There is nothing wrong with praying for rescue. God has provided the rescue plan for us! Jesus is our Rescue. He fulfilled the ultimate rescue mission when He came down to the earth, set aside His deity to take on the form of a man, lived a sinless life, and became the ultimate Sacrifice for our sins. He defeated sin, death, hell, and the grave. He ransomed us out of a situation that we could never have gotten out of on our own.

Rescue is something Jesus did for us when we were powerless to save ourselves. Romans 5:6-8 (NIV) encourages us, *"You see, at just the right time, when we were still powerless, Christ died for the ungodly. Very rarely will anyone die for a righteous person, though for a good person someone might possibly dare to die. But God demonstrates his own love for us in this: While we were still sinners, Christ died for us."* Through His death and resurrection, Christ has already completed God the Father's rescue plan of redemption for us.

Jesus is the Warrior that has come down from on high to rescue us out of the war zone of sin and eternal separation from God. Your Heavenly Father has already done that for you. Rescue power is alive and well. You can call on the name of Jesus and that ultimate rescue power is there immediately for you. There are times in our lives when we are powerless in our human strength to change a situation. You or a family member may receive a difficult diagnosis; Jesus is your Rescue! You may face a natural disaster, like a hurricane, tornado, or earthquake; Jesus is your Rescue! You may face a devastating heartbreak and you need the Lord to ease your pain; Jesus is your Rescue!

Rescue and breakthrough are two different things. Rescue is what Jesus did for us at the cross. Breakthrough, on the other hand, is something we do. It is an act of warfare. Some battles we have to fight. We have to take territory. We have to beat back the circumstances.

Jesus is our Rescue. Breakthrough is warfare.

To strengthen you, God will allow circumstances to exist and to continue in your life that you need to battle through. He doesn't drop into the circumstance and dramatically lift you up and out. He keeps you on the battlefield, but He strengthens you to fight and WIN. We learn the right mindset for breakthrough from King David.

Psalm 144:1-2 (NLT) proclaims, *"Praise the Lord, who is my rock. He trains my hands for war and gives my fingers skill for battle. He is my loving ally and my fortress, my tower of safety, my rescuer. He is my shield, and I take refuge in him. He makes the nation submit to me."*

Psalm 18:34-36 (NLT) tells us, *"He trains my hands for battle; he strengthens my arm to draw a bronze bow. You have given me your shield of victory. Your right hand supports me; your help has made me great. You have made a wide path for my feet to keep them from slipping."*

Often, your Heavenly Father will keep you in a situation and use it to teach you how to war. The resistance makes you stronger. You develop faith, tenacity, perseverance, and endurance. You learn to use the weapons of our warfare. You become a skilled warrior with the Word of God. 2 Timothy 2:3 (NKJV) encourages us, *"You therefore must endure hardship as a good soldier of Jesus Christ."* As the Body of Christ, we must learn to stand our ground in difficult circumstances, enforce the victory, occupy territory, and forcefully advance using the delegated authority we have in Jesus.

Let's look at the definition of breakthrough. A breakthrough is 1) an act of overcoming or penetrating an **obstacle** or **restriction**; 2) a **military offensive** that penetrates an enemy's lines of defense; and 3) a **major achievement** or success that permits further progress.

When you battle for breakthrough, you are standing your ground in the spiritual and natural realms, taking down strongholds, breaking through barriers, and overcoming obstacles. Breakthrough is a military offensive – it is violent. It is combat. It is warfare. You are violently opposing the obstacles in your mindset, overcoming the resistance of the enemy, and attacking the presence of negative circumstances in your life. You are occupying your position, forcefully advancing, and taking new territory, until you reach your Promised Land.

We cannot sit back and wait for financial breakthrough to come to us. Breakthrough is something we push forward to accomplish. You lay hold of it. We forcefully advance the breakthrough! You will worship the Lord and honor Him in your life. You will seek first the Kingdom of God, and everything else shall be added. You will declare the promises of God over your life and activate them by faith.

You will do battle with the sword of the Spirit, which is the Word of God. You will stop the attack of the enemy – he is under your feet. You will not tolerate the trespass! You will trample on serpents and scorpions and over all the power of the enemy and nothing shall by any means hurt you. You will discern the deceptions and distractions of the devil. You will renew your mind and change your actions. You will submit to God, resist the devil, and he must flee! You will employ wisdom, knowledge, and understanding in your financial decisions. You will use everything the Lord has given you to enforce your victory and bring forth the breakthrough! You will take hold of the promises of God for your life, starting now.

Your Heavenly Father extends grace to you to cover what you cannot do. Where you are weak, He will show Himself strong and mighty on your behalf. You are not alone. He always goes before you. His grace is sufficient for you. He will not give you more than you can bear. It is perfectly fine to call on the rescue power of the Lord Jesus Christ. God will meet you at your place of faith. You must also do your part. If the Lord does not rescue you up and out of your situation, you still stand strong in your victory, recognizing you are fully equipped to battle for your breakthrough. The weapons of our warfare are not carnal but mighty in God for pulling down strongholds. In the next chapter, we will study your mighty weapons!

13 | the weapons of our warfare

For though we walk in the flesh, we do not war according to the flesh. For the weapons of our warfare are not carnal but mighty in God for pulling down strongholds, casting down arguments and every high thing that exalts itself against the knowledge of God, bringing every thought into captivity to the obedience of Christ, and being ready to punish all disobedience when your obedience is fulfilled.
2 Corinthians 10:3-6 (NKJV)

The enemy comes to steal, kill, and destroy, but we are by no means powerless in this situation! Quite to the contrary, we have all power in Jesus Christ to stop these attacks and trespasses. Jesus has defeated all of the enemy's attacks, plans, and schemes at the cross, but we must know the Word of the Lord, be on the offensive, and use the weapons we have been given to enforce the victory we already have in each area of life. Jesus won the victory at the cross. Since the day of His resurrection, and until the day of Christ's triumphal return, all believers are commissioned with the responsibility to stay on the battlefield and occupy the territory that has been won. When Christ returns, the enemy's rampage against

240

the Body of Christ will cease. Until then, we must use our enforcement strategy, empowered by the Word of God, the name of Jesus, and the blood of Jesus. The blood of Jesus is a hedge of protection around you that the enemy cannot cross.

We must be on the offensive by using the weapons of our warfare to fight for our financial breakthrough on a daily basis. In a natural war, the soldiers have a multitude of different weapons in their arsenal. They have trained endless hours in a variety of scenarios and exercises, so they are fully prepared for anything and everything that can come. When they enter the theater of actual combat, they are so well-trained, they can use their mighty arsenal and move from weapon to weapon, quickly, effortlessly, and automatically without thinking about it. The Army of the Lord is to be the same way! We must learn the weapons of our warfare and train *now* so we are thoroughly equipped, and fully capable of subduing any spiritual opposition that rises against us from the enemy.

When attacked, many believers panic or are paralyzed. When they encounter resistance, a fiery dart, or a wicked scheme of the evil one, they are stunned and stricken with fear. God has not given you a spirit of fear, but of power, love, and a sound mind (2 Timothy 1:7). Greater is He that is in you than he that is in the world (1 John 4:4). If God is for you, who can stand against you (Romans 8:31)? You are an overcomer born of God (1 John 5:4). There is no reason to panic or be paralyzed with fear.

Many believers panic because they are not prepared. They have not learned their weapons, they have not practiced the drills, and they have not completed the daily training exercises. They can't find their combat boots, they don't know where their ammunition is housed, and they don't know how to operate their powerful weapons while skillfully maneuvering in combat. So when the evil day of danger presents itself, and it is time to defend their position, enforce the victory, and win, they have no idea where to start or what to do. Forgive us, Lord, for this lack of preparation! It is time for the Army of the Lord to rise up, get trained, and get equipped to battle for breakthrough!

God has given us a multitude of powerful weapons to secure our victory! You have many different ways to honor the Lord, submit to God, and resist the devil so he *must* flee from you. In the following table, I will share 40 spiritual weapons in seven different areas you can use to defeat the enemy every day of your life! Start out by learning just one or two, and add them to your arsenal. Add prayer to your morning routine every day. Memorize a scripture each day. Write down a power promise from the Word of God and read it out loud several times a day throughout the day. Declare the Word of God over your circumstances. Start taking Holy Communion on a daily basis. Praise God in advance for the victory. Over time, add more. Get skillful. Let the Lord train your hands for battle.

To change your financial circumstances and bring about complete financial breakthrough, you will need to become very effective in using all of these spiritual weapons. You are well able to possess your Promised Land. The enemy has absolutely no chance of keeping you from your abundant financial inheritance if you will dedicate yourself to becoming a skillful warrior, adept in using the following weapons already given and guaranteed effective!

I have divided the 40 weapons into seven categories. The seven focus areas are:

- The Word of God

- The Name of Jesus

- The Blood of Jesus

- Prayer

- Praise, Worship, and Thanksgiving

- Acting on the Word, and

- Enduring in the Word.

Let's take a brief look at each category.

The Word of God. The Word of God is the one offensive weapon listed in the full armor of God in Ephesians Chapter 6. Ephesians 6:17 (NIV) tells us, *"Take the helmet of salvation and the sword of the Spirit, which is the word of God."* God's Word will not return to Him void. Isaiah 55:11 (AMP) declares, *"So shall My word be that goes forth out of My mouth: it shall not return to Me void [without producing any effect, useless], but it shall accomplish that which I please and purpose, and it shall prosper in the thing for which I sent it."*

God has exalted two things above all else – His name and His word, and He has magnified His word even above His name (Psalm 138:2)! If God has said it, you can stand on it – it will come to pass. You have His word on it! Change the focus and substance of your prayer life from your words to God's Word. Memorize the Word of God and speak it into every situation in your life! Stop talking *about* the circumstances and speak *to* the circumstances with the Word of God.

The Name of Jesus. All of the Word of God is summarized in one name: **Jesus**. John 1:1-5 (AMP) explains that, *"In* *the beginning [before all time] was the Word (Christ), and the Word was with God, and the Word was God Himself. He was present originally with God. All things were made and came into existence through Him; and without Him was not even one thing made that has come into being. In Him was Life, and the Life was the Light of men. And the Light shines on in the darkness, for the darkness has never overpowered it [put it out or absorbed it or appropriated it, and is unreceptive to it]."*

Jesus is the Word of God. The name of Jesus holds all power and authority in the universe (Matthew 28:18-20 AMP). Spiritual darkness can never overpower Him. When we speak the name of Jesus over our circumstances, pray in the authority of the name of Jesus, and take authority over any demonic presence and spiritual wickedness in the name of Jesus, we are assured of the victory. Jesus' name is the totality of the Word of God; therefore, Jesus name is above every name. Every knee must bow to the name of Jesus.

Philippians 2:9-11 (NIV) states, *"Therefore God exalted him to the highest place and gave him the name that is above every name, that at the name of Jesus every knee should bow, in heaven and on earth and under the earth, and every tongue acknowledge that Jesus Christ is Lord, to the glory of God the Father."* The name of Jesus has complete authority in every realm. Speak the name of Jesus over your situation and operate in the authority of Jesus Christ every day.

The Blood of Jesus. The enemy cannot penetrate the blood of Jesus over your life. It is vitally important that you apply the blood of Jesus over every aspect of your life every day. Study the account of the first Passover in Exodus Chapters 12-14. Just as the Israelites applied the blood of the Passover lamb to their doorposts so that the death angel had to pass over their homes and not kill the firstborn, we have the complete fulfillment of that protection now by the blood of Jesus, the Lamb of God. Revelation 12:11 (NIV) instructs us that, *"They triumphed over him by the blood of the Lamb and by the word of their testimony; they did not love their lives so much as to shrink from death."* We will live in triumph over the evil one when we apply the blood of Jesus over our lives. We do this by taking Holy Communion on a frequent basis (see Luke 22:17-20 and 1 Corinthians 11:23-26). One of the greatest weapons you have is to appropriate the blood of Jesus over your life, your family, your health, your work, your purpose, and your provision. We will discuss this in detail in an upcoming chapter.

Prayer. Ephesians 6:10-18 teaches us how to be strong in the Lord and in the power of His might. Ephesians 6:11 (NKJV) tells us to, *"Put on the whole armor of God, that you may be able to stand against the wiles of the devil."* Once we are properly clothed for battle and equipped with the sword of the Spirit, which is the Word of God, we must use the Word effectively in prayer. Ephesians 6:18 (AMP) admonishes us to, *"Pray at all times (on every occasion, in every season) in the Spirit, with all [manner of] prayer and entreaty. To that end keep alert and watch with strong purpose and perseverance, interceding in behalf of all the saints (God's consecrated people)."*

We must not react to circumstances with fear or panic, but with prayer. Philippians 4:6-7 (NKJV) instructs us, *"Be anxious for nothing, but in everything by prayer and supplication, with thanksgiving, let your requests be made known to God; and the peace of God, which surpasses all understanding, will guard your hearts and minds through Christ Jesus."* The most effective prayer is to pray the specific Word of God;

pray the power promises related to the circumstance. God's Word will accomplish what He sent it to do!

Praise, worship, and thanksgiving. The commitment to remain thankful in all situations, including difficulty and adversity, is a master key to experiencing God's mighty power in your life (see Philippians 4:4-13). When you praise and worship the Lord, your attention is focused completely on the Father, Son, and Holy Spirit. The enemy covets and craves the worship of God (Matthew 4:8-10). He desires to divert your attention to him. By praising and worshiping the Lord, you are also resisting the devil and driving him and all demonic forces to flee far away from you.

Praise and worship brings confusion to the camp of the enemy (2 Chronicles 20:22). Walls must come down! (See Joshua 6:1-20.) Strongholds must come down! Prison doors are opened and shackles are loosed (Acts 16:23-31)! Remember that before he was cast out, Lucifer led the worship of the angels before God in Heaven. Praise, worship, and thanksgiving are powerful weapons to magnify the Lord and keep the enemy under your feet. No demon can stay in your presence when you praise and worship the Lord!

To *praise* God is to speak or sing in praise of God, to laud, or to tell of His goodness (see Psalm 103 (NKJV) and Psalm 150(NIV)). To *worship* God is to express honor and reverence, to render service to God, and to stand in awe before God. Worship is direct acknowledgment to God of His nature, His ways, and His attributes (see Psalm 139 and Psalm 18:1). *Thanksgiving* is to give thanks and express heartfelt gratitude to God, to acknowledge the blessings of God, and to celebrate the goodness of God, specifically in your life (see 1 Corinthians 1:4, Ephesians 1:15-16, and Philippians 1:3-6). Stay in a thankful, praise-filled, worshipful attitude at all times and you will experience victory!

Acting on the Word. When you take action and obey the Word of God, keeping the commandments, you are submitting to God, resisting the devil, and he must flee from you (James 4:7). Obedience is an act of worship. Jesus tells us in John 14:15 (AMP), *"If you [really] love Me, you will keep (obey) My commands."* Obedience is a tremendous tool of warfare.

Commit to being a doer of the Word, not just a hearer only. James 1:22 (NLT) challenges us, *"But don't just listen to God's word. You must do what it says. Otherwise, you are only fooling yourselves."* Your actions in the natural realm must line up with what you are praying and commanding in the spiritual realm. If you pray but never change your actions, you will not see results. Faith without accompanying works is dead (James 2:26)!

You have the power to change your actions, choices, and decisions regarding your finances and in every area of life. When you repent, renew your mind, resist temptation, and change your daily actions, you are defeating the schemes of the enemy in your life. When you work hard with diligence and determination, using the specific strategies outlined in the Word of God, you are battling for your financial breakthrough and you will see results!

Enduring in the Word. Your mental posture in warfare must be to stand strong and never give up. You can never back up or back down. The enemy is relentless in his attack. You must be more committed to your breakthrough than he is to defeating you. Victory lives in you. You must make the decision to be on the offensive and keep coming. Get the mindset that you will never give up and you will never give in. God's Word will not return void, it will accomplish what He sent it to do, and you will stand strong with faith, endurance, tenacity, and perseverance until the complete victory is manifested in your life. It's not over until you WIN. Period. You have to stand and keep standing. Having done all, stand!

Ephesians 6:13 (AMP) encourages us, *"Therefore put on God's complete armor, that you may be able to resist and stand your ground on the evil day [of danger], and, having done all [the crisis demands], to stand [firmly in your place]."* We must be steadfast, immovable, always abounding in the work of the Lord (1 Corinthians 15:58). Remember the encouragement of Galatians 6:9, which tells us, *"Let us not become weary in doing good, for at the proper time we will reap a harvest if we do not give up."*

THE 40 WEAPONS OF OUR WARFARE

THE WORD OF GOD	
Pray the Word of God over every situation	Isaiah 55:8-11 (AMP)
	Psalm 107:20 (AMP)
Meditate on and memorize scripture day and night	Joshua 1:8 (NKJV)
	Psalm 1:2 (AMP)
	Psalm 119:48 (AMP)
	Philippians 4:8 (NKJV)
Declare God's promises in the circumstance – speak to the mountain	Mark 11:22-24 (NIV)
Change the confession of your mouth to align with the Word of God	Luke 6:45 (NKJV)
	Matthew 10:32-33 (AMP)
	Hebrews 10:23 (AMP)
THE NAME OF JESUS	
Declare the name of Jesus – every knee must bow	Philippians 2:9-11 (NIV)
Pray in the name of Jesus	John 14:12-14 (NKJV)
	Mark 16:17-19 (NIV)

THE NAME OF JESUS	
Use your delegated authority in the name of Jesus to bind and loose spiritual forces	Luke 10:19 (NKJV) Matthew 16:19 (NIV) Matthew 18:18 (NIV)
Walk in your identity as co-heir with Christ	Romans 8:16-17 (NIV)
THE BLOOD OF JESUS	
Declare the blood of Jesus covers you – your sins are forgiven	Matthew 26:28 (AMP) Ephesians 1:7 (NKJV) 1 John 1:7 (NKJV)
Take Holy Communion often	Luke 22:17-20 (NIV) 1 Corinthians 11:23-26 (NIV)
Declare the seven protections of Holy Communion – the word of your testimony	Revelation 12:11 (NIV)
PRAYER – POWER OF THE WORD	
Put on the full armor of God	Ephesians 6:11-17 (NKJV)
Pray the Word of God over every situation	Ephesians 6:18 (AMP)
Pray in the Spirit	Romans 8:26 (AMP) 1 Corinthians 14:14-15 (NIV)
Bind and loose spiritual forces	Matthew 16:19 (NIV) Matthew 18:18 (NIV)
Bind the Strongman	Matthew 12:29 (NIV)
Pray in agreement	Matthew 18:19 (NIV)
Rebuke the devil and demons	Luke 9:1 (NKJV) Mark 16:17-19 (NIV)
Enforce scriptural punishments	2 Corinthians 10:6 (NKJV)
Claim spiritual restitutions	Proverbs 6:30-31 (NKJV)
Release and ask for the assistance of ministering angels	Hebrews 1:14 (AMP)

PRAISE, WORSHIP, AND THANKSGIVING	
Praise the Lord	Psalm 103
	Psalm 150
	Psalm 118:1-7 (NIV)
Worship God	Psalm 5:7 (AMP)
	Psalm 95:6-7 (NIV)
	Psalm 99:5 (AMP)
Put on the garment of praise for the spirit of heaviness	Isaiah 61:3 (NKJV)
Sing psalms, hymns, and spiritual songs	Acts 16:23-31 (NIV)
	Ephesians 5:18-19 (NKJV)
Give thanks in all circumstances	1 Thessalonians 5:16-18 (NIV)
	Ephesians 5:20 (NKJV)
	Philippians 4:4 (NKJV)
ACTING ON THE WORD	
Repent	Matthew 4:17 (NIV)
	John 8:10-11 (NIV)
Renew your mind	Romans 12:1-2 (NKJV)
	Ephesians 4:23 (NKJV)
Resist temptation	1 Corinthians 10:13 (NIV)
Obey the Word of God	John 14:15 (AMP)
	James 1:22 (NLT)
Forgive others	Matthew 5:23-24 (NKJV)
	Matthew 6:12 (AMP)
Tithe (God will rebuke the Devourer)	Malachi 3:10-12 (AMP)
Give	Luke 6:38 (NIV)
	Proverbs 11:24-26 (NKJV)
Gain wisdom, knowledge, and understanding	Proverbs 4:4-7 (NIV)
Make right decisions — choose life	Deuteronomy 30:19-20 (NKJV)

ACTING ON THE WORD	
Work diligently	Proverbs 10:4 (NIV)
	Proverbs 15:19 (NLT)
	Proverbs 22:29 (AMP)
Resist the devil	James 4:7 (NKJV)
Seek wise counsel	Proverbs 11:14 (NKJV)
ENDURING IN THE WORD	
Stand against the wiles of the devil	Ephesians 6:11-12 (AMP)
Having done all, stand in the evil day of danger	Ephesians 6:13 (AMP)
Do not grow weary and give up	Galatians 6:9 (NIV)

As you can now see, you have many powerful weapons to use as you press forward to break through financially. In the following chapters, I will focus on four of these areas to give you some specific tools you can begin to use right away. We will concentrate on the Word of God, the name of Jesus, the blood of Jesus, and acting on the Word. I want you to recognize you are fully equipped to win! Choose two new weapons you can begin to use now and add them to your personal arsenal. Together, we will expand your knowledge of the Word of God so you can declare the scriptures over your life and into your situation every day. This is breakthrough!

14 | power of the word

God's Word is all powerful and will change your circumstances. Over the next 90 days, you will press forward for your financial breakthrough. All true liberation begins with a spiritual liberation. John 8:36 (AMP) encourages us, *"So if the Son liberates you [makes you free men], then you are really and unquestionably free."* We are seeking permanent change. I want you to lay hold of everything the Lord has promised you.

I want to empower you to elevate to the level of financial liberation, wholeness, wellness, abundance, and overflow the Lord has promised you in His Word. That is why we are not starting with financial management techniques and strategies. We are beginning with the Word of God regarding your finances. Everything in the natural realm begins and is continually held together in the spiritual realm. When your spirit is liberated and your mind is renewed, and you take dominion and subdue all opposing forces in the spiritual realm, you will see permanent, radical change in your life. You will pray the Word over your circumstances and into your situation. You will elevate your money mindset to align with the Word of God. Then by faith, you will align your actions in the natural realm with what you are speaking, praying, believing, and declaring in the spiritual realm.

The foundation of your breakthrough is prayer. James 5:16 (AMP) tells us, *"The earnest (heartfelt, continued) prayer of a righteous man makes tremendous power available [dynamic in its working]."* The key to effective, dynamic prayer is praying the Word of God.

God's Word will not return void – it will accomplish what the Lord has sent it to accomplish. If God has said it, it will come to pass (Isaiah 55:8-11).

The Word of God is the strongest power of the universe and created the very earth we live in. John 1:3 (AMP) states, *"In the beginning [before all time] was the Word (Christ), and the Word was with God, and the Word was God Himself. He was present originally with God. All things were made and came into existence through Him; and **without Him was not even one thing made that has come into being.**"* What you create must begin with the Word.

You have been given delegated authority to use the power of God's Word in the name of Jesus. When you speak the Word of God by faith, with a pure heart, in the name of Jesus, and by the power and authority of Jesus Christ, it has the same force and effect as if God Almighty is speaking (Mark 16:17, Luke 10:17).

Read the following scriptures *out loud* each day. Faith comes by hearing, and by hearing the Word of God (Romans 10:17). Hearing it has a different impact on you than just reading it. Hearing the Word of God and hearing your own personal declaration of the Word will make a tremendous difference in your life of faith. Don't just casually read over the following scriptures; speak the Word of the Lord into the atmosphere to create an environment of faith. Read these scriptures daily to build your faith in God's Word!

THE INTEGRITY OF GOD'S WORD

God is not a man, so he does not lie. He is not human, so he does not change his mind. Has he ever spoken and failed to act? Has he ever promised and not carried it through?
Numbers 23:19 (NLT)

As for God, His way is perfect! The word of the Lord is tested and tried; He is a shield to all those who take refuge and put their trust in Him.
Psalm 18:30 (AMP)

The counsel of the Lord stands forever, the thoughts of His heart through all generations.
Psalm 33:11 (AMP)

This is my comfort and consolation in my affliction: that Your word has revived me and given me life.
Psalm 119:50 (AMP)

Forever, O Lord, Your word is settled in heaven [stands firm as the heavens].
Psalm 119:89 (AMP)

I will worship toward Your holy temple and praise Your name for Your loving-kindness and for Your truth and faithfulness; for You have exalted above all else Your name and Your word and You have magnified Your word above all Your name!
Psalm 138:2 (AMP)

The Lord will perfect that which concerns me; Your mercy, O Lord, endures forever; Do not forsake the works of Your hands.
Psalm 138:8 (NKJV)

The grass withers, the flower fades, But the word of our God stands forever.
Isaiah 40:8 (NKJV)

As the rain and the snow come down from heaven, and do not return to it without watering the earth and making it bud and flourish, so that it yields seed for the sower and bread for the eater, so is my word that goes out from my mouth: It will not return to me empty, but will accomplish what I desire and achieve the purpose for which I sent it.
Isaiah 55:10-11 (NIV)

Then said the Lord to me, You have seen well, for I am alert and active, watching over My word to perform it.
Jeremiah 1:12 (AMP)

For I am the Lord, I do not change;
Malachi 3:6 (NKJV)

Every Scripture is God-breathed (given by His inspiration) and profitable for instruction, for reproof and conviction of sin, for correction of error and discipline in obedience, [and] for training in righteousness (in holy living, in conformity to God's will in thought, purpose, and action), So that the man of God may be complete and proficient, well fitted and thoroughly equipped for every good work.
2 Timothy 3:16-17 (AMP)

Jesus Christ is the same yesterday and today and forever.
Hebrews 13:8 (NIV)

Every good and perfect gift is from above, coming down from the Father of the heavenly lights, who does not change like shifting shadows.
James 1:17 (NIV)

EQUIPPED FOR SPIRITUAL WARFARE

The following scriptures will equip you in the area of spiritual warfare. Use this list as a starting point and add to it as you study the Word of God. Read these scriptures daily as you pray.

There is no wisdom, no insight, no plan that can succeed against the Lord.
Proverbs 21:30 (NIV)

"No weapon formed against you shall prosper, And every tongue which rises against you in judgment You shall condemn. This is the heritage of the servants of the Lord, And their righteousness is from Me," Says the Lord.
Isaiah 54:17 (NKJV)

"Not by might nor by power, but by My Spirit," Says the Lord of hosts.
Zechariah 4:6 (NKJV)

From the days of John the Baptist until now, the kingdom of heaven has been forcefully advancing, and forceful men lay hold of it.
Matthew 11:12 (NIV)

I will give you the keys of the kingdom of heaven; whatever you bind on earth will be bound in heaven, and whatever you loose on earth will be loosed in heaven.
Matthew 16:19 (NIV)

I have told you these things, so that in Me you may have [perfect] peace and confidence. In the world you have tribulation and trials and distress and frustration; but be of good cheer [take courage; be confident, certain, undaunted]! For I have overcome the world. [I have deprived it of power to harm you and have conquered it for you.]
John 16:33 (AMP)

I saw Satan fall like lightning from heaven. Behold, I give you the authority to trample on serpents and scorpions, and over all the power of the enemy, and nothing shall by any means hurt you.
Luke 10:18-19 (NKJV)

What then shall we say to these things? If God is for us, who can be against us?
Romans 8:31 (NKJV)

Yet amid all these things we are more than conquerors and gain a surpassing victory through Him Who loved us.
Romans 8:37 (AMP)

For I am persuaded beyond doubt (am sure) that neither death nor life, nor angels nor principalities, nor things impending and threatening nor things to come, nor powers, Nor height nor depth, nor anything else in all creation will be able to separate us from the love of God which is in Christ Jesus our Lord.
Romans 8:38-39 (AMP)

For though we walk in the flesh, we do not war according to the flesh. For the weapons of our warfare are not carnal but mighty in God for pulling down strongholds, casting down arguments and every high thing that exalts itself against the knowledge of God, bringing every thought into captivity to the obedience of Christ, and being ready to punish all disobedience when your obedience is fulfilled.
2 Corinthians 10:3-6 (NKJV)

Finally, my brethren, be strong in the Lord and in the power of His might. Put on the whole armor of God, that you may be able to stand against the wiles of the devil. For we do not wrestle against flesh and blood, but against principalities, against powers, against the rulers of the darkness of this age, against spiritual hosts of wickedness in the heavenly

places. Therefore take up the whole armor of God, that you may be able to withstand in the evil day, and having done all, to stand. Stand therefore, having girded your waist with truth, having put on the breastplate of righteousness, and having shod your feet with the preparation of the gospel of peace; above all, taking the shield of faith with which you will be able to quench all the fiery darts of the wicked one. And take the helmet of salvation, and the sword of the Spirit, which is the word of God; praying always with all prayer and supplication in the Spirit, being watchful to this end with all perseverance and supplication for all the saints— and for me, that utterance may be given to me, that I may open my mouth boldly to make known the mystery of the gospel, for which I am an ambassador in chains; that in it I may speak boldly, as I ought to speak.
Ephesians 6:10-20 (NKJV)

So be subject to God. Resist the devil [stand firm against him], and he will flee from you.
James 4:7 (AMP)

Be well balanced (temperate, sober of mind), be vigilant and cautious at all times; for that enemy of yours, the devil, roams around like a lion roaring [in fierce hunger], seeking someone to seize upon and devour. Withstand him; be firm in faith [against his onset—rooted, established, strong, immovable, and determined], knowing that the same (identical) sufferings are appointed to your brotherhood (the whole body of Christians) throughout the world. And after you have suffered a little while, the God of all grace [Who imparts all blessing and favor], Who has called you to His [own] eternal glory in Christ Jesus, will Himself complete and make you what you ought to be, establish and ground you securely, and strengthen, and settle you.
1 Peter 5:8-10 (AMP)

Little children, you are of God [you belong to Him] and have [already] defeated and overcome them [the agents of the antichrist], because He Who lives in you is greater (mightier) than he who is in the world.
1 John 4:4 (AMP)

They triumphed over him by the blood of the Lamb and by the word of their testimony; they did not love their lives so much as to shrink from death.
Revelation 12:11 (NIV)

15 | power of the blood

> T hey triumphed over him by the blood of the Lamb
> and by the word of their testimony; they did not love
> their lives so much as to shrink from death.
> **Revelation 12:11 (NIV)**

I believe that taking Holy Communion is one of the most
underutilized weapons of our warfare. The enemy cannot
penetrate the blood of Jesus over your life. You may participate
in Holy Communion in your church services, but you may
not have considered partaking in Communion on your own
or with your family. In 1 Corinthians 11:23-26 (NKJV), the
Apostle Paul tells us, *"The Lord Jesus on the same night
in which He was betrayed took bread; and when He had
given thanks, He broke it and said, 'Take, eat; this is My
body which is broken for you; do this in remembrance of
Me.' In the same manner He also took the cup after supper,
saying, 'This cup is the new covenant in My blood. This do,
as often as you drink it, in remembrance of Me.' For as often
as you eat this bread and drink this cup, you proclaim the
Lord's death till He comes."*

As often as you choose to take Holy Communion, eating the
bread and drinking the cup, you are remembering the Lord's

sacrifice, reaffirming the power of the blood of Jesus over your life, reinforcing the blood line that sanctifies you and sets you apart, and resisting the enemy who cannot cross that spiritual threshold into your life. You can do it as often as you choose! I choose to do it daily. I have been taking Holy Communion on a daily basis for several years now, and I have experienced tremendous benefits in all aspects of my life, particularly my physical health.

As I was preparing for this writing, the Holy Spirit showed me seven areas of **protection** that we have in the blood of Jesus, and He gave me a prayer outline to declare these protections each time I take Holy Communion. This is what I pray on a daily basis.

We see a picture of protection by the blood in the Old Testament. Exodus 12:23 (NIV) tells us, *"When the Lord goes through the land to strike down the Egyptians, he will see the blood on the top and sides of the doorframe and will pass over that doorway, and he will not permit the destroyer to enter your houses and strike you down."* Just as the Israelites applied the blood of the Passover lamb to their doorposts so that the destroyer saw the blood and passed over their homes, we have the complete fulfillment of that protection now by the blood of Jesus, the Lamb of God. Revelation 12:11 (NIV) tells us, *"They triumphed over him by the blood of the Lamb and by the word of their testimony."*

When you take Holy Communion, you are remembering the Lord's sacrifice which has already paid the price for the remission of your sin. You are forgiven. You are also establishing a perimeter around your life, marking it with the blood of Jesus. In the spiritual realm, that is a visible protection that tells the devil and all of his demon forces, "Back off! You have absolutely no access or authority here. I am covered by the blood of Jesus. I am protected, my family is protected, and all that the Lord has given me is protected in the name of Jesus." The second half of this promise says they overcome *"by the word of their testimony."* What you declare as you take Holy Communion and apply the blood to protect your life is very important. Declare the Word of God over your life.

As we pray for your financial breakthrough, I want you to be able to protect every blessing the Lord sends to you. The enemy cannot *stop* your blessings from coming forth, so his strategy is to *steal* them. Your job is to get on the offensive, anticipate that attack, and protect every blessing coming to you from the onset. By faith, reinforce the covering over your life. Shut off every access point to you, your family, and your finances! I declare the Word of God and claim the protection of the blood of Jesus in seven areas, as outlined to me by the Holy Spirit.

The Seven Areas of Protection

The seven areas of protection covered by the blood of Jesus are:

- Your Person
- Your Purpose
- God's Plan for your life
- Your Paternity
- Your Property
- Your Provision, and
- Your Promise.

Let's look at each one of these individually. I encourage you to read Isaiah Chapter 53 in its entirety before we begin.

Your Person. The blood of Jesus protects your spirit, soul, and body. Affirm that you are saved and your sins are forgiven. Your spirit is protected for all eternity. Declare that you are protected from sickness and disease, injury, accidents, and all other manifestations of illness (see Chapter 2, The Trifold Attack). You walk in divine health and healing by the blood of Jesus. I declare 1 Peter 2:24 (NIV) which states, *"He himself bore our sins,' in his body on the cross, so that we might die to sins and live for righteousness; 'by his wounds you have been healed.'"* I also declare Romans 12:1-2, that my body is a living sacrifice, holy and acceptable to God, and I am transformed by the renewing of my mind so that I may prove what is the good, pleasing, and perfect will of God. I declare that I have the mind of Christ, and hold the thoughts, feelings, and purposes of His heart (1 Corinthians 2:16 AMP).

Your Purpose. The blood of Jesus protects the purpose and mission assignment for your life. Jeremiah 1:5 (NIV) tells us, *"Before I formed you in the womb I knew you, before you were born I set you apart; I appointed you as a prophet to the nations."* Likewise, before the Lord formed you in your mother's womb, He knew you, He set you apart, and He gave you a specific purpose for your life. I declare that my purpose is protected by the blood of Jesus. I declare that I am confident that He who began a good work in me will carry it on to completion until the day of Jesus Christ (Philippians 1:6).

God's Plan for Your Life. The blood of Jesus protects God's plan for your life. Not only did the Lord give you a specific purpose and mission assignment for your life, He also gave you a specific plan to carry it out. Jeremiah 29:11 (NIV) encourages us, *"'For I know the plans I have for you,' declares the Lord, 'plans to prosper you and not to harm you, plans to give you hope and a future.'"* I declare that God's divine plan for my life is protected by the blood of Jesus. The devil cannot stop it, delay it, or thwart it in any way. I also pray Proverbs 16:3 (AMP) which states, *"Roll your works upon the Lord [commit and trust them wholly to Him; He will cause your thoughts to become agreeable to His will, and] so shall your plans be established and succeed."* I encourage you to cover all aspects of God's plan for your life so that your plans may be established and succeed!

Your Paternity. Pray that the blood of Jesus protects all members of your family lineage. Call out the names of your family members before the Lord. Declare according to Joshua 24:15 (NKJV), *"As for me and my house, we will serve the Lord."*

Be especially mindful to protect your unsaved family members who do not yet know the Lord. Call out the names of your unsaved loved ones in your family and extended family and cover them with the blood of Jesus. 2 Peter 3:9 (AMP) tells us, *"The Lord does not delay and is not tardy or slow about what He promises, according to some people's conception of slowness, but He is long-suffering (extraordinarily patient) toward you, not desiring that any should perish, but that all should turn to repentance."*

Ask the Lord of the Harvest to send laborers specifically to your family members (Matthew 9:38). You want to protect your unsaved family members from the evil one so they are covered until they come into the saving knowledge of Christ for themselves. Then believe by faith according to Acts 16 that your whole household will be saved! Acts 16:29-31 (NIV) tells us, *"The jailer called for lights, rushed in and fell trembling before Paul and Silas. He then brought them out and asked, 'Sirs, what must I do to be saved?' They replied, 'Believe in the Lord Jesus, and you will be saved—you and your household.'"* I pray for and cover every unsaved family member by name.

Your Property and Possessions. Pray that the blood of Jesus protects all that you own including your home, your vehicles, your possessions, and all that you have worked hard to earn. Establish a perimeter around your property. Protect your dwelling. Psalm 91:9-11 (NKJV) tells us, *"Because you have made the Lord, who is my refuge, Even the Most High, your dwelling place, No evil shall befall you, Nor shall any plague come near your dwelling; For He shall give His angels charge over you, To keep you in all your ways."*

The Lord has given you a powerful promise regarding your home. Isaiah 32:18 (NIV) states, *"My people will live in peaceful dwelling places, in secure homes, in undisturbed places of rest."* Protect the security of your home with the blood of Jesus. Cancel any schemes of the wicked one for theft, robbery, burglary, break-ins, accidents, fires, flooding, or other property damage. When I pray, I will often walk the physical perimeter of my property and reestablish the protection of the blood over my property and possessions in Jesus' name. Also pray for the protection of your vehicles. Pray that you and your passengers travel safely without accident, incident, or breakdown. Finally, pray that you own your home and all that is contained within it without debt. Declare that your home is paid in full.

Your Provision. Your provision is protected by the blood of Jesus. Pray that all of your income sources are protected. Make sure that you are returning the tithe to the Lord promptly; He promises to rebuke the Devourer for your sake (Malachi 3:8-11).

Give your offerings and stay in the cycle of blessing (see Chapter 6).

Declare that all of your needs are met. Philippians 4:19 (AMP) states, *"And my God will liberally supply (fill to the full) your every need according to His riches in glory in Christ Jesus."* Declare Psalm 23:1 (NIV) over your life, *"The Lord is my shepherd, I lack nothing."*

Pray that the Lord bless all the work of your hands and all that you undertake according to Deuteronomy 28:8. Pray that your ideas and intellectual property are protected. I speak the names of each of my income sources and I declare that the blood of Jesus protects each one. Bind the enemy and cancel all manifestations of income interruptions — layoffs, furloughs, decreased hours, business downturns, lost contracts, delayed compensation, and slow-paying or non-paying clients. Call forth new income sources, new clients for your businesses, promotions, raises, and bonuses.

Declare that you are debt free and protected against debt slavery (Proverbs 22:7). Conclude by declaring 1 Corinthians 9:8 (AMP) over your finances: *"And God is able to make all grace (every favor and earthly blessing) come to you in abundance, so that you may always and under all circumstances and whatever the need be self-sufficient [possessing enough to require no aid or support and furnished in abundance for every good work and charitable donation]."*

Your Promise. The blood of Jesus protects the promise of your future. The enemy will attempt to delay and detain you, but you have a promised destination for your life. When the Lord delivered the children of Israel, He took them from **Poverty** (slavery to the Egyptians), to **Provision** (manna in the wilderness), to the **Promised Land** (a land overflowing with milk and honey). Do not stop at the place of your provision: Needs Met. The Israelites needs were met in the wilderness, but they were not in the place of *promise.*

Ezekiel 20:6 (NIV) states, *"On that day I swore to them that I would bring them out of Egypt into a land I had searched out for them, a land flowing with milk and honey, the most beautiful of all lands."* Your promise, the culmination of your mission assignment on the earth, your place of abundance and overflow, your place of fulfillment where you are living in the fullness of your purpose and plan of God, is yours to achieve. Be thankful and protect your provision, but do not *stop* at the place of provision.

Have the same attitude as Joshua and Caleb regarding your promise. Numbers 13:30 (NIV) tells us, *"Then Caleb silenced the people before Moses and said, 'We should go up and take possession of the land, for we can certainly do it.'"* We see the fulfillment in Joshua 21:45 (NKJV) which states, *"Not a word failed of any good thing which the LORD had spoken to the house of Israel. All came to pass."* Cover the vision the Lord has given you with the blood of Jesus. Cover your Promised Land. As I conclude my prayer time, I declare the vision the Lord has given me, cover it with the blood of Jesus, and protect it.

When you have taken Holy Communion and declared the seven protections over your life, praise! Praise the Lord it is done. You overcome by the blood of the Lamb and the word of your testimony. Praise God you are protected and you will fulfill all that He has called you to do.

The following chart summarizes the seven protections of Holy Communion and a few of the scripture references applicable to each one. Take time to research and add to this list.

SUMMARY OF THE SEVEN PROTECTIONS

PROTECTION	COVERS	SCRIPTURES
Person	Your spirit, soul, and body – remission of sin Physical health, wellness and protection Mental and emotional health Thought life	Isaiah 53:4-6 (NKJV) 1 Peter 2:24 (NKJV) Romans 12:1-2 (NKJV) 1 Corinthians 2:16 (AMP) Revelation 12:11 (NIV)
Purpose	Divine purpose and mission assignment	Jeremiah 1:5 (NIV) Romans 8:28 (NIV) Philippians 1:6 (NIV)
Plan	God's plan for your life	Jeremiah 29:11 (NIV) Proverbs 16:3 (AMP)
Paternity	Your family lineage: immediate and extended family Saved and unsaved family members	Joshua 24:15 (NKJV) Matthew 9:38 (NIV) Acts 16:29-31 (NIV) 2 Peter 3:9 (AMP)
Property and Possessions	Land, homes, cars, all possessions in your home and properties, pets; real property and intellectual property	Isaiah 32:18 (NIV) Psalm 91:9-11 (NKJV)
Provision	All of your income sources, savings and investments Jobs and businesses Clients and contracts Raises, promotions, bonuses Being debt free	Malachi 3:8-11 (NKJV) Psalm 23:1 (NIV) Proverbs 22:7 (NKJV) Philippians 4:19 (AMP) 1 Corinthians 9:8 (AMP) All scriptures in Part III: 90 Days of Prayer
Promise	Fulfillment of your mission assignment on the earth Your place of abundance and overflow	Exodus 6:8 (AMP) Deuteronomy 27:3 (NIV) Numbers 13:30 (NIV) All scriptures in Part III: 90 Days of Prayer

Final Instructions

When you begin to take Holy Communion on a daily basis, it is very important that you take measures to handle the Lord's Supper with reverence. 1 Corinthians 11:27-31 (NIV) warns us, *"So then, whoever eats the bread or drinks the cup of the Lord in an unworthy manner will be guilty of sinning against the body and blood of the Lord. Everyone ought to examine themselves before they eat of the bread and drink from the cup. For those who eat and drink without discerning the body of Christ eat and drink judgment on themselves. That is why many among you are weak and sick, and a number of you have fallen asleep. But if we were more discerning with regard to ourselves, we would not come under such judgment."* This is a vital component of your worship and your warfare. You must prepare for it and handle it properly.

Consecrate the emblems. I choose to use 100% grape juice and a flatbread cracker for my emblems of Holy Communion. You can use what the Lord places on your heart. The most important thing is that you pray and *consecrate* what you are using to represent the body and the blood of Jesus Christ, sanctify and set these apart, and under no circumstances use them for regular food or drink. Ensure your family members are aware these items are for Holy Communion only. Clearly mark them and place them in a secure place so no one mistakenly eats from them as food.

Consecrate the service items. I use a china cup and small plate. Use what the Holy Spirit places on your heart. Once again, I have consecrated these for use for Holy Communion only. I do not eat or drink out of these items. They are stored separately from the kitchen items used for regular meals.

Prevent interruptions. Set apart a quiet place and a time when you will not be interrupted. Holy Communion is a sacred time of prayer and worship. Make sure you are in a quiet place in your home and you can complete the service uninterrupted. Turn off the television and your cell phone. I have dedicated a specific room in my home for prayer. You may have a favorite place to pray. You may use a bedroom or a den. Whatever room you choose, make sure you have uninterrupted prayer time. Put a note on the door asking to not be disturbed for fifteen minutes.

Confirm salvation. Make sure participating family members are born again. If you choose to serve Holy Communion to other members of your family, make sure they have received Jesus Christ as their personal Lord and Savior. Do not serve Holy Communion to small children who do not understand and are not of age to confess Jesus Christ as Lord. They are covered by your prayers. Do not force family members to participate who do not want to do so. It would be better to pray alone with faith and cover those family members until such time as they have matured in their faith and want to participate with you.

Confess your sin. Take a few minutes before you begin to examine yourself and confess your sin to the Lord. Allow the Holy Spirit to bring whatever needs to be addressed to your mind. Then you can enter your prayer time with a clean heart and a clear conscience, and your prayers will not be hindered. 1 John 1:9 (AMP) tells us, *"If we [freely] admit that we have sinned and confess our sins, He is faithful and just (true to His own nature and promises) and will forgive our sins [dismiss our lawlessness] and [continuously] cleanse us from all unrighteousness [everything not in conformity to His will in purpose, thought, and action]."*

Begin with a Scripture. Begin your prayer time with a reading from the scripture. I always read Isaiah 53 in its entirety. I use different translations throughout the week. I also read 1 Corinthians 11:23-26 (NKJV) or Luke 22:17-20 (NKJV). Use what the Holy Spirit places on your heart.

I find it takes me about fifteen minutes each morning to complete this prayer. The benefits are immeasurable. As you begin the process of pressing forward for financial breakthrough, it is vitally important that you protect yourself and your family. Remember that breakthrough is warfare. The demonic forces over poverty and lack are ruling, high ranking demons. When you are stopping the cycle of stealing, taking back your blessings, demanding restitution, and pressing forward to achieve the levels of wealth, riches, abundance, and overflow the Lord has for you, you will encounter strong opposition. That is why I am devoting an entire section of this writing to the weapons of our warfare. You must be prepared for this resistance.

I encourage you to take fifteen minutes each morning to declare the protection of the blood of Jesus over your life. The blood of Jesus protects your Person, Purpose, Plan, Paternity, Property, Provision, and Promise! You are completely protected and you have the victory in Christ!

16 | power of the name

> *herefore God exalted him to the highest place and gave him the name that is above every name, that at the name of Jesus every knee should bow, in heaven and on earth and under the earth, and every tongue acknowledge that Jesus Christ is Lord, to the glory of God the Father.*
> **Philippians 2:9-11 (NIV)**

One of the biggest barriers that most people struggle with is **identity**. If you do not fully understand who you are in Christ, you will live far below your birthright. Many Christians struggle with feeling inadequate, inferior, and unworthy of the blessings of their Heavenly Father. We must not become arrogant and think more highly of ourselves than we ought to think, but we cannot fulfill our mission on the earth if we are haunted by limiting beliefs of inferiority and unworthiness. To embrace your inheritance in the Lord, you must understand who you are and accept the fullness of your new identity in Christ.

Imagine for a moment that you were born a Kennedy. If you were born into the Kennedy family, you would enter the world with unprecedented political power, presence, and prestige.

The family lineage of the Kennedys speaks of a long line of respected political leaders, visionaries, and world changers. To carry the surname of Kennedy brings honor, favor, and respect. You are politically powerful, and your contributions to society are highly anticipated. There is power in the name. It is your birthright.

Certain names are loaded with political power and prestige, longstanding financial wealth, and socioeconomic status. Consider the surnames of Rockefeller, Carnegie, Gates, Buffett, Hilton, or Walton. Imagine being an heir to Bill Gates or Sam Walton. Your bloodline secures your birthright and blessing. If you are an heir to any of these prestigious estates, you represent generational wealth, entrepreneurial power, ingenuity, and innovation. You are an heir to extraordinary family wealth and privilege. There are certain rights and privileges associated with the name itself. Your rights as an heir are not earned – you are born into it. Your name can open doors for you. There is favor and blessing in your name. There is power in your name. It is your birthright.

If you carry the name Spielberg, you have the keys to kingdom of Hollywood. If you carry the name Manning, you have the keys to the kingdom of the National Football League (NFL). Born into the athletic lineage of the Manning family, there is a high expectation of an NFL career for you. It is the blessing of the bloodline.

Whether you are born into the family, adopted, or joined by marriage, taking on a powerful societal name beckons in certain expectations. Imagine you are born into a family with distinguished historical significance such as the King family. Though others may stand in awe of your lineage, your powerful father is simply Dad to you. Yet, you are born with a powerful voice of social justice to combat oppression and lift humanity that others do not have. To continue the cause of fighting social injustice is your cross to carry. It is your natural responsibility. It is the responsibility of the bloodline. It is your birthright. There is power in your name.

We have a worldwide fascination with the British Royal Family. Who will ascend to the throne? The young princes must be educated not only on the power of their lineage, but also on the responsibilities of being heir to the throne. They must understand and properly wield the tremendous power they hold in society.

As an heir to any of the aforementioned families – Kennedy, Carnegie, or King – you would be educated on your family lineage, the patriarchs in your bloodline, and the powerful benefits associated with your name. You do not earn your right as an heir – it is your inheritance – you are born into it. Yet you must learn to walk in your inheritance with the proper posture. There is tremendous power in your name.

Yet with all of the worldly power, prestige, and precedence wielded by these powerful names, there is **one name** that will forever surpass them all. As a believer, your bloodline is more powerful than the Kennedy, Carnegie, King, Gates, Rockefeller, Walton, Hilton, Buffett, Manning, and all royal families *combined*. The name of Jesus carries all power, rule, and authority in the universe. Far beyond political power, socioeconomic status, and worldly wealth, it is the only name by which men may be saved, reconciled to God, and transformed for all eternity. Every knee shall bow to the name of Jesus. As a believer, now that you are born again, you carry the most powerful name in the universe. It is your bloodline. It is your birthright. There is ultimate and supreme power in your name!

Jesus approached and, breaking the silence, said to them, **All authority (all power of rule) in heaven and on earth has been given to Me.** *Go then and make disciples of all the nations,* **baptizing them into the name** *of the Father and of the Son and of the Holy Spirit, Teaching them to observe everything that I have commanded you, and behold, I am with you all the days (perpetually, uniformly, and on every occasion), to the [very] close and consummation of the age. Amen (so let it be).* **Matthew 28:18-20 (AMP)**

Therefore God exalted him to the highest place and gave him **the name that is above every name,** *that at the name of Jesus every knee should bow, in heaven and on earth and under the earth, and every tongue acknowledge that Jesus Christ is Lord, to the glory of God the Father.* **Philippians 2:9-11 (NIV)**

Royal families carry the name of their kingdom in their titles – Prince of Wales, Duchess of Cambridge, etc. To a far greater extent, so do you! You are a child of the Most High God. You are a Christian. You carry the name of the Lord Jesus Christ and you carry the identity of God Himself. You are a member of the Kingdom of God. You are part of the ultimate Royal Family.

This means that anyone who belongs to Christ has become a new person. The old life is gone; a new life has begun! **2 Corinthians 5:17 (NLT)**

But you are a chosen people, a royal priesthood, a holy nation, God's special possession, that you may declare the praises of him who called you out of darkness into his wonderful light. **1 Peter 2:9 (NIV)**

Yet this is only the beginning. You are not merely a subject in the kingdom – you are a child of the King! God is no longer solely your Lord, the Creator of the Universe, or the Lord God Almighty. He is your Heavenly Father! You are a child of the Most High God. You are adopted into the family of God and you carry the favor, blessings, birthright, and inheritance of a son. You cannot earn it. You cannot work for it – the blessings of God are appropriated to you **through grace by faith** in Jesus Christ *alone*.

*See what great love the Father has lavished on us, that we should be called **children of God**! And that is what we are!* ***1 John 3:1 (NIV)***

*For those who are led by the Spirit of God are the **children of God**. The Spirit you received does not make you slaves, so that you live in fear again; rather, the Spirit you received brought about your **adoption to sonship**. And by him we cry, "**Abba, Father.**" The Spirit himself testifies with our spirit that we are **God's children**.* ***Romans 8:14-16 (NIV)***

When you were born again, you took on the identity of your Lord and Savior Jesus Christ, with all of the power, authority, and Kingdom rights His name carries in the universe. You were born into the family of God Himself!

When you were born again, your **identity** changed. Your **name** changed. Your **lineage** changed. Your **birthright** changed. Your **blessings** changed. Your **inheritance** changed. You are an **heir** of God and **co-heir** with Christ!

*So in Christ Jesus you are all children of God through faith, for all of you who were baptized into Christ have clothed yourselves with Christ. There is neither Jew nor Gentile, neither slave nor free, nor is there male and female, for you are all one in Christ Jesus. **If you belong to Christ, then you are Abraham's seed, and heirs according to***

the promise.
Galatians 3:26-29 (NIV)

Now if we are children, then we are heirs—heirs of God and co-heirs with Christ, if indeed we share in his sufferings in order that we may also share in his glory.
Romans 8:17 (NIV)

Many members of the Body of Christ operate far below their birthright in the Kingdom of God. Why? First, they do not know what their inheritance is in the Lord, and second, they do not fight to enforce their covenant blessings secured for them at the cross. They unknowingly allow the enemy to deceive, cheat, and trick them out of their birthright with planned attacks and schemes designed to steal, kill, and destroy what is rightfully their own. I do not want this to happen to you any longer.

It is time for you to begin to walk in the fullness of the favor, blessings, and the abundance of your bloodline. It is time to embrace your sonship. It is time for you to walk in the enormity of your inheritance. It is time to operate in the bounty of your birthright that you may be blessed, and a blessing to others. It is time to use your authority in Christ to subdue the attacks of the enemy and enforce your right to freedom as a child of the Most High! It is time for you to take on the full responsibilities of your name, and execute those responsibilities with power, justice, and authority on the earth.

Just as a child born into a royal family must be educated on their position and the rights and responsibilities that come with their name, how much more should we, as children of the Most High God! You must learn the full extent of your birthright to walk in it.

You have a rich inheritance in the Lord which includes your eternal life with your Heavenly Father, and an abundant life **right now** in this time through Christ Jesus. Divine protection and covering are yours now (Psalm 91). Divine health and healing are your covenant blessings and your inheritance now (1 Peter 2:24). Righteousness, peace, and joy in the Holy Spirit are yours now (Romans 14:17). Financial wellness, wholeness, and abundance are yours now (1 Corinthians 9:8).You must lay hold of your sonship. You must defend your blessings from the attack of the enemy. You must understand your rights and responsibilities and walk in them.

You must grasp the enormity of your identity in Christ. It is time to come of age, and walk in the fullness of your inheritance as a child of God. You do not have to live as a slave to your circumstances. You do not have to live entrapped by spiritual forces of wickedness that desire to deceive you out of your Kingdom power and position. By the grace of God and faith in Jesus Christ, you are an **heir** to your Heavenly Father, the Lord God Almighty, Creator of All Heaven and Earth.

**There is no reason to live another day
below your birthright.**

---

*What I am saying is that **as long as an heir is underage, he is no different from a slave, although he owns the whole estate**. The heir is subject to guardians and trustees until the time set by his father. So also, when we were underage, we were in slavery under the elemental spiritual forces of the world. But when the set time had fully come, God sent his Son, born of a woman, born under the law, to redeem those under the law, that **we might receive adoption to sonship**. Because you are his sons, God sent*

*the Spirit of his Son into our hearts, the Spirit who calls out, "Abba, Father." **So you are no longer a slave, but God's child; and since you are his child, God has made you also an heir.***
Galatians 4:1-7 (NIV)

You are more than a conqueror through Christ who loves you (Romans 8:37). You can do all things through Christ who strengthens you (Philippians 4:13). Greater is He that is in you than he that is in the world (1 John 4:4). If God be for you, who can stand against you (Romans 8:31)? Who can bring a charge against God's elect (Romans 8:33)? God always causes you to triumph in Him (2 Corinthians 2:14). In Christ, this is your bloodline. This is your birthright.

Far beyond any earthly name, there is supernatural power in the name of Jesus! It is the name above every name. If you have not yet been engrafted into the family of God, do not fear or fret. It is not something you must earn. You can become a member of God's family right now, by receiving Jesus Christ as your personal Lord and Savior by faith.

(See pages 442 – 445 for a special invitation and prayer to join the family of God).

17 acting on the word

*B*ut don't just listen to God's word. You must do what it says. Otherwise, you are only fooling yourselves. For if you listen to the word and don't obey, it is like glancing at your face in a mirror. You see yourself, walk away, and forget what you look like. But if you look carefully into the perfect law that sets you free, and if you do what it says and don't forget what you heard, then God will bless you for doing it.
James 1:22-25 (NLT)

As you pray over the next 90 days, the following Financial Wellness Action Plan will help you implement what you have learned from the Word of God. Your Financial Wellness Action Plan will help you renew your money mindset, conquer debt, restore your health, and create wealth, using the wealth generation strategies in the Word.

Read through the entire Action Plan now. Mark the items you have completed or have already begun. Make a specific plan to implement all of the actions. Faith without accompanying works is dead (James 2:26)! Be a doer of the Word (James 1:22)!

280

Your Financial Wellness Action Plan – Figure 1

RENEW YOUR MONEY MINDSET
❑ Begin memorizing one **power promise** per day
❑ Begin **daily prayer** for financial breakthrough
❑ Trust God as your Source for all your needs
❑ Begin warfare prayer for your finances
❑ Declare the power promises out loud each day
❑ Return the **tithe** to the Lord; God will rebuke the Devourer
❑ Write your **vision** for your finances; long-term financial goals
❑ Achieve debt-free status
❑ Provide for yourself and family; extended family
❑ Prepare for the unexpected (6-12 months cash reserve)
❑ Plan for the future
❑ Provide an inheritance for children and grandchildren
❑ Build the Kingdom of God
❑ Share the gospel
❑ Give generously to others
❑ Enjoy your life on the earth – lifestyle desires
❑ Evaluate the **current state** of your finances; full inventory
❑ Debt Level
❑ Income Sources
❑ Expenses
❑ Net Income
❑ Assets
❑ Liabilities
❑ Net Worth
❑ Create a **monthly budget**
❑ Is your budget balanced?
❑ Determine if you have a net income deficit or surplus
❑ Identify self-sabotaging financial habits
❑ Eliminate unnecessary expenses or overspending
❑ Focus on increasing income sources

RENEW YOUR MONEY MINDSET
❑ Create an **Emergency Fund** – begin building to $500
❑ Determine your **free-will giving**; offering to the Lord
❑ Complete Part III: 90 Days of Prayer for Financial Breakthrough

CONQUER DEBT
❑ **Stop creating new debt**
❑ Challenge all purchases requiring debt
❑ Plan a Rapid Debt Reduction strategy for essential new debt
❑ Declare daily that you are debt free
❑ Take a complete **debt inventory**; all interest-bearing loans
❑ Create a list of your debts from smallest to largest
❑ **Start Rapid Debt Reduction Plan**
❑ Define net income amount you can apply to debt reduction
❑ Start wherever you are: $10, $50, $100, $500, $1,000, etc.
❑ Assign to budget as a line item: Debt Reduction
❑ Apply 1/2 to 2/3 to consumer debt — Use Debt Eraser strategy
❑ Apply 1/2 to 1/3 to mortgage debt — begin to apply Mortgage Multiplier strategy
❑ Apply consumer debt reduction amount to smallest bill first
❑ Apply mortgage debt reduction to principal monthly
❑ **Consumer Debt Reduction — Debt Eraser**
❑ Apply consumer debt reduction amount to smallest bill first; repeat monthly
❑ Pay off smallest bill first
❑ Add the retired monthly payment for smallest bill to the consumer debt reduction amount; do not absorb into budget
❑ Apply new consumer debt reduction amount to second bill on your list
❑ Pay off second bill — add retired payment to debt reduction
❑ Repeat payoff cycle until all consumer debt is paid in full
❑ Add consumer debt reduction to mortgage debt reduction
❑ Apply full Rapid Debt Reduction budget as a *principal-only* additional payment, on top of monthly mortgage payment

CONQUER DEBT

- ☐ **Mortgage Debt Reduction — Mortgage Multiplier**
  - ☐ Obtain the Amortization Schedule for your mortgage
  - ☐ Check availability online from mortgage lender or request by mail
  - ☐ Identify next *principal-only* payment amount
  - ☐ Apply mortgage debt reduction amount to next payment principal, preferably covering the full principal of next payment due; practice monthly
  - ☐ Continue paying additional principal payments until mortgage is paid in full

- ☐ **Achieve debt-free status**
  - ☐ Consumer debt paid in full
  - ☐ Mortgage debt paid in full

- ☐ **Debt-free Purchase Account** — Savings/Money Market
  - ☐ Begin designated savings account for future debt-free purchases (e.g. car purchase)
  - ☐ Make monthly payments to savings/money market account
  - ☐ Complete designated purchase debt free
  - ☐ Believe God to stay out of debt

RESTORE HEALTH

- ☐ **Return the tithe** — the Lord will rebuke the Devourer for your sake
- ☐ **Sow seed** through free-will giving; practice generosity
- ☐ Declare the **seven protections** of Holy Communion
- ☐ Command the **sevenfold restitution** on all that has been stolen
- ☐ Create an **Emergency Fund**
  - ☐ Milestone 1: $500
  - ☐ Milestone 2: $1,000
  - ☐ Milestone 3: 1 month of expenses
  - ☐ Milestone 4: 3 months of expenses
  - ☐ Milestone 5: 6-12 months of expenses

RESTORE HEALTH
❑ Create your **Savings and Investment Plan**
❑ Consult a faith-based financial advisor for best investment strategy for your situation
❑ Communicate your commitment to returning the tithe/ giving offerings
❑ Communicate your commitment to debt-free living
❑ Complete Part III: 90 Days of Prayer for Financial Breakthrough

CREATE WEALTH
❑ Declare the 10 **Wealth Strategies** in the Word daily
❑ Complete Part III: 90 Days of Prayer for Financial Breakthrough
❑ Implement **Rapid Debt Reduction** Plan
❑ Pay off all consumer debt
❑ Pay off mortgage debt
❑ Achieve debt-free status
❑ List your **current income sources**; income-generating assets
❑ Prioritize adding **second income source** if you have a single source of income; keep your job — build a business
❑ **Position for Promotion**: Assess current job/businesses for income potential (contact us for assistance)
❑ Assess actions needed to position yourself for increase
❑ Improve work performance/increase productivity?
❑ Enroll in educational courses/degree program?
❑ Take additional training courses?
❑ Complete certifications?
❑ Propose new solutions/new position of responsibility?
❑ Complete **Talent Portfolio** to ascertain your highest level gifts and talents (contact us for assistance)
❑ Evaluate potential businesses for additional income (contact us for assistance)
❑ **Select/start side business** for additional income source (contact us for assistance)
❑ **Maximize teamwork**: add a team-based business to portfolio (contact us for assistance)

CREATE WEALTH
❑ Get profitable in first business before adding the second
❑ Create **multiple streams of income** (contact us for assistance)
❑ Objective: seven to eight income streams
❑ **Diversify** your income sources (contact us for assistance)
❑ Establish plan for **land, home, property**, and intellectual property ownership
❑ Expand ownership of **real property, intellectual property, and businesses**
❑ Begin legacy planning for **multi-generational wealth**
❑ Implement legacy plan for multi-generational wealth

RAPID DEBT REDUCTION METHOD #1: CONSUMER DEBT ERASER

To help you with your debt reduction goals, let's review two easy, rapid debt reduction strategies you can begin to use right away. To aid with eliminating consumer (non-mortgage) debt, I encourage you to apply the following technique we will call the Debt Eraser. Once you have determined your monthly net income (income – expenses), designate a specific amount of your available funds for debt reduction. Add "Debt Reduction" as a line item to your monthly budget. In this example, we will assume you have $150 available for debt reduction per month. Designate one-half to two-thirds of your Debt Reduction budget for consumer debt, and the remaining portion to mortgage debt, if you own a home. If you do not have a mortgage, use your full Debt Reduction budget to rapidly retire your consumer debt. In our example, let's assume you will apply two-thirds of your Debt Reduction budget to consumer debt or $100/month.

Secondly, make a list of all of your debts from smallest to largest. Instead of adding a little bit to each of your debt payments, concentrate you full consumer Debt Reduction budget — $100 — on one bill only, to eliminate it as quickly as possible. You will target the smallest debt first to eliminate it as soon as possible. Let's assume your smallest bill is a credit card, with a minimum payment of $25 and a current card balance of $300. For rapid debt reduction, you will pay the minimum payment ($25), along with your Debt Reduction payment ($100) for a total payment of $125. Assuming your minimum payment is covering predominantly your interest and a small amount of principal, using your Debt Reduction strategy, you will eliminate your first debt within three months. Your Debt Reduction budget has now increased to $125 ($100 + $25 retired minimum payment).

Let's assume the next bill on your list is an installment loan of $1,500. You make a minimum monthly payment of $75. Using the Debt Eraser strategy, you will apply your original Debt Reduction budget ($100), the minimum payment from the first credit card you have paid off ($25), and your normal minimum payment of $75 to the installment loan. You will now apply a total of $200 per month to your installment loan until it is paid in full. Your Debt Reduction budget has now doubled to $200 per month. Now that your installment loan is paid in full, you will turn to the third bill on your list.

Let's assume it is your car payment. Your monthly car payment is $300, and your remaining balance is $10,000. You will add your Debt Reduction budget of $200/month to your normal car payment for a total payment of $500/month to rapidly pay off the remaining balance on your car. Once your car note is paid in full, you will have $500 available in Rapid Debt Reduction funds. You have paid off three debts and quintupled your Debt Reduction budget. These funds will now be applied to rapidly reduce your mortgage.

I am using simplistic numbers in this example to make it easy for you to grasp the basic concept. Start wherever you are. If your budget allows for $25 for Debt Reduction, start there. If you have $500 available, start there. The Debt Eraser strategy will work for you whatever your situation may be.

To apply the Debt Eraser technique:

1. Calculate your net income (income −expenses)

2. Designate a portion of your net income for Debt Reduction

3. List your debts from smallest to largest

4. Apply your Debt Reduction budget to your smallest debt until paid in full

5. Add the retired payment to your Debt Reduction budget

6. Apply new Debt Reduction budget to your next debt until paid in full

7. Repeat steps 4-6 until all consumer debt is paid off

8. Once consumer debt is paid in full, concentrate full Debt Reduction budget on your mortgage payment.

RAPID DEBT REDUCTION METHOD #2: MORTGAGE MULTIPLIER

There are many different strategies for rapid mortgage reduction. I want to quickly introduce just one to get you started. We will call this technique the Mortgage Multiplier. You will need to obtain the amortization schedule for your mortgage. An **amortization schedule** is the schedule of payments for paying off a loan. An amortization schedule breaks down the payments into interest and principal, which is helpful because with an amortized loan these amounts vary with each payment. Typically, an amortization schedule will also include additional information such as the amount of interest and principal paid, as well as the remaining principal balance. Amortization schedules are most frequently used with mortgages (courtesy of www.investwords.com).

The amortization schedule shows you the blend of interest and principal you are paying with each payment. At the beginning of the mortgage term, your mortgage payments are front-loaded with predominantly interest payments, with very little principal reduction. Over time, the principal amount covered in each payment will slowly increase. Once an amount of principal is paid, you are no longer charged additional interest on that amount. By aggressively paying ahead on your principal balance early in your loan term, you can significantly reduce the overall term of your loan.

Let's look at a hypothetical snapshot of an amortization schedule for a 30-year fixed rate mortgage over six periods.

Amortization Schedule – Figure 2

PERIOD	INTEREST	PRINCIPAL	BALANCE
1	$583.33	$191.97	$99,808.03
2	$582.21	$193.09	$99,614.95
3	$581.09	$194.21	$99,420.74
4	$579.95	$195.34	$99,225.39
5	$578.81	$196.48	$99,028.91
6	$577.67	$197.63	$98,831.28

Again, we will make the numbers very simplistic so you can grasp the basic technique with minimal financial jargon. In this example, the principal and interest portion of the mortgage payment is $775.30. The monthly mortgage payment may also include taxes, insurance, and other fees. In Period 1, you will pay $583.33 of interest, and $191.97 on the principal, the actual balance of the home value at purchase. The total payment is $775 but the principal is decreasing by only $192. In Period 2, you see a slight change, with the principal amount increasing slightly. When you make an additional principal-only payment earlier than scheduled, you are essentially eliminating the interest penalty scheduled to be charged on that principal amount. Let's say for simplicity, if you make the payments as scheduled for Periods 1, 2, and 3, you would pay $2,325.90 to reduce the principal balance by only $579.27. You are paying over $1,746 in just three months on interest alone — the penalty the world system charges on lack. Do you see why the Lord does not want you subjected to this system?

Yes, mortgage interest is tax deductible, reducing your tax burden to the federal government; however, you are by no means recouping dollar for dollar the full amount of the overwhelming interest penalty you are paying. (Consult your tax professional for advice on your specific situation.)

One straightforward method to reduce the interest penalty is to pay ahead on the principal balance of your mortgage. In Period 1, if you pay the principal and interest, and you ADD the Period 2 **principal-only** amount, you are prepaying the Period 2 principal, and effectively eliminating the Period 2 interest penalty. Using the Mortgage Multiplier strategy, you are essentially paying two principal payments in one. In Period 1, you would pay:

$775.30 (P/I for P.1) + $193.09 (Principal Only for P.2)
= $968.39

Since the principal for Period 2 has already been paid ahead of schedule, you would eliminate $582.21 in interest penalty. By paying an additional $193.09 in principal you have cleared **two** mortgage payments.

In the second month, you would be ready to pay Period 3 (not P.2). You are a month ahead. Let's assume you do the same thing and pay the Period 3 regular payment, plus Period 4 principal only.

$775.30 (P/I for P.3) + $195.34 (Principal Only for P.4)
= $970.64

Since the principal for Period 4 has already been paid, you would eliminate $579.95 in interest penalty. By paying an additional $195.34 in principal you have cleared **two** mortgage payments.

In the third month, you are now two payments ahead. You are ready to pay Period 5. Let's assume you do the same thing one more time. You pay the regular Period 5 payment, plus the Period 6 principal only.

$775.30 (P/I for P.5) + $197.63 (Principal Only for P.6)
= $972.93

In three months, by simply adding the *principal only* for the *next payment* due, you have essentially paid six mortgage payments. You have paid all six principal payments, and eliminated three interest penalties. Using the Mortgage Multiplier strategy, let's look at your savings.

Conventional Payments (CP):.............................. $4,651.80

Principal Reduction: $1,168.72

Mortgage Multiplier Payments (MMP): $2,911.96

Principal Reduction: $1,168.72

Savings (CP-MMP):....................................**$1,739.84**
in three months!

If you apply the Mortgage Multiplier strategy over the life of your mortgage loan, you can significantly reduce the term of the mortgage by 10 to 15 years, depending on the term of the mortgage and when you start the plan. I encourage you to access the amortization schedule for your mortgage loan, and begin to put this strategy to work for you. Using the Debt Eraser strategy, you will free up funds to apply to your Mortgage Multiplier. Use these two techniques together to rapidly reduce your debt.

Consult your Financial Wellness Action Plan daily as you complete Part III: 90 Days of Prayer for Financial Breakthrough. Commit to being a doer of the Word!

PART III

90 DAYS OF PRAYER

FOR FINANCIAL BREAKTHROUGH

day 1

seek first the kingdom

power promise

But seek (aim at and strive after) first of all His kingdom and His righteousness (His way of doing and being right), and then all these things taken together will be given you besides.
Matthew 6:33 (AMP)

Father, I seek You first and foremost above all things. As I seek first Your Kingdom and Your righteousness, I know everything else shall be added. Lord, You are my Shepherd; I shall not want (Psalm 23:1). I thank You that no good thing will You withhold from those who walk uprightly (Psalm 84:11). I will not be conformed to this world, but I will be transformed by the renewing of my mind, so that I may prove what is the good and acceptable and perfect will of God (Romans 12:2). I cast all my cares upon You, Lord, knowing that You care for me, and You will help me (1 Peter 5:7). In the name of Jesus I pray, AMEN.

day 2

faithful and just

power promise

If we [freely] admit that we have sinned and confess our sins, He is faithful and just (true to His own nature and promises) and will forgive our sins [dismiss our lawlessness] and [continuously] cleanse us from all unrighteousness [everything not in conformity to His will in purpose, thought, and action].

1 John 1:9 (AMP)

Father, Your Word says that if I freely admit and confess my sin, You are faithful and just to forgive my sin, and cleanse me of all unrighteousness. Create in me a clean heart, O God, and renew a steadfast spirit within me (Psalm 51:10). Father, I lay before you now all financial mistakes I have made in the past. I ask for Your forgiveness for any wrong decisions, wrong motives, or wrong attitudes I have had previously. I ask for forgiveness for all financial choices and habits that have not aligned with Your Word or Your will for my life.

Father, I lay aside every weight, and the sin which so easily ensnares, and I run with endurance the race that is set before me, looking unto Jesus, the Author and Finisher of my faith (Hebrews 12:1-2). Father, I believe according to Your Word that as far as the east is from the west, that is how far You have removed my transgressions from me (Psalm 103:12). Thank You, Father, that You pardon my sin and forgive my transgressions. You will again have compassion on me. You will trample my transgressions underfoot and hurl all my iniquities into the depths of the sea (Micah 7:18-19). Thank You, Lord, that You will forgive my wickedness and remember my sins no more (Hebrews 8:12).

Now Father, I forgive myself and let go of all past mistakes, knowing You have completely forgiven me and cleansed me. I release the past — I let it go and put it behind me. One thing I do: forgetting what is behind and straining toward what is ahead, I press on toward the goal to win the prize for which You have called me heavenward in Christ Jesus (Philippians 3:14-15). I submit myself to You. I resist the devil, knowing he must flee from me (James 4:7).

Now Father, I fearlessly and confidently and boldly draw near to the throne of grace that I may receive mercy and find grace to help in good time for every need. I thank You for appropriate and well-timed help, coming just when I need it (Hebrews 4:16 AMP). I set my mind and keep it set on what is above, the higher things, not on the things that are on the earth (Colossians 3:2 AMP).

I reject the voice of the accuser (Revelation 12:10). You are the Good Shepherd (John 10:14). I know Your voice and I will follow You (John 10:27). Thank You for a fresh new start and complete financial victory! In the name of Jesus, AMEN.

day 3

good success

power promise

This Book of the Law shall not depart from your mouth, but you shall meditate in it day and night, that you may observe to do according to all that is written in it. For then you will make your way prosperous, and then you will have good success.

Joshua 1:8 (NKJV)

Father, Your Word is a lamp to my feet and a light to my path (Psalm 119:105). Your Word shall not depart from my mouth, but I shall meditate in it day and night, so that I may observe to do all that is written in it. Then I will make my way prosperous and I will have good success (Joshua 1:8). My delight is in the law of the Lord, and in Your law I meditate day and night. I shall be like a tree planted by rivers of water, that brings forth its fruit in its season, whose leaf also shall not wither. Whatever I do shall prosper (Psalm 1:2-3).

Father, I believe that all Scripture is God-breathed and is useful for teaching, rebuking, correcting and training in righteousness, so that I may be thoroughly equipped for every good work (2 Timothy 3:16-17). I declare, according to Isaiah 55:11, that Your Word shall not return to You void, but it shall accomplish what You please. It shall prosper in the thing for which You sent it.

Therefore, Father, I fix my mind on Your Word. I know that You are alert and active, watching over Your Word to perform it (Jeremiah 1:12). Whatever things are true, whatever things are noble, whatever things are just, whatever things are pure, whatever things are lovely, whatever things are of good report, if there is any virtue and if there is anything praiseworthy—I meditate on these things (Philippians 4:8). Father, I renew my mind with Your Word daily. I will not conform to the pattern of this world, but I am transformed by the renewing of my mind (Romans 12:2).

I do not doubt in my heart, but I believe that those things that I say will be done. Therefore, I will have what I speak in accordance with Your Word (Mark 11:23). I declare Your Word over my life that I am prospering and I will have good success in all that I set my hand to do (Joshua 1:8). I speak good success over my family. I speak good success over my finances. I speak good success over my health. I speak good success over my career, my business, and my ministry to others. I speak good success over my ideas and opportunities.

Father, I am a doer of the Word (James 1:22). Because I am a doer of the work, I am blessed in what I do (James 1:25). I am diligent, disciplined, and determined. I am more than a conqueror through Christ who loves me (Romans 8:37). In the name of Jesus I pray, AMEN.

day 4

the power to produce

power promise

But remember the Lord your God, for it is he who gives you the ability to produce wealth, and so confirms his covenant, which he swore to your forefathers, as it is today.

Deuteronomy 8:18 (NIV)

Remember the Lord your God. He is the one who gives you power to be successful, in order to fulfill the covenant he confirmed to your ancestors with an oath.

Deuteronomy 8:18 (NLT)

Thank You, Father, for giving me the power and ability to produce wealth in order to establish Your covenant (Deuteronomy 8:18). I have strength for all things in Christ Who empowers me. I am ready for anything and equal to anything through Him Who infuses inner strength into me; I am self-sufficient in Christ's sufficiency (Philippians 4:13 AMP). The power to produce is already in me, along with every gift and talent I need to succeed.

Thank You, Father, that Your gifts and Your call on my life are under full warranty—never canceled, never rescinded (Romans 11:29 MSG). I will stir up the gift of God that is in me (2 Timothy 1:6). Right now, I place a demand on the gifts, talents, skills, and abilities You have given me. I will use my gifting with diligence today! Your Word says that lazy hands make for poverty, but diligent hands bring wealth (Proverbs 10:4).

Father, I position myself for promotion to produce wealth. I distinguish myself because an excellent spirit is found in me (Daniel 6:3). I let my light so shine before men that they may see my good works and glorify my Father in heaven (Matthew 5:16). Thank You, Father, that I am created in Your image and in Your likeness (Genesis 1:26). I have the power to create. I call forth the creative ideas, inventions, innovations, and the intellectual property that You have placed within me to produce wealth. I have the power to be successful. I have the ability to produce wealth (Deuteronomy 8:18). I declare that I am wealthy. I am prosperous. I am debt free. I am generous. I am blessed to be a blessing.

No weapon formed against me shall prosper (Isaiah 54:17). I bind the enemy and cancel every scheme of the evil one to distract me from my purpose or delay my blessings of wealth. As I prosper and succeed, I know that it is not my power that has produced this wealth for me (Deuteronomy 8:17). I give You all the honor and glory that is due to Your name! Now to Him who is able to do exceedingly abundantly above all that I could ask or think, according to the power that works within me, to Him be glory in the church by Christ Jesus to all generations, forever and ever. AMEN (Ephesians 3:20-21).

day 5

the earth is the Lord's

power promise

The earth is the Lord's, and everything in it, the world, and all who live in it.

Psalm 24:1 (NIV)

Yours, O Lord, is the greatness, the power, the glory, the victory, and the majesty. Everything in the heavens and on earth is Yours, O Lord, and this is Your Kingdom. I adore You as the one who is over all things. Wealth and honor come from You alone, for You rule over everything. Power and might are in Your hand, and at Your discretion people are made great and given strength (1 Chronicles 29:11-12). I declare the earth is the Lord's and everything in it, the world, and all who live in it (Psalm 24:1). For every beast of the forest is Yours, and the cattle on a thousand hills (Psalm 50:10).

Father, Your resources are infinite! As Your child, my resources are infinite in You. I seek first Your Kingdom and Your righteousness, and everything else shall be added (Matthew 6:33). I declare this day according to Psalm 23:1, the Lord is my Shepherd. I shall not want or lack for anything. In You, there is no insufficiency. Everything in and upon the earth is Yours. I am abundantly supplied. I trust in You alone as my Source. I declare according to Philippians 4:19, my God shall supply all my need according to Your riches in glory by Christ Jesus. According to Psalm 67:6, the earth will yield its harvests, and God, our God, will richly bless us. Father, I believe the earth is yielding its harvest to me right now. I am richly blessed in the name of Jesus. You crown the year with a bountiful harvest; even the hard pathways overflow with abundance (Psalm 65:11).

Whatever I bind on earth will be bound in heaven, and whatever I loose on earth will be loosed in heaven (Matthew 16:19). Right now, I bind all demonic attacks against my resources. I cancel all manifestations of shortage, scarcity, drought, and insufficiency. I come against all manifestations of debt and lack. I declare that all debt is paid in full. I will let no debt remain outstanding (Romans 13:8). I am debt free.

Father, I believe You are commanding the blessing on me in my storehouse and in all to which I set my hand (Deuteronomy 28:8). I am abundantly supplied. I walk in abundance and overflow. Father, I believe You shall cause me to have a surplus of prosperity (Deuteronomy 28:11 AMP). I have more than enough for every good work. I am a faithful steward over the abundant resources You have entrusted to me. I am a cheerful giver (2 Corinthians 9:7). I am blessed to be a blessing.

Now Lord, I give You all the honor and all the praise due to Your holy name! In the name of Jesus I pray, AMEN.

day 6

bring all the tithes

power promise

"Bring all the tithes into the storehouse, That there may be food in My house, And try Me now in this," Says the Lord of hosts, "If I will not open for you the windows of heaven And pour out for you such blessing That there will not be room enough to receive it. "And I will rebuke the devourer for your sakes, So that he will not destroy the fruit of your ground, Nor shall the vine fail to bear fruit for you in the field," Says the Lord of hosts; "And all nations will call you blessed, For you will be a delightful land," Says the Lord of hosts.

Malachi 3:10-12 (NKJV)

Father, Your way is perfect! The Word of the Lord is tested and tried; You are a shield to all those who take refuge and put their trust in You (Psalm 18:30 AMP). I seek first Your Kingdom and Your righteousness, knowing everything else shall be added (Matthew 6:33). Father, Your Word says to

304

bring all the tithes into the storehouse, that there may be food in Your house (Malachi 3:10). Your Word decrees that a tithe of everything belongs to You; it is holy to the LORD (Leviticus 27:30).

I declare that I am a tither. I honor You with the tithe. I honor You, Lord, with my possessions, and with the firstfruits of all my increase (Proverbs 3:9). Now Father, I believe according to Your Word that all of my increase is blessed and not cursed. I believe that You are opening for me the windows of Heaven, and You are pouring out such blessing that there will not be room enough to receive it. Lord of Hosts, I believe that You are right now rebuking the Devourer for my sake, so that he will not destroy the fruit of my ground, nor shall my vine fail to bear fruit in its time (Malachi 3:8-11). I know You are alert and active, watching over Your Word to perform it (Jeremiah 1:12 AMP).

SATAN, you are rebuked. I cancel all demonic plans and schemes set against my finances now in the name of Jesus. I take up the shield of faith, with which I extinguish all the flaming arrows of the evil one (Ephesians 6:16). I cancel all manifestations of debt, lack, and shortage. I cancel all demonic schemes to delay, detour, and devour my income. No weapon formed against me shall prosper (Isaiah 54:17).

Father, I declare overflow in my life now. My barns will be filled with plenty, and my vats will overflow with new wine (Proverbs 3:10). All nations will call me blessed because Your presence and blessing are evident in my life (Malachi 3:11). I give You all the honor and praise due to Your holy name. In the name of Jesus, AMEN.

day 7

life in abundance

power promise

The thief comes only in order to steal and kill and destroy. I came that they may have and enjoy life, and have it in abundance (to the full, till it overflows).

John 10:10 (AMP)

Father, Your Word says there is no wisdom, no insight, and no plan that can succeed against the Lord (Proverbs 21:30). The thief comes only in order to steal and kill and destroy, but Jesus has come that I may have and enjoy life, and have it in abundance, to the full, till it overflows (John 10:10). I declare I am of God — I belong to You — therefore I have already defeated and overcome the agents of the antichrist, because He Who lives in me is greater and mightier than he who is in the world (1 John 4:4).

Father, today I declare complete victory through Jesus Christ over the enemy's Trifold Attack on my life. I declare complete and total victory over Poverty and Lack, Sickness and Disease, and Sexual Immorality and Relationship Fracture. I decree complete healing and divine health in my finances, my physical health, and in all of my relationships. Jesus disarmed the powers and authorities, making a public spectacle of them, triumphing over them by the cross (Colossians 2:15). I enforce the victory of the cross in my life now, in the mighty name of Jesus. Amid all these things I am more than a conqueror and I gain a surpassing victory through Jesus Christ who loves me (Romans 8:37).

Whatever I bind on earth will be bound in heaven, and whatever I loose on earth will be loosed in heaven (Matthew 18:18). SATAN, I command you and all demonic forces to cease and desist. I bind every demonic spirit on assignment against me, and I cancel all attacks, schemes, and manifestations of debt, lack, shortage, sickness, disease, infirmity, and relationship strife in my life. The Devourer is rebuked. I bind the Strongman and spoil his goods in Jesus' name (Matthew 12:29). I bind the Spirit of Infirmity, the Spirit of Heaviness, and the Lying Spirit. I submit to God, I resist you, and command you to flee in the name of Jesus (James 4:7).

Father, I thank You for and I receive the abundant life Jesus has provided for me — I live my life to the full, till it overflows. I declare increase, abundance, prosperity, and divine favor over my life now. I am debt free. I am blessed to be a blessing. I am blessed and cannot be cursed (Numbers 23:8, 20)! The blessing of the Lord makes me rich, and You add no sorrow to it (Proverbs 10:22). Now thanks be to God who always leads us in triumph in Christ (2 Corinthians 2:14). I give You all the honor, praise, and glory that is due to Your holy name. In the name of Jesus I pray. AMEN.

day 8

prosper in all things

power promise

Beloved, I pray that you may prosper in all things and be in health, just as your soul prospers.

3 John 2 (NKJV)

Father, Your way is perfect! The Word of the Lord is tested and tried; You are a shield to all those who take refuge and put their trust in You (Psalm 18:30 AMP). I pray that I will prosper in all things and be in health, even as my soul prospers (3 John 2). Father, I will not copy the behavior and customs of this world; I will be transformed by the renewing of my mind so that I may live out Your good, pleasing, and perfect will for my life (Romans 12:2). As my soul prospers and my mind is renewed, my actions will continually align with Your will and Your Word. Your Word shall not depart from my mouth, but I shall meditate in it day and night, that I may observe to do according to all that is written in it. For then

I will make my way prosperous, and then I will have good success (Joshua 1:8).

Father, Your Word declares, what good will it be for someone to gain the whole world, yet forfeit their soul (Matthew 16:26)? Therefore, I seek first Your Kingdom and Your righteousness, and everything else shall be added (Matthew 6:33). I rejoice that my name is written in Heaven (Luke 10:20). I am blessed with righteousness, peace, and joy in the Holy Spirit (Romans 14:17).

As I seek You first, I declare today that I am prospering spiritually, mentally, physically, emotionally, and financially. The blessing of the Lord makes me rich, and You add no sorrow to it (Proverbs 10:22). Father, I thank You that your blessings upon my life are holistic. I am blessed in my spirit, soul, and body. Your blessings are spiritual, natural, and material. I pray that I will prosper in all things and be in health (3 John 2). Father, Your Word declares it is a good thing to receive wealth from God and the good health to enjoy it. This is a gift from God (Ecclesiastes 5:19). I walk in abundant prosperity and divine health. I am blessed with a full life span (Exodus 23:26). My family is whole and abundantly blessed. My children will be mighty in the land; the generation of the upright will be blessed. Wealth and riches are in my house, and my righteousness endures forever (Psalm 112:2-3).

I prosper in wisdom, knowledge, and understanding. Lord, I declare that I am the head and not the tail; I shall be above only, and not be beneath, because I heed the commandments of the Lord and I am careful to observe them (Deuteronomy 28:13). Everything I set my hand to do, I do it unto the Lord, and I will prosper and succeed! I pray these things in the name of Jesus. AMEN.

day 9

running over

power promise

Give, and it will be given to you. A good measure, pressed down, shaken together and running over, will be poured into your lap. For with the measure you use, it will be measured to you.

Luke 6:38 (NIV)

Heavenly Father, I enter Your gates with thanksgiving and Your courts with praise! I give thanks to You and bless Your name (Psalm 100:4). Bless the Lord, O my soul; And all that is within me, bless His holy name! Bless the Lord, O my soul, and forget not all His benefits: Who forgives all my iniquities, Who heals all my diseases, Who redeems my life from destruction, Who crowns me with lovingkindness and tender mercies, Who satisfies my mouth with good things, So that my youth is renewed like the eagle's (Psalm 103:1-5).

Father, I thank You for all of Your abundant blessings upon my life. You so loved the world that You gave Your only begotten

Son, that whoever believes in Him should not perish but have everlasting life (John 3:16). I give thanks and worship You with a cheerful heart! I am a cheerful giver (2 Corinthians 9:7). As You have given so generously, now I give generously.

Father, I continually participate in Your cycle of blessing. According to Malachi 3:10, I bring all the tithes into the storehouse, that there may be food in Your house. I declare according to Your Word that the windows of Heaven are open to me, and You are pouring out such blessing that there will not be room enough to receive it. You have rebuked the Devourer for my sake. I cancel all manifestations of debt and lack in the name of Jesus.

Now Father, I cheerfully and thankfully give my free-will offering. I declare according to Luke 6:38 that as I give, it will be given to me: a good measure, pressed down, shaken together and running over, will be poured into my lap. For with the same measure I use, it will be measured back to me. I sow generously, and I will therefore reap generously (2 Corinthians 9:6). The blessings of God are running over in my life. I live in Your abundance. I live in Your overflow. Jesus has come that I may have and enjoy life, and have it in abundance, to the full, till it overflows (John 10:10 AMP). I thank You now, that You will liberally supply and fill to the full my every need according to Your riches in glory in Christ Jesus (Philippians 4:19 AMP). The Lord is my Shepherd, to feed, guide, and shield me; I shall not lack (Psalm 23:1 AMP). I am debt free. I rejoice in Your abundant, overflowing blessings that are running over!

In the name of Jesus, AMEN.

day 10

i shall not lack

power promise

The Lord is my Shepherd [to feed, guide, and shield me], I shall not lack.

Psalm 23:1 (AMP)

Forever, O Lord, Your Word is settled in Heaven (Psalm 119:89). Father, Your Word declares that You are my Shepherd, to feed, guide, and shield me; I shall not lack (Psalm 23:1). You, Lord, are my Source for everything. You shall supply all of my need according to Your riches in glory by Christ Jesus (Philippians 4:19). I stand on Your Word in Psalm 34:10, that those who trust in the Lord will lack no good thing.

Father, Your Word says the blameless spend their days under the Lord's care, and their inheritance will endure forever. In times of disaster I will not wither; in days of famine I will enjoy plenty (Psalm 37:18-19). I shall not lack or want for anything in You. I am abundantly supplied. I am fully equipped for every good work. I thank You, Father, that according to Deuteronomy 28:12, You will open the heavens, the storehouse of Your bounty, to send rain on my land in season, and to bless all the work of my hands. I will lend to many nations, but will borrow from none. My cup runs over (Psalm 23:5). I am in overflow.

Now, in the authority of Jesus Christ, I declare the Devourer has been rebuked. I cancel every demonic assignment and manifestation of debt, lack, stealing, shortage, and insufficiency set in motion against me, my family, and extended family. I cancel all satanic delays, distractions, detours, and diversions that are hindering any aspect of our financial increase. SATAN, I command you and all demonic forces to STOP NOW! Behold, Jesus has given me the authority to trample on serpents and scorpions, and over all the power of the enemy, and nothing shall by any means hurt me (Luke 10:19).

Heavenly Father, I believe as Abraham believed, that You are our God who gives life to the dead and calls those things which do not exist as though they did (Romans 4:17). Therefore, I call all debt in my family paid in full: all mortgages on homes, land, and commercial properties are paid in full, all car loans are paid in full, business loans are paid in full, student loans are paid in full, credit card debts and all consumer loans are paid in full. All interest-bearing loans are paid in full now in the name of Jesus. I am debt free and will remain debt free. The Son has set me free; I am free indeed (John 8:36). I thank You, Father, that you are Jehovah Jireh, *The Lord Who Sees and Provides*. You are *El Shaddai, The All Sufficient One, Who Nourishes, Supplies, and Satisfies* me.

I decree all shall be done according to Your Word. I praise You now! In the name and authority of Jesus Christ, AMEN.

day 11

fill to the full

power promise

And my God will liberally supply (fill to the full) your every need according to His riches in glory in Christ Jesus.

Philippians 4:19 (AMP)

Father, I come to You in the name of Jesus. I know that You will perfect that which concerns me (Psalm 138:8). I give all my worries and cares to You, knowing that You care about me (1 Peter 5:7). I thank You that my every need is met — filled to the full — according to Your riches in glory in Christ Jesus (Philippians 4:19). You are my Shepherd, to feed, guide, and shield me; I shall not lack (Psalm 23:1). I believe Your Word that You are able to make all grace — every favor and earthly blessing — come to me in abundance, so that I may always, and under all circumstances, and whatever the need, be self-sufficient, possessing enough to require no aid or support and furnished in abundance for every good work and charitable donation (2 Corinthians 9:8 AMP). I declare that I have more than enough now in the name of Jesus. I declare I am fully able to meet all of my financial obligations. I am liberally supplied and self-sufficient. I am debt free. I generously provide for my family and extended family. I am prepared for the unexpected because I wisely build my house on the Rock. Though the rain descends, the floods come, and the winds blow and beat on the house, it will not fall, for it was founded on the Rock (Matthew 7:24-25). I will provide a rich inheritance for my children's children (Proverbs 13:22). Every need is met.

Father, I bring my whole tithe into the storehouse. I believe according to Malachi 3:10 that You are opening the windows of Heaven for me, and You are pouring out such blessing that I will not have room enough to receive it. I generously give to build the Kingdom of God. I give generously to the needs of widows and orphans, and those who are in distress (James 1:27). Your Word says to give, and it will be given to me: a good measure, pressed down, shaken together and running over, will be poured into my lap. For with the measure I use, it will be measured back to me (Luke 6:38). I believe Your Word for blessings that are pressed down, shaken together, and running over!

Yes, the Lord pours down His blessings. Our land will yield its bountiful harvest (Psalm 85:12). I expand my faith for a bountiful harvest now, in the name of Jesus. I extend my faith for riches, abundance, overflow, and more than enough. Thank You, Father, that You will liberally supply and fill to the full my every need according to Your riches in glory in Christ Jesus. I call it done now in the name of Jesus. AMEN.

day 12

blessings shall overtake you

power promise

Now it shall come to pass, if you diligently obey the voice of the Lord your God, to observe carefully all His commandments which I command you today, that the Lord your God will set you high above all nations of the earth. And all these blessings shall come upon you and overtake you, because you obey the voice of the Lord your God...

Deuteronomy 28:1-2 (NKJV)

Heavenly Father, thank You for Your Word. The law of the Lord is perfect, refreshing the soul. The statutes of the Lord are trustworthy, making wise the simple. The precepts of the Lord are right, giving joy to the heart. The commands of the Lord are radiant, giving light to the eyes. The fear of the Lord is pure, enduring forever. The decrees of the Lord are firm, and all of them are righteous. They are more precious than gold, than much pure gold; they are sweeter than honey, than honey from the honeycomb. By them Your servant is warned;

in keeping them there is great reward (Psalm 19:7-11). Jesus said, "If you love Me, keep My commandments." (John 14:15). I love the Lord Jesus and I willingly obey His commands.

Father, Your Word promises that if I diligently obey the voice of the Lord my God, to observe carefully all Your commandments, that You will set me high above all nations of the earth. And the blessings of God shall come upon me and overtake me, because I obey Your voice (Deuteronomy 28:1-2). Father, I thank You that Your blessings of obedience are coming upon me and overtaking me now. I believe Your Word that if I am willing and obedient, I shall eat the good of the land (Isaiah 1:19). Faith without accompanying works is dead (James 2:26). I am a doer of the Word (James 1:22). I diligently obey Your voice. I stay on the path that You have commanded me to follow. Therefore, I will live a long and prosperous life (Deuteronomy 5:33).

You will cause my enemies who rise against me to be defeated before my face; they shall come out against me one way and flee before me seven ways. You will command the blessing on me in my storehouses and in all to which I set my hand, and will bless me in the land which You are giving me (Deuteronomy 28:7-8).

Father, I declare that You will grant me plenty of goods. You will open to me Your good treasure, the heavens, to bless all the work of my hand. I shall lend and not borrow (Deuteronomy 28:11-12). I am the head and not the tail; I shall be above only, and not be beneath, because I heed the commandments of the Lord (Deuteronomy 28:13). In the mighty name of Jesus I pray, AMEN.

317

day 13

favor upon favor

power promise

For out of His fullness (abundance) we have all received [all had a share and we were all supplied with] one grace after another and spiritual blessing upon spiritual blessing and even favor upon favor and gift [heaped] upon gift. For while the Law was given through Moses, grace (unearned, undeserved favor and spiritual blessing) and truth came through Jesus Christ.

John 1:16-17 (AMP)

Father, thank You that I am Your child. You made Him who knew no sin to be sin for me, that I might become the righteousness of God in Christ (2 Corinthians 5:21). Surely, Lord, You bless the righteous; You surround them with your favor as with a shield (Psalm 5:12). Thank You that Your divine favor surrounds me. You alone have blessed me with one grace after another, spiritual blessing upon spiritual blessing, and even favor upon favor, and gift heaped upon gift through Jesus Christ my Lord (John 1:16-17)! I recognize it is unearned and undeserved. It is through faith in Jesus Christ.

Father, Your Word says a good man obtains favor from the Lord (Proverbs 12:2). Remember me, Lord, when You show favor to Your people. Let me share in the prosperity of Your chosen ones. Let me rejoice in the joy of Your people; let me praise You with those who are Your heritage (Psalm 106:4-5). Thank You, Father, for divine favor in my employment. I receive favor in hiring decisions, promotions, raises, and bonuses. I declare Your favor upon my businesses. I receive Your divine favor in new business development, sales, negotiations, selection decisions, and new contract awards. Thank You for favor upon my proposals, quotes, bids, and offers. Thank You for new clients, preferred clients, and loyal clients. I declare Your favor with government officials for expansion, zoning, and permits. I believe for Your divine favor in legal decisions, righteous judgments, and vindication.

Father, thank You for Your divine favor upon my family. My offspring shall be known among the nations and my descendants among the peoples. All who see them in their prosperity will recognize and acknowledge that they are the people whom the Lord has blessed (Isaiah 61:9).

Father, I give all honor, all praise, and all glory to You for Your divine favor upon my life. I am becoming progressively acquainted with and recognizing more strongly and clearly the grace of my Lord Jesus Christ, His kindness, His gracious generosity, His undeserved favor and spiritual blessing, in that though He was so very rich, yet for my sake He became so very poor, in order that by His poverty I might become enriched and abundantly supplied (2 Corinthians 8:9 AMP). I receive it now in the mighty name of Jesus! AMEN.

day 14

firstfruits of your increase

power promise

Honor the Lord with your possessions, And with the firstfruits of all your increase; So your barns will be filled with plenty, And your vats will overflow with new wine.
Proverbs 3:9-10 (NKJV)

Yours, O Lord, is the greatness, the power, the glory, the victory, and the majesty. Everything in the heavens and on earth is Yours, O Lord, and this is Your Kingdom. I adore You as the One who is over all things. Wealth and honor come from You alone, for You rule over everything. Power and might are in Your hand, and at Your discretion people are made great and given strength (1 Chronicles 29:11-12).

Father, I honor You with my possessions, and with the firstfruits of all my increase (Proverbs 3:9). I bring all the tithes — the whole tenth of my income — into the storehouse, that there may be food in Your house. Your Word says, "And prove Me now by it," says the Lord of hosts, "if I will not open the windows of heaven for you and pour you out a blessing, that there shall not be room enough to receive it. And I will rebuke the Devourer — insects and plagues — for your sake and he shall not destroy the fruits of your ground, neither shall your vine drop its fruit before the time in the field," says the Lord of hosts (Malachi 3:10-11 AMP).

Father, You are not a man, so You do not lie. You are not human, so You do not change Your mind. Have You ever spoken and failed to act? Have You ever promised and not carried it through? (Numbers 23:19). I am a tither. I honor You with the firstfruits of all my increase. Therefore I stand confidently, boldly, and with certainty, knowing the windows of Heaven are now open to me. The Devourer is rebuked in the name of Jesus. I cancel all schemes, plans, and fiery darts of the wicked one sent to steal and consume my provision.

I am a child of Zion; I rejoice in the Lord my God. I thank You for the former rain and the latter rain. My floors shall be full of wheat, and my vats shall overflow with the wine and oil of Your abundance and increase. Thank You, Father, You are restoring to me the years that the locust had eaten, the cankerworm, and the caterpillar, and the palmerworm (Joel 2:23-25). All that the Devourer has consumed has been restored now in the name of Jesus. My barns will be filled with plenty, and my vats will overflow with new wine (Proverbs 3:10). I am debt free. I am wealthy. I am prosperous. I am in overflow. I am blessed to be a blessing. Thank you, Father, that You shall make me have a surplus of prosperity (Deuteronomy 28:11 AMP). I pray these things in the name of Jesus. AMEN.

day 15

sow generously

power promise

[Remember] this: he who sows sparingly and grudgingly will also reap sparingly and grudgingly, and he who sows generously [that blessings may come to someone] will also reap generously and with blessings.

2 Corinthians 9:6 (AMP)

Father, thank You for Your Word. The counsel of the Lord stands forever, the thoughts of Your heart through all generations (Psalm 33:11). I seek the Kingdom of God above all else, and live righteously, knowing You will give me everything I need (Matthew 6:33 NLT). Every good and perfect gift is from above, coming down from the Father of the heavenly lights, who does not change like shifting shadows (James 1:17). Thank You, Father, for giving me the ability to produce wealth, confirming Your covenant (Deuteronomy 8:18). Your Word says whatever I sow, that I will also reap (Galatians 6:7). With thanksgiving in my heart, I sow generously, that blessings may come to someone (2 Corinthians 9:6). I give as I have purposed in my heart, not reluctantly or sorrowfully or under compulsion, for You love, take pleasure in, prize above other things, and are unwilling to abandon or to do without, a cheerful, joyous, "prompt to do it" giver whose heart is in his giving (2 Corinthians 9:7). I am a cheerful, joyous, "prompt to do it" giver! I am extravagantly generous (1 Timothy 6:18 MSG). I purpose in my heart to do good, that I may be rich in good works, ready to give, and willing to share, storing up a good foundation for the time to come, that I may lay hold on eternal life (1 Timothy 6:18-19). I gather and heap up and store treasures in Heaven, where neither moth nor rust nor worm consume and destroy, and where thieves do not break through and steal; for where my treasure is, there my heart will be also (Matthew 6:20-21 AMP).

Father, thank You for the blessing of wealth that is upon my giving. I sow generously, therefore, I will also reap generously (2 Corinthians 9:6). As I give, it will be given to me. A good measure, pressed down, shaken together and running over, will be poured into my lap. For with the measure I use, it will be measured to me (Luke 6:38). Your Word declares that a generous person will prosper; whoever refreshes others will be refreshed (Proverbs 11:25).

Thank You, Father, that You are able to make all grace — every favor and earthly blessing — come to me in abundance, so that I may always, and under all circumstances, and whatever the need, be self-sufficient, possessing enough to require no aid or support and furnished in abundance for every good work and charitable donation (2 Corinthians 9:8 AMP). I pray these things in the name of Jesus. AMEN.

day 16

diligent hands bring wealth

power promise

Lazy hands make for poverty, but diligent hands bring wealth.

Proverbs 10:4 (NIV)

Father, I ask You to fill me with the knowledge of Your will through all the wisdom and understanding that the Spirit gives, so that I may live a life worthy of You, Lord, and please You in every way: bearing fruit in every good work, growing in the knowledge of God, and being strengthened with all power according to Your glorious might so that I may have great endurance and patience (Colossians 1:9-11). Father, Your Word is a lamp to my feet and a light to my path (Psalm 119:105). Your Word says lazy hands make for poverty, but diligent hands bring wealth (Proverbs 10:4). Thank You for the blessing of wealth upon my diligence. I am hard-working, industrious, diligent, and productive. I am focused, strategic, disciplined, and determined. I am organized and effective.

Whatever I do, I do it heartily, as to the Lord and not to men, knowing that from the Lord I will receive the reward of the inheritance; for I serve the Lord Christ (Colossians 3:23-24).

Your Word declares that the hand of the diligent will rule, but the lazy man will be put to forced labor (Proverbs 12:24). I am the head and not the tail; I shall be above only, and not be beneath (Deuteronomy 28:13). I am diligent and skillful in my business. Therefore I will stand before kings; I will not stand before obscure men (Proverbs 22:29).

The appetite of the sluggard craves and gets nothing, but the appetite of the diligent is abundantly supplied (Proverbs 13:4). I watch over the ways of my household; I do not eat the bread of idleness (Proverbs 31:27). I am very careful, how I live—not as unwise but as wise, redeeming the time and making the most of every opportunity, because the days are evil. I am not foolish, but understand what Your will is (Ephesians 5:15-17). I thank You, Father, that You shall liberally supply — fill to the full — my every need according to Your riches in glory in Christ Jesus (Philippians 4:19).

Your Word declares that all hard work brings a profit, but mere talk leads only to poverty (Proverbs 14:23). I am a doer of the Word (James 1:22). I am positioned for promotion. My businesses are highly profitable. I am steadfast, immovable, always abounding in the work of the Lord, knowing that my labor is not in vain in the Lord (1 Corinthians 15:58). Father, I thank You for blessing my diligence with increase, wealth, riches, abundance, and overflow. In the name of Jesus I pray, AMEN.

day 17

no debt outstanding

power promise

Let no debt remain outstanding, except the continuing debt to love one another, for whoever loves others has fulfilled the law.

Romans 13:8 (NIV)

Heavenly Father, I praise You for the wisdom of Your Word. Blessed are those who find wisdom, those who gain understanding, for she is more profitable than silver and yields better returns than gold. She is more precious than rubies; nothing I desire can compare with her. Long life is in her right hand; in her left hand are riches and honor. (Proverbs 3:13-16).

Father, Your Word commands me to let no debt remain outstanding, except the continuing debt to love one another, for whoever loves others has fulfilled the law (Romans 13:8). The rich rule over the poor, and the borrower is slave to the lender (Proverbs 22:7). Therefore I declare I AM DEBT FREE.

Father, thank You for divine favor and protection on all of my income sources. Thank You, Lord, for accelerating my ability to pay off all debts and interest-bearing loans. I have more than enough to meet every need. Surely, Lord, You bless the righteous; You surround me with Your favor as with a shield (Psalm 5:12). The blessing of the Lord makes me rich, and You add no sorrow with it (Proverbs 10:22).

I cancel all manifestations of debt, lack, shortage, and insufficiency. The Lord is my Shepherd, to feed, guide, and shield me; I shall not lack (Psalm 23:1). The earth is the Lord's, and everything in it, the world, and all who live in it (Psalm 24:1). I have more than enough to meet every need. All debt is PAID IN FULL now, in Jesus' name. I will lend, but I will not borrow (Deuteronomy 28:12).

I will keep out of debt and owe no man anything (Romans 13:8 AMP). Therefore, I call all debt in my family paid in full: all mortgages on homes, land, and commercial properties are paid in full, all car loans are paid in full, business loans are paid in full, student loans are paid in full, credit card debts and all consumer loans are paid in full.

Though I walk in the flesh, I do not war according to the flesh. For the weapons of my warfare are not carnal but mighty in God for pulling down strongholds (2 Corinthians 10:3-4). I pull down the stronghold of debt now in the name of Jesus. The Devourer is rebuked. SATAN, you must cease and desist. All manifestations of debt are revoked now in the name of Jesus. I AM DEBT FREE. I am strong in the Lord and in the power of His might (Ephesians 6:10). In the name of Jesus I pray, AMEN.

day 18

thirty, sixty, hundredfold

power promise

And those sown on the good (well-adapted) soil are the ones who hear the Word and receive and accept and welcome it and bear fruit – some thirty times as much as was sown, some sixty times as much, and some [even] a hundred times as much.

Mark 4:20 (AMP)

Heavenly Father, I will meditate on Your precepts, and contemplate Your ways. I will delight myself in Your statutes; I will not forget Your Word (Psalm 119:15-16). I declare today that my heart is good, fertile, and well-adapted soil for Your Word. I hear the Word, receive it, accept it, welcome it, and bear fruit—thirty, sixty, and even a hundred times as much as was sown (Mark 4:20). I am focused. I am productive. I am a doer of the Word (James 1:22). I declare a thirty, sixty, and a hundredfold return on all my labor now in the name of Jesus.

Now that I belong to Christ, I am a true child of Abraham. I am his heir, and I thank You, Father, that Your promise to Abraham belongs to me (Galatians 3:29). Your Word says that Isaac sowed in that land, and reaped in the same year a hundredfold; and the Lord blessed him (Genesis 26:12). Therefore, as Abraham's seed and heir to the promise, I believe Your Word for a hundredfold return on my labor in this same year, in Jesus' name.

Father, Your Word declares a lazy person's way is blocked with briers, but the path of the upright is an open highway (Proverbs 15:19). I am diligent. I am disciplined. Thank You that my path is an open highway full of opportunity, full of blessing, full of increase, and full of abundance. You crown the year with a bountiful harvest; even the hard pathways overflow with abundance (Psalm 65:11). Yes, the Lord pours down His blessings. Our land will yield its bountiful harvest (Psalm 85:12).

SATAN, I command you and all principalities, powers, rulers of the darkness of this age, and spiritual hosts of wickedness in the heavenly places to STOP all attacks and schemes against my harvest now in the name of Jesus. I cancel all satanic delay, distractions, detours, deceptions, detainment, and diversions sent to hinder and steal my harvest. I forbid you to operate any longer in my life. There is no wisdom, no insight, no plan that can succeed against the Lord (Proverbs 21:30). No weapon formed against me shall prosper (Isaiah 54:17).

I can do all things through Christ who strengthens me (Philippians 4:13). I am strong in You, Lord, and in the power of Your might (Ephesians 6:10). In the name and authority of Jesus Christ I pray, AMEN.

day 19

more will be given

power promise

*To those who use well what they are given, even more will
be given, and they will have an abundance.*

Matthew 25:29 (NLT)

Father, I thank You that I am in Christ, and I am a new
creation. Old things have passed away; behold, all things
have become new (2 Corinthians 5:17). Thank You that I am
created in Your image, and after Your likeness, and I have
dominion (Genesis 1:26). Your Word shall not depart from
my mouth, but I shall meditate in it day and night, that I may
observe to do according to all that is written in it. For then
I will make my way prosperous, and then I will have good
success (Joshua 1:8).

Father, I remember that it is You Who has given me the
ability to produce wealth (Deuteronomy 8:18). Before You
formed me in the womb You knew me; before I was born,
You sanctified me and ordained me to my purpose (Jeremiah

1:5). You have given me multiple talents, according to my ability (Matthew 25:15).

Father, Your Word says that to those who use well what they are given, even more will be given, and they will have an abundance (Matthew 25:29). I will multiply every gift and talent You have given me to fulfill my purpose, create wealth, and expand my territory. I put every talent into action now in Jesus' name. Your Word says that to whom much is given, from him much will be required (Luke 12:48). I declare today, because I use well what I have been given, even more will be given, and I will have an abundance (Matthew 25:29).

Father, Your Word says that lazy hands make for poverty, but diligent hands bring wealth (Proverbs 10:4). The appetite of the sluggard craves and gets nothing, but the appetite of the diligent is abundantly supplied (Proverbs 13:4). I declare I am diligent. I am productive. I am abundantly supplied.

My testimony shall be "Lord, You delivered to me five talents; look, I have gained five more talents besides them" (Matthew 25:20). I am resourceful. I am creative. Million dollar ideas, inventions, and innovations come forth from my mind. I am responsible. I am a trustworthy steward over Your resources. I am a doer of the Word (James 1:22). I hear the Word, receive it, accept it, welcome it, and bear fruit – thirty, sixty, and even a hundred times as much as was sown (Mark 4:20). I seek first the Kingdom of God and Your righteousness, and all these things shall be added to me (Matthew 6:33).

Thank You, Father, that as I am faithful over a few things, You will make me ruler over many things (Matthew 25:21). More will be given, and I will have an abundance. I am more than a conqueror and gain a surpassing victory through Christ Who loves me (Romans 8:37 AMP). In the name of Jesus I pray, AMEN.

day 20

command
the blessing

power promise

The Lord will command the blessing on you in your storehouses and in all to which you set your hand, and He will bless you in the land which the Lord your God is giving you.

Deuteronomy 28:8 (NKJV)

Heavenly Father, I praise You for the integrity of Your Word. Forever, O Lord, Your Word is settled in Heaven (Psalm 119:89). My delight is in the law of the Lord, and in Your law I meditate day and night. I shall be like a tree planted by the rivers of water, that brings forth its fruit in its season, whose leaf also shall not wither; and whatever I do shall prosper (Psalm 1:2-3). Thank You, Father, that You are alert and active, watching over Your Word to perform it (Jeremiah 1:12). I stand on Your promise that if I diligently obey Your voice, to observe carefully all of Your commandments, blessings shall come upon me and overtake me (Deuteronomy 28:1- 2). You

332

will command the blessing on me in my storehouses and in all to which I set my hand, and You will bless me in the land which You are giving me (Deuteronomy 28:8).

Father, I believe that right now, You are commanding the blessing upon me in my employment. You are commanding the blessing upon my businesses. You are commanding the blessing upon each of my income sources. You are commanding the blessing upon my creative works. You are commanding the blessing upon my real property and intellectual property. You are commanding the blessing upon my bank accounts, investments, stocks, bonds, and securities. You are commanding the blessing upon all to which I set my hand. You are commanding the blessing upon lands and properties you have designated for me. I thank You and praise You now that these blessings shall come upon me and overtake me. You have given the command to bless me, and no one can reverse it (Numbers 23:20).

I declare, Father, according to Your Word that You will open the heavens, the storehouse of Your bounty, to send rain on my land in season and to bless all the work of my hands. I will lend to many nations but will borrow from none (Deuteronomy 28:12). Surely, Lord, you bless the righteous; you surround me with your favor as with a shield (Psalm 5:12). It is not by my might nor by my power, but by Your Spirit (Zechariah 4:6).

SATAN, I bind you and all demonic forces in the authority of Jesus Christ (Matthew 18:18). I trample on serpents and scorpions, and over all the power of the enemy, and nothing shall by any means hurt me (Luke 10:19).

If God is for me, who can be against me? (Romans 8:31). Now thanks be to God who always leads me in triumph in Christ (2 Corinthians 2:14). Hallelujah! In the name of Jesus, AMEN.

day 21

the answer
for everything

power promise

A feast is made for laughter, and wine makes life merry, but money is the answer for everything.

Ecclesiastes 10:19 (NKJV)

Father, thank You for the wisdom of Your Word. Your Word has revived me and given me life (Psalm 119:50). I get skillful and godly Wisdom, and I get understanding — discernment, comprehension, and interpretation; I will not forget and I will not turn back from the words of Your mouth (Proverbs 4:5 AMP). Father, Your Word declares that a feast is made for laughter, and wine makes life merry, but money is the answer for everything (Ecclesiastes 10:19). I shall have an answer for those who taunt and reproach me, for I lean on, rely on, and trust in Your Word (Psalm 119:42).

Father, I believe You will liberally supply and fill to the full my every need according to Your riches in glory in Christ

Jesus (Philippians 4:19). My spiritual, natural, and material needs are all met in Jesus' name. I believe You are able to make all grace — every favor and earthly blessing — come to me in abundance, so that I may always, and under all circumstances, and whatever the need, be self-sufficient, possessing enough to require no aid or support and furnished in abundance for every good work and charitable donation (2 Corinthians 9:8 AMP).

Father, Your Word says I do not have because I do not ask God (James 4:2). Therefore I confidently ask for supernatural favor upon my employment, businesses, properties, investments, and all the work of my hand. I declare a thirty, sixty, and a hundredfold return on all my labor now in the name of Jesus (Mark 4:20). Your Word says that all hard work brings a profit, but mere talk leads only to poverty (Proverbs 14:23). Lazy people want much but get little, but those who work hard will prosper (Proverbs 13:4). I am diligent. I am strategic. I am focused. I am productive. I am wealthy. I have an abundance of money to answer every need, because money answers everything.

SATAN, I bind and declare unlawful any presence of debt, lack, or shortage in my life (Matthew 18:18). I resist the devil and you must flee from me (James 4:7).

I have more than enough to answer every debt "PAID IN FULL". I shall let no debt remain outstanding, except the continuing debt to love one another, for whoever loves others has fulfilled the law (Romans 13:8). I AM DEBT FREE. I declare that I have more than enough money to answer every need, for money is the answer to everything (Ecclesiastes 10:19). Father, I give You all the praise, honor, and glory! In the name of Jesus I pray, AMEN.

day 22

truly rich

power promise

The blessing of the Lord—it makes [truly] rich, and He adds no sorrow with it [neither does toiling increase it].

Proverbs 10:22 (AMP)

Father, Your Word is true for all eternity. The grass withers, the flower fades, but the Word of our God stands forever (Isaiah 40:8). Your Word declares the blessing of the Lord makes me truly rich, and You add no sorrow with it — neither does toiling increase it (Proverbs 10:22 AMP). I will not strive, overwork, or toil for wealth. I will not allow the worries of this life, the deceitfulness of wealth, and the desires for other things come in and choke the Word, making it unfruitful (Mark 4:18-19). I pray that I may prosper in every way and that my body may keep well, even as my soul keeps well and prospers (3 John 2 AMP).

Unless the LORD builds a house, the work of the builders is wasted. Unless the LORD protects a city, guarding it with sentries will do no good. It is useless for me to work so hard from early morning until late at night, anxiously working for food to eat; for God gives rest to his loved ones (Psalm 127:1-2 NLT). I will not wear myself out trying to get rich. I am wise enough to know when to stop (Proverbs 23:4).

Father, I do not worry about my life saying, "What will I eat? What will I drink? What will I wear?" These things dominate the thoughts of unbelievers, but You are my Heavenly Father, and You already know all my needs. Therefore I seek the Kingdom of God above all else, and live righteously, and You will give me everything I need (Matthew 6:31-33).

Now it shall come to pass, because I diligently obey the voice of the Lord my God, You will set me high above all nations of the earth, and Your blessings shall come upon me and overtake me (Deuteronomy 28:1-2). Father, I believe You are commanding the blessing on me in my storehouses and in all to which I set my hand (Deuteronomy 28:8). It is not by might nor by power, but by Your Spirit (Zechariah 4:6). Surely, Lord, you bless the righteous; you surround me with Your favor as with a shield (Psalm 5:12).

SATAN, I quench every fiery dart and cancel all satanic delay, distractions, detours, deceptions, detainment, and diversions sent to stop my wealth. I am already blessed and cannot be cursed (Numbers 23:8, 20).

I believe according to Proverbs 22:29, that I am diligent and skillful, therefore, I will stand before kings; I will not stand before obscure men. Thank You, Father. I decree these things in the name of Jesus. AMEN.

day 23

teaches you to profit

Thus says the Lord, your Redeemer, the Holy One of Israel: I am the Lord your God, Who teaches you to profit, Who leads you in the way that you should go.

Isaiah 48:17 (AMP)

Praise the Lord, who is my Rock. You train my hands for war and give my fingers skill for battle (Psalm 144:1). Father, Isaiah 48:17 declares, "Thus says the Lord, your Redeemer, the Holy One of Israel: I am the Lord your God, Who teaches you to profit, Who leads you in the way that you should go." Thank You, Father, that You teach me how to profit in Your Word. I trust in You, Lord, with all my heart, and lean not on my own understanding; in all my ways I acknowledge You, and You shall direct my path (Proverbs 3:5-6).

As the heavens are higher than the earth, Father, so are Your ways higher than my ways, and Your thoughts higher than my thoughts (Isaiah 55:9). I align my thoughts with Your thoughts and I elevate my ways to Your ways. I declare the wealth strategies from the Word over my life. Faith comes by hearing, and hearing by the Word of God (Romans 10:17).

I will get out and stay out of debt. The rich rule over the poor, and the borrower is slave to the lender (Proverbs 22:7). I am debt free.

I will use multiplication for income growth. I receive a thirty, sixty, and a hundredfold return on all my labor (Mark 4:20).

I am positioned for promotion. I have divine favor for raises, promotions, bonuses, new clients, and advancement opportunities (Genesis 41:38-41, Psalm 5:12).

I own my own business. I am a successful business owner (Proverbs 31:16, 18, 24).

I am creating multiple streams of income. I have seven, yes eight streams of income. I own multiple businesses and income-generating assets (Ecclesiastes 11:2, 6).

I am diversifying my income (Ecclesiastes 11:2, 6).

I own land, homes, real property, and intellectual property (Proverbs 31:16).

I use my highest level gifting to create wealth (1 Peter 4:10 AMP).

I will use leverage, not time, to create wealth and abundance (Mark 12:1-2).

I will maximize teamwork (Ecclesiastes 4:9-12).

Father, I believe You are commanding the blessing on me now in my storehouses and in all to which I set my hand (Deuteronomy 28:8). Hallelujah! I decree these things in the name of Jesus. AMEN.

day 24

slave to the lender

power promise

The rich rule over the poor, and the borrower is slave to the lender.

Proverbs 22:7 (NIV)

Father, You train my hands for battle; You strengthen my arm to draw a bronze bow. You have given me Your shield of victory (Psalm 18:34-35). Lord, I heed Your warning in Proverbs 22:7 — the rich rule over the poor, and the borrower is slave to the lender. The Spirit which I have now received is not a spirit of slavery to put me once more in bondage to fear, but I have received the Spirit of adoption — the Spirit producing sonship (Romans 8:15 AMP). So I am no longer a slave, but Your child; and since I am Your child, You have made me also an heir (Galatians 4:7). I declare war on all debt and debt slavery. I renounce all debt and declare my freedom. I am debt free.

Father, Jesus said, "The Spirit of the Lord is on me, because he has anointed me to proclaim good news to the poor. He has sent me to proclaim freedom for the prisoners and recovery of sight for the blind, to set the oppressed free, to proclaim the year of the Lord's favor." (Luke 4:18-19). Therefore, I declare that I am completely and permanently free of the prison and oppression of debt. I proclaim total freedom and supernatural favor. The Son has set me free; I am free indeed (John 8:36).

Father, Your Word says to keep out of debt and owe no man anything, except to love one another (Romans 13:8 AMP). I expand my income sources. I accelerate the payoff of all outstanding debt. I call all debt paid in full: all mortgages, car loans, business loans, student loans, credit card debts, consumer loans, and any other interest-bearing loans are PAID IN FULL in the name of Jesus. I am debt free and I will remain debt free.

Father, I believe You have opened to me Your good treasure, the heavens, to bless all the work of my hand. I shall lend, but I shall not borrow (Deuteronomy 28:12). I am abundantly supplied.

Father, Your Word says to be sober, be vigilant; because my adversary the devil walks about like a roaring lion, seeking whom he may devour. I forbid the Devourer from consuming and wasting away any of my provision through debt and interest. I resist him, steadfast in the faith (1 Peter 5:8-9). The thief does not come except to steal, and to kill, and to destroy. Jesus came that I may have life, and that I may have it more abundantly (John 10:10). I revoke all access to my provision through debt and interest. I AM DEBT FREE.

I decree these things in the name of Jesus. AMEN.

day 25

arise and build

power promise

"The God of Heaven Himself will prosper us; therefore we His servants will arise and build...

Nehemiah 2:20 (NKJV)

Father, I thank You for the power of Your Word. For the Word that God speaks is alive and full of power making it active, operative, energizing, and effective; it is sharper than any two-edged sword (Hebrews 4:12). I take up the sword of the Spirit, which is the Word of God (Ephesians 6:17). Father, I declare Your Word over my life. The God of Heaven Himself will prosper me; therefore I will arise and build (Nehemiah 2:20)! Father, You are the Lord my God, Who teaches me to profit, Who leads me in the way that I should go (Isaiah 48:17). I believe by faith You will abundantly prosper me; I will arise and build according to Your Word.

I am a doer of the Word (James 1:22). Faith by itself, if it is not accompanied by action, is dead (James 2:17). Therefore,

I take action now by faith. I fan into flame the gift of God, which is in me (2 Timothy 1:6). I will use my gifting to create wealth to fulfill my mission assignment, provide for my family, share the gospel, and build the Kingdom of God.

I will arise and build the Kingdom of God. For the sake of the house of the Lord my God, I will seek Your prosperity (Psalm 122:9). Father, I will arise and build a successful family. I will arise and build people. I will arise and build teams of people working together for Your mission and purpose. I will arise and build leaders. I will arise and build the future generation.

I will arise and build a successful career. I will arise and build my own business. I will arise and build multiple businesses and multiple income streams for wealth and abundance. Father, Your Word instructs me to invest in seven ventures, yes, in eight; I do not know what disaster may come upon the land. I sow my seed in the morning, and at evening I will not let my hands be idle, for I do not know which will succeed, whether this or that, or whether both will do equally well (Ecclesiastes 11:2, 6). Therefore, I will arise and build multiple, diversified income sources.

Father, I believe that You — the God of Heaven Himself — will prosper me. I believe that right now, You are throwing open the floodgates of Heaven and pouring out so much blessing that there will not be room enough to store it (Malachi 3:10). You are rebuking the Devourer now for my sake (Malachi 3:11). Praise the name of the Lord! I decree these things in the name of Jesus. AMEN.

day 26

invest in

seven ventures

power promise

*Invest in seven ventures, yes, in eight; you do not know
what disaster may come upon the land. Sow your seed in
the morning, and at evening let your hands not be idle, for
you do not know which will succeed, whether this or that,
or whether both will do equally well.*

Ecclesiastes 11:2, 6 (NIV)

Father, I thank You for the wisdom of Your Word. I will study
Your commandments and reflect on Your ways (Psalm 119:15).
To acquire wisdom is to love oneself; people who cherish
understanding will prosper (Proverbs 19:8). Father, You are
the Lord my God, Who teaches me to profit, Who leads me in
the way that I should go (Isaiah 48:17). Therefore, I will invest
in seven ventures, yes, in eight; I do not know what disaster
may come upon the land. I sow my seed in the morning, and
at evening I will not let my hands be idle, for I do not know
which will succeed, whether this or that, or whether both will

do equally well (Ecclesiastes 11:2, 6). I am a doer of the Word (James 1:22). I am strategically implementing Your Word to create multiple, diversified sources of income so that I am protected from disaster. Father, Your Word says the blameless spend their days under the Lord's care, and their inheritance will endure forever. In times of disaster I will not wither; in days of famine I will enjoy plenty (Psalm 37:18-19).

Holy Spirit, The Word declares that You will guide me into all the truth. You will not speak on Your own; You will speak only what You hear, and You will tell me what is yet to come (John 16:13). Holy Spirit, I listen closely for Your instruction. I ask You to lead me to the correct income sources. Show me what is to come. Guide my selection of business ventures, properties, investments, and employment opportunities. I ask for clarity in each investment. Show me where to invest my time, talent, and treasury. Show me which businesses are worthy of my investment. I will increase my income sources first from one to two, then from two to three. With Your guidance, I will invest in seven ventures, yes, in eight. I believe the God of Heaven Himself will prosper me; I will arise and build (Nehemiah 2:20)!

SATAN, whatever I bind on earth will be bound in heaven (Matthew 18:18). I bind you and all demonic forces. I cancel every planned scheme and extinguish every flaming arrow of deception, delay, distraction, detour, detainment, and diversion sent to stop, steal, or disrupt my income sources. No weapon formed against me shall prosper (Isaiah 54:17).

Praise the Lord! I decree these things in the name of Jesus. AMEN.

day 27

for the sake of the house

power promise

For the sake of the house of the Lord our God, I will seek your prosperity.

Psalm 122:9 (NIV)

Father, I was glad when they said unto me, let us go into the house of the LORD (Psalm 122:1). Your Word declares the righteous will flourish like a palm tree, they will grow like a cedar of Lebanon; planted in the house of the Lord, they will flourish in the courts of our God (Psalm 92:12-13). For the sake of the house of the Lord our God, I will seek Your prosperity (Psalm 122:9).

Father, when Jesus saw the multitudes, He was moved with compassion for them, because they were weary and scattered, like sheep having no shepherd. The Lord Jesus said, "The harvest truly is plentiful, but the laborers are few. Therefore pray the Lord of the harvest to send out laborers into His harvest." (Matthew 9:36-37). Father, Your Word declares that

346

whoever calls on the name of the Lord shall be saved. How then shall they call on Him in whom they have not believed? And how shall they believe in Him of whom they have not heard? And how shall they hear without a preacher? And how shall they preach unless they are sent? As it is written: "How beautiful are the feet of those who preach the gospel of peace, Who bring glad tidings of good things!" (Romans 10:13-15). Father, I seek Your prosperity so laborers may be sent into the harvest, and many will hear the gospel and be saved for all eternity.

I seek the Kingdom of God above all else, and live righteously, knowing You will give me everything I need (Matthew 6:33). I do not seek Your prosperity for selfish gain. For the love of money is a root of all kinds of evil. Some people, eager for money, have wandered from the faith and pierced themselves with many griefs (1 Timothy 6:10).

Father, Your Word says do not lay up for yourselves treasures on earth, where moth and rust destroy and where thieves break in and steal; but lay up for yourselves treasures in heaven, where neither moth nor rust destroys and where thieves do not break in and steal. For where your treasure is, there your heart will be also (Matthew 6:19-21). I willingly participate in the cycle of blessing to save souls! I store up treasure in Heaven. Father, You are not slow in keeping Your promise. Instead You are patient, not wanting anyone to perish, but everyone to come to repentance (2 Peter 3:9).

As You prosper me, Lord, I pray that Your Kingdom will advance and many will be saved. For the sake of the house of the Lord our God, I will seek Your prosperity (Psalm 122:9). In Jesus' name, AMEN.

day 28

the generous soul

power promise

There is one who scatters, yet increases more; And there is one who withholds more than is right, But it leads to poverty. The generous soul will be made rich, And he who waters will also be watered himself. The people will curse him who withholds grain, But blessing will be on the head of him who sells it.

Proverbs 11:24-26 (NKJV)

Heavenly Father, the sum of Your Word is truth; and every one of Your righteous decrees endures forever (Psalm 119:160). Since I have been raised with Christ, I set my heart on things above, where Christ is, seated at the right hand of God. I set my mind on things above, not on earthly things. For I died, and my life is now hidden with Christ in God (Colossians 3:1-3). Father, Your Word promises that there is one who scatters, yet increases more; and there is one who withholds more than is right, but it leads to poverty. The generous soul will be made rich, and he who waters will also be watered himself (Proverbs 11:24-25). I don't copy the behavior and customs of this world. I let Your Word transform me into a new person by changing the way I think (Romans 12:2). I will not withhold, hoard, or hold back when it is within my power to give. I am a vessel of blessing. I am extravagantly generous (1 Timothy 6:18 MSG). As I bless others, I will be abundantly blessed and amply supplied. Your Word declares that he who sows sparingly and grudgingly will also reap sparingly and grudgingly, and he who sows generously — that blessings may come to someone — will also reap generously and with blessings (2 Corinthians 9:6 AMP). Holy Spirit, show me where I may be a God-sent blessing today. As I sow generously, I will also reap generously and with blessings. I am a cheerful giver (2 Corinthians 9:7)!

Father, I follow Your Word to do good, to be rich in good works, ready to give, willing to share, storing up a good foundation for the time to come, that I may lay hold on eternal life (1 Timothy 6:18-19). I stand on Your promise that as I give, it will be given to me. A good measure, pressed down, shaken together and running over, will be poured into my lap. For with the measure I use, it will be measured to me (Luke 6:38).

Father, Your Word promises that blessing will be upon the head of him who sells (Proverbs 11:26). I receive the blessing now. I speak increase, growth, abundance, divine favor, and multiplied blessings upon my businesses in accordance with Your Word. You crown the year with a bountiful harvest; even the hard pathways overflow with abundance (Psalm 65:11). In the name of Jesus, AMEN.

day 29

hard work brings profit

power promise

All hard work brings a profit, but mere talk leads only to poverty.

Proverbs 14:23 (NIV)

Father, I give You praise for the wisdom of Your Word. Let the wise listen and add to their learning, and let the discerning get guidance (Proverbs 1:5). I am wise and discerning. Thank You, Father, that you are my Redeemer, the Holy One of Israel: You are the Lord my God, Who teaches me to profit, Who leads me in the way that I should go (Isaiah 48:17). I listen and apply Your Word to my life.

All hard work brings a profit, but mere talk leads only to poverty (Proverbs 14:23). I am focused, hard-working, and strategic. I am positioned for promotion. My businesses, creative works, and investments are highly profitable. Lazy people want much but get little, but those who work hard will prosper (Proverbs 13:4). I am firm, steadfast, and immovable, always abounding in the work of the Lord — always being superior, excelling, doing more than enough in the service of the Lord, knowing and being continually aware that my labor in the Lord is not futile. It is never wasted or to no purpose (1 Corinthians 15:58 AMP).

Father, Your Word declares that a wise youth harvests in the summer, but one who sleeps during harvest is a disgrace (Proverbs 10:5). Your Word warns, "Go to the ant, you sluggard; consider its ways and be wise! It has no commander, no overseer or ruler, yet it stores its provisions in summer and gathers its food at harvest. A little sleep, a little slumber, a little folding of the hands to rest — and poverty will come on you like a thief and scarcity like an armed man." (Proverbs 6:6-11). I am self-motivated and industrious. I am productive, organized, and effective. I make the very most of the time, buying up each opportunity, because the days are evil (Ephesians 5:16).

Father, Your Word declares that good planning and hard work lead to prosperity, but hasty shortcuts lead to poverty (Proverbs 21:5). I will not be deceived by the devil's trickery to lure me into hasty shortcuts as counterfeits of Your favor. Get behind me, Satan. I recognize shortcuts as your trap to ensnare me. I reject your schemes. I cancel all diversions sent to stop my hard work and steal my profit. I trample on serpents and scorpions, and over all the power of the enemy, and nothing shall by any means hurt me (Luke 10:19).

Thank You, Father, for Your favor. For out of Your abundance I have received one grace after another and spiritual blessing upon spiritual blessing and even favor upon favor and gift heaped upon gift through Jesus Christ (John 1:16-17 AMP). Praise the Lord! In the name of Jesus, AMEN.

day 30

two are better than one

power promise

Two are better than one, because they have a good return for their labor: If either of them falls down, one can help the other up. But pity anyone who falls and has no one to help them up.

Ecclesiastes 4:9-10 (NIV)

Thank You, Father for the wealth strategies in Your Word. You are my Redeemer, the Holy One of Israel: You are the Lord my God, Who teaches me to profit, Who leads me in the way that I should go (Isaiah 48:17). Father, Your Word declares that two are better than one, because they have a good return for their labor: if either of them falls down, one can help the other up. But pity anyone who falls and has no one to help them up (Ecclesiastes 4:9-10). A person standing alone can be attacked and defeated, but two can stand back-to-back and conquer. Three are even better, for a triple-braided cord is not easily broken (Ecclesiastes 4:12).

So let us then definitely aim for and eagerly pursue what makes for harmony and for mutual upbuilding, edification, and development of one another (Romans 14:19). I am a team builder. I am a strong team leader. I will maximize teamwork to build wealth in ways that are mutual beneficial and edifying for everyone on the team.

Jesus said, "Again I say to you that if two of you agree on earth concerning anything that they ask, it will be done for them by My Father in heaven. For where two or three are gathered together in My name, I am there in the midst of them." (Matthew 18:19-20). Through the power of agreement we will accomplish Your will. Father, Your Word declares that five will chase a hundred, and a hundred will chase ten thousand! All our enemies will fall beneath our sword (Leviticus 26:8). Through teamwork, unity, and the power of agreement, we will defeat the attack of the enemy.

SATAN, I command you and all principalities, powers, rulers of the darkness of this age, and spiritual hosts of wickedness in the heavenly places to STOP all attacks and schemes against my relationships now, in the name of Jesus (Ephesians 6:12). I bind Satan, the Lying Spirit, the Spirit of Jealousy, and all other demons, and I cancel all schemes, attacks, and manifestations of anger, strife, wrath, argument, angry outbursts, upsets, hurts, offenses, wounds, injuries, jealousy, envy, rivalry, unforgiveness, grudges, and bitterness. I will not let the devil get a foothold (Ephesians 4:27). I command you to STOP. I command you to go to dry places and I forbid you to return.

Father, I decree that there be no divisions among us, but that we will be perfectly united in mind and thought (1 Corinthians 1:10). Praise the Lord! In the name of Jesus, AMEN.

day 31

proverbs 31
entrepreneur

power promise

She considers a field and buys it; out of her earnings she plants a vineyard. She sets about her work vigorously; her arms are strong for her tasks. She sees that her trading is profitable, and her lamp does not go out at night. She opens her arms to the poor and extends her hands to the needy. She makes linen garments and sells them, and supplies the merchants with sashes. She is clothed with strength and dignity; she can laugh at the days to come.

Proverbs 31:16-18, 20, 24-25 (NIV)

Father, I seek out the wisdom of Your Word. Your Word declares, "Blessed are all who fear the Lord, who walk in obedience to him. You will eat the fruit of your labor; blessings and prosperity will be yours." (Psalm 128:1-2). Thank You, Father, for giving me the ability to produce wealth (Deuteronomy 8:18). I use my ability to build multiple businesses. I use my ability to produce creative works. I use

354

my ability to make smart investments. I follow the path of the Proverbs 31 entrepreneur.

Your Word says that she considers a field and buys it; out of her earnings she plants a vineyard (Proverbs 31:16). I am a smart investor as the Holy Spirit guides me. She sets about her work vigorously; her arms are strong for her tasks. She sees that her trading is profitable, and her lamp does not go out at night (Proverbs 31:17-18). Your Word says all hard work brings a profit, but mere talk leads only to poverty (Proverbs 14:23). I work hard with diligence and discipline.

She opens her arms to the poor and extends her hands to the needy (Proverbs 31:20). Yes, there is one who scatters, yet increases more; and there is one who withholds more than is right, but it leads to poverty. The generous soul will be made rich, and he who waters will also be watered himself (Proverbs 11:24-25). I sow generously that blessings may come to someone (2 Corinthians 9:6).

She makes linen garments and sells them, and supplies the merchants with sashes (Proverbs 31:24). According to Your Word, I will invest in seven ventures, yes, in eight; I do not know what disaster may come upon the land. I sow my seed in the morning, and at evening my hands will not be idle, for I do not know which will succeed, whether this or that, or whether both will do equally well (Ecclesiastes 11:2, 6).

She is clothed with strength and dignity; she can laugh at the days to come (Proverbs 31:25). Father, You crown the year with a bountiful harvest; even the hard pathways overflow with abundance (Psalm 65:11). I am a Proverbs 31 entrepreneur. I thank You now for prosperous businesses, profitable investments, increase, abundance, and overflow. In the name of Jesus, AMEN.

day 32

willing and obedient

power promise

If you are willing and obedient, You shall eat the good of the land.

Isaiah 1:19 (NKJV)

Father, Your Word has revived me and given me life (Psalm 119:50). I speak the following faith confessions of Your Word over my life. I am willing and obedient; I shall eat the good of the land (Isaiah 1:19). I meditate in Your Word day and night, that I may observe to do according to all that is written in it. I make my way prosperous, and I have good success (Joshua 1:8). I have the power to produce wealth. I have Your God-given ability to be successful (Deuteronomy 8:18). I will prosper and be in health, even as my soul prospers (3 John 2). The blessings of God come upon me and overtake me (Deuteronomy 28:2). I am debt free. Every need is met. I am abundantly supplied. I am in overflow. In the name of Jesus, AMEN.

day 33

give cheerfully

power promise

You must each decide in your heart how much to give. And don't give reluctantly or in response to pressure. "For God loves a person who gives cheerfully."

2 Corinthians 9:7 (NLT)

Father, I am a cheerful, joyous, "prompt to do it" giver whose heart is in my giving (2 Corinthians 9:7 AMP). For the sake of the house of the Lord our God, I will seek Your prosperity (Psalm 122:9). I honor You, Lord, with my possessions, and with the firstfruits of all my increase; my barns are filled with plenty, and my vats overflow with new wine (Proverbs 3:9-10). I sow generously — that blessings may come to someone — and I reap generously and with blessings (2 Corinthians 9:6). I am extravagantly generous (1 Timothy 6:18 MSG). The generous soul will be made rich, and he who waters will also be watered himself (Proverbs 11:25). I am abundantly supplied. Thank you, Father! In the name of Jesus, AMEN.

day 34

the promise
of blessings

power promise

God did not reveal it to previous generations, but now by his Spirit he has revealed it to his holy apostles and prophets. And this is God's plan: Both Gentiles and Jews who believe the Good News share equally in the riches inherited by God's children. Both are part of the same body, and both enjoy the promise of blessings because they belong to Christ Jesus.

Ephesians 3:5-6 (NLT)

Father, what great love You have lavished on me, that I should be called a child of God (1 John 3:1)! Anyone who belongs to Christ has become a new person. The old life is gone; a new life has begun (2 Corinthians 5:17)! I believe the good news of the gospel of Jesus Christ. Your Word promises that both Gentiles and Jews who believe the Good News share equally in the riches inherited by God's children. Both are part of the same body, and both enjoy the promise of blessings because we belong to Christ Jesus (Ephesians 3:5-6).

We are a chosen people, a royal priesthood, a holy nation, God's special possession, that we may declare the praises of Him who called us out of darkness into His wonderful light (1 Peter 2:9). I enjoy the promise of blessings now because I belong to Christ Jesus.

I was in slavery under the elemental spiritual forces of the world. But when the set time had fully come, You sent Your Son, born of a woman, born under the law, to redeem those under the law, that we might receive adoption to sonship. You have sent the Spirit of Your Son into my heart, the Spirit who calls out, "Abba, Father." So I am no longer a slave, but Your child; and since I am Your child, You have also made me an heir (Galatians 4:1-7). My adoption to sonship is sealed with the Holy Spirit.

Those who are led by the Spirit of God are the children of God. The Spirit I received does not make me a slave, so that I live in fear again; rather, the Spirit I received brought about my adoption to sonship. By him I cry, "Abba, Father." The Spirit Himself testifies with my spirit that I am Your child. Now if I am Your child, then I am Your heir — an heir of God and co-heir with Christ, if indeed I share in his sufferings in order that I may also share in his glory (Romans 8:14-17). Father, I proclaim that I am Your child. I am Your heir — I am an heir of God and co-heir with Christ.

Father, I know who I am in Christ. I am no longer deceived by the lies of the evil one. I will not live another day below my birthright. HALLELUJAH! In the name of Jesus, AMEN.

day 35

favor shall surround you

power promise

Surely, Lord, you bless the righteous; you surround them with your favor as with a shield.

Psalm 5:12 (NIV)

Father, thank You for Your divine favor upon my life. Surely, Lord, You bless the righteous; You surround me with Your favor as with a shield (Psalm 5:12). Your supernatural favor surrounds me and protects me. All grace — every favor and earthly blessing — comes to me in abundance (2 Corinthians 9:8 AMP). Out of Your abundance I have received one grace after another and spiritual blessing upon spiritual blessing and even favor upon favor and gift heaped upon gift. Grace — unearned, undeserved favor and spiritual blessing — and truth have come through Jesus Christ (John 1:16-17 AMP). Jesus came that I may have and enjoy life, and have it in abundance, to the full, till it overflows (John 10:10 AMP). Praise the Lord! In the name of Jesus, AMEN.

day 36

richly blesses all

power promise

For there is no difference between Jew and Gentile—the same
Lord is Lord of all and richly blesses all who call on him...
Romans 10:12 (NIV)

Father, today I give thanks for the blessing of birthright. For there is no difference between Jew and Gentile—the same Lord is Lord of all and You richly bless all who call on You (Romans 10:12). I am a new creation in Christ. My old life is gone; all things have become new (2 Corinthians 5:17)! I enjoy the promise of blessings because I belong to Christ Jesus (Ephesians 3:6). Those who trust in You, Lord, will lack no good thing (Psalm 34:10). You surround me with Your favor as with a shield (Psalm 5:12). The Spirit I received brought about my adoption to sonship. By Him I cry, "Abba, Father." I am Your child. I am an heir of God and co-heir with Christ (Romans 8:14-17). Thank You, Father! In the name of Jesus, AMEN.

day 37

children of Abraham

power promise

"And now that you belong to Christ, you are the true children of Abraham. You are his heirs, and God's promise to Abraham belongs to you."

Galatians 3:29 (NLT)

Father, I give thanks for the blessing of bloodline. The counsel of the Lord stands forever, the thoughts of Your heart through all generations (Psalm 33:11). Your Word says that now that I belong to Christ, I am a true child of Abraham. I am his heir, and Your promise to Abraham belongs to me (Galatians 3:29 NLT). Your Word declares that Christ has redeemed us from the curse of the law, having become a curse for us (for it is written, "Cursed is everyone who hangs on a tree"), that the blessing of Abraham might come upon the Gentiles in Christ Jesus, that we might receive the promise of the Spirit through faith (Galatians 3:13-14). So in Christ Jesus I am a child of God through faith, for I was baptized into Christ and I have clothed myself with Christ. There is neither Jew nor Gentile, neither slave nor free, nor is there male and female, for we are all one in Christ Jesus. I belong to Christ, therefore I am Abraham's seed, and an heir according to the promise (Galatians 3:26-29).

Thank You, Father, I am saved by grace through faith (Ephesians 2:8). My sins are forgiven by grace through faith. I am abundantly blessed by grace through faith. I am becoming progressively acquainted with and recognizing more strongly and clearly the grace of my Lord Jesus Christ, in that though He was so very rich, yet for my sake He became so very poor, in order that by His poverty I might become enriched and abundantly supplied (2 Corinthians 8:9 AMP).

Father, I believe I am Abraham's seed. I receive all of the blessing of Abraham by faith. Your Word says that Abram was extremely rich in livestock and in silver and in gold (Genesis 13:2 AMP). Father, You greatly blessed him; he became a wealthy man. You gave him flocks of sheep and goats, herds of cattle, a fortune in silver and gold, and many male and female servants and camels and donkeys (Genesis 24:34-35). The blessing came to Isaac. Isaac sowed in that land, and reaped in the same year a hundredfold; and You blessed him. Isaac began to prosper, and continued prospering until he became very prosperous (Genesis 26:12-13). The blessing came to Jacob. Jacob became very wealthy, with large flocks of sheep and goats, female and male servants, and many camels and donkeys (Genesis 30:43). Your Word says "For I am the Lord, I do not change." (Malachi 3:6). Just as You prospered Abraham, Isaac and Jacob, I receive the same blessing now in this time. I am wealthy. I am prosperous. Thank You, Father! AMEN.

day 38

in silver and gold

power promise

Abram had become very wealthy in livestock and in silver and gold.

Genesis 13:2 (NIV)

Father, thank You for the blessing of bloodline. Now that I belong to Christ, I am a true child of Abraham. I am his heir, and Your promise to Abraham belongs to me. I am Abraham's seed, and an heir according to the promise (Galatians 3:29). I receive the full blessing of Abraham by faith. I am very wealthy in silver and in gold (Genesis 13:2). I am exceedingly fruitful (Genesis 17:6). As I sow, I will reap a hundredfold return in the same year. I will prosper and will continue prospering until I become very prosperous (Genesis 26:12-13). There is no difference between Jew and Gentile—the same Lord is Lord of all and You richly bless all who call on You (Romans 10:12). I am very wealthy. I am prosperous. Father, I give You all the praise and glory. In the name of Jesus, AMEN.

day 39

favor from the Lord

power promise

A good man obtains favor from the Lord, But a man of wicked intentions He will condemn.

Proverbs 12:2 (NKJV)

Father, thank You for Your divine favor. A good man obtains favor from the Lord (Proverbs 12:2). For the sake of the house of the Lord our God, I will seek Your prosperity (Psalm 122:9). I seek first the Kingdom of God and Your righteousness, and all these things shall be added (Matthew 6:33). True humility and fear of the Lord lead to riches, honor, and long life (Proverbs 22:4). Surely, Lord, You bless the righteous; You surround me with Your favor as with a shield (Psalm 5:12). The godly are showered with blessings (Proverbs 10:6). I receive one grace after another and spiritual blessing upon spiritual blessing and even favor upon favor and gift heaped upon gift through Jesus Christ (John 1:16-17 AMP). Thank You, Father for supernatural favor, blessings, riches, honor, and long life. In the name of Jesus, AMEN.

day 40

seven protections

power promise

They triumphed over him by the blood of the Lamb and by the word of their testimony; they did not love their lives so much as to shrink from death.

Revelation 12:11 (NIV)

Father, Your Word says to be sober, be vigilant; because my adversary the devil walks about like a roaring lion, seeking whom he may devour. I resist him, steadfast in the faith (1 Peter 5:8-9). I triumph over him by the blood of the Lamb and by the word of my testimony (Revelation 12:11). Holy Spirit, lead and guide me into all truth (John 16:13). I declare the seven protections of the blood of Jesus over my life.

The blood of Jesus protects my Person, spirit, soul, and body. I am saved by grace through faith (Ephesians 2:8). I am protected from sickness and disease, injury, accidents, and all other manifestations of illness. I walk in divine health

366

by the blood of Jesus. Jesus Himself bore my sin in His body on the cross, so that I might die to sin and live for righteousness; by His wounds I have been healed (1 Peter 2:24). I offer my body as a living sacrifice, holy and pleasing to God—this is my true and proper worship. I do not conform to the pattern of this world, but I am transformed by the renewing of my mind (Romans 12:1-2). I have the mind of Christ, and hold the thoughts, feelings, and purposes of His heart (1 Corinthians 2:16 AMP).

The blood of Jesus protects my Purpose. Father, before You formed me in the womb, You knew me, before I was born You set me apart; You appointed me to my divine purpose (Jeremiah 1:5). You have begun a good work in me and will carry it on to completion until the day of Jesus Christ (Philippians 1:6).

The blood of Jesus protects Your Plan for my life. Father, Your Word says, "'For I know the plans I have for you,' declares the Lord, 'plans to prosper you and not to harm you, plans to give you hope and a future.'" (Jeremiah 29:11). The devil cannot stop it, delay it, or thwart it in any way. I roll my works upon You Lord — commit and trust them wholly to You; You will cause my thoughts to become agreeable to Your will — and so shall my plans be established and succeed (Proverbs 16:3 AMP).

The blood of Jesus protects my Paternity and all members of my family lineage. As for me and my house, we will serve the Lord (Joshua 24:15). Lord, You do not delay and You are not tardy or slow about what You promise, but You are long-suffering and extraordinarily patient toward us, not desiring that any should perish, but that all should turn to repentance (2 Peter 3:9 AMP). Father, as the Lord of the Harvest, I ask You now to send laborers specifically to my family members (Matthew 9:38). I believe by faith according to Acts 16:31, "Believe in the Lord Jesus, and you will be saved—you and your household." I pray for and cover every unsaved family member in my family, now, in Jesus' name.

The blood of Jesus protects my Property and Possessions. All that I own — including my home, vehicles, and possessions — is protected now in the name of Jesus. I establish a perimeter around my property and protect my dwelling by the blood of Jesus. Because I have made the Lord, who is my refuge, even the Most High, my dwelling place, no evil shall befall me, nor shall any plague come near my dwelling; for You shall give Your angels charge over me, to keep me in all my ways (Psalm 91:9-11). Father, Your Word declares, "My people will live in peaceful dwelling places, in secure homes, in undisturbed places of rest." (Isaiah 32:18). I protect the security of my home with the blood of Jesus. I own my home and all that is contained within it without debt. I am debt free.

SATAN and all demonic forces, I cancel any schemes now for theft, robbery, burglary, break-ins, accidents, fires, flooding, or other property damage. My family, home, vehicles, and all of my possessions are protected now by the blood of Jesus. You cannot cross the bloodline protecting my family and my home. You have no access whatsoever to my dwelling. I command you to go to dry places and I forbid your return.

The blood of Jesus protects my Provision. All of my income sources are protected now by the blood of Jesus. I am a tither. Thank You, Father, that You rebuke the Devourer for my sake (Malachi 3:8-11). I give generously and stay in the cycle of blessing. My God will liberally supply and fill to the full my every need according to His riches in glory in Christ Jesus (Philippians 4:19 AMP). The Lord is my Shepherd;

I shall not lack (Psalm 23:1). Those who trust in the Lord will lack no good thing (Psalm 34:10). I am debt free and protected against debt slavery (Proverbs 22:7).

Whatever I bind on earth will be bound in heaven, and whatever I loose on earth will be loosed in heaven (Matthew 16:19). SATAN, I bind you and cancel all manifestations of income interruptions — layoffs, furloughs, decreased hours, business downturns, lost contracts, delayed compensation, and slow-paying or non-paying clients. I cancel all satanic delay and detainment of my income. I loose and call forth new income sources, new clients for my businesses, promotions, raises, and bonuses.

Father, I believe that You are commanding the blessing on me in my storehouses and in all to which I set my hand (Deuteronomy 28:8). My ideas and intellectual property are protected by the blood of Jesus. I believe now that You are able to make all grace — every favor and earthly blessing — come to me in abundance, so that I may always, and under all circumstances, and whatever the need, be self-sufficient, possessing enough to require no aid or support and furnished in abundance for every good work and charitable donation (1 Corinthians 9:8 AMP).

The blood of Jesus protects my Promise for the future. I have a promised destination for my life. Lord, when you delivered the children of Israel, You took them from Poverty (slavery to the Egyptians), to Provision (manna in the wilderness), to the Promised Land (a land overflowing with milk and honey). Father, I believe that You are bringing me out into a land You have searched out for me, a land flowing with milk and honey, the most beautiful of all lands (Ezekiel 20:6). Father, thank You for my provision. Thank You that I will arrive at the promise. I will go up and take possession of the land, for I can certainly do it (Numbers 13:30). I cover the vision You have given me with the blood of Jesus. I cover my Promised Land.

SATAN, I command you and all principalities, powers, rulers of the darkness of this age, and spiritual hosts of wickedness in the heavenly places to STOP YOUR TRESPASS NOW IN THE NAME OF JESUS. You cannot cross the bloodline of Jesus Christ. You have no access to me or any aspect of my life. I overcome by the blood of the Lamb and by the word of my testimony. My Person, Purpose, Plan, Paternity, Property, Provision, and Promise are all protected now by the blood of Jesus.

Hallelujah! Father, I praise Your name for You are worthy to be praised! Thank You, Jesus, for Your precious shed blood. Thank You, Holy Spirit, for infilling me with power, and leading and guiding me into all truth. I praise the Lord it is done! I praise You, Father, that I am fully protected, and I will fulfill all that You have called me to do. I decree all of these things in the mighty name of Jesus, AMEN AND SO BE IT.

day 41

no good thing

power promise

Taste and see that the Lord is good. Oh, the joys of those who take refuge in him! Fear the Lord, you his godly people, for those who fear him will have all they need. Even strong young lions sometimes go hungry, but those who trust in the Lord will lack no good thing.

Psalm 34:8-10 (NLT)

Forever, O Lord, Your Word is settled in Heaven (Psalm 119:89). Father, Your Word says those who trust in the Lord will lack no good thing. I will have all I need (Psalm 34:9-10). The Lord is my Shepherd, to feed, guide and shield me; I shall not lack (Psalm 23:1). Money is the answer for everything (Ecclesiastes 10:19). The blessing of the Lord brings wealth, without painful toil for it (Proverbs 10:22). My God will liberally supply and fill to the full my every need according to His riches in glory in Christ Jesus (Philippians 4:19 AMP). I am debt free. Thank you, Father! In Jesus' name, AMEN.

day 42

my cup overflows

power promise

You prepare a feast for me in the presence of my enemies. You honor me by anointing my head with oil. My cup overflows with blessings.

Psalm 23:5 (NLT)

Thank You, Father, my cup overflows with blessings. You prepare a feast for me in the presence of my enemies (Psalm 23:5). You have given the command to bless me, and no one can reverse it (Numbers 23:20). The blessings of God shall come upon me and overtake me, because I obey Your voice (Deuteronomy 28:2). The LORD will cause my enemies who rise against me to be defeated before my face; they shall come out against me one way and flee before me seven ways. The LORD will command the blessing on me in my storehouses and in all to which I set my hand (Deuteronomy 28:7-8). If God is for me, who can be against me? (Romans 8:31). I have total and complete victory today. In the name of Jesus, AMEN.

day 43

abundantly supplied

power promise

The appetite of the sluggard craves and gets nothing, but the appetite of the diligent is abundantly supplied.
Proverbs 13:4 (AMP)

Father, Your Word promises the appetite of the sluggard craves and gets nothing, but the appetite of the diligent is abundantly supplied (Proverbs 13:4). Lazy hands make for poverty, but diligent hands bring wealth (Proverbs 10:4). I am diligent. I am strategic. I am creative. I am productive. I am wealthy. The God of Heaven Himself will prosper me; therefore I will arise and build (Nehemiah 2:20). No weapon formed against me shall prosper (Isaiah 54:17). Satan, I bind you and all demonic forces sent to stop me. I cancel every scheme to stop my progress. No distractions, no delays, and no detours will impact me. Father, Your Word says all hard work brings a profit, but mere talk leads only to poverty (Proverbs 14:23). My businesses are profitable. I am abundantly supplied! In the name of Jesus, AMEN.

day 44

the fruit of your labor

power promise

Blessed are all who fear the Lord, who walk in obedience to him. You will eat the fruit of your labor; blessings and prosperity will be yours.

Psalm 128:1-2 (NIV)

Father, Your Word is a lamp to my feet and a light to my path (Psalm 119:105). I speak Your Word over my life. Blessed are all who fear the Lord, who walk in obedience to You. I will eat the fruit of my labor; blessings and prosperity will be mine (Psalm 128:1-2). The blessings of God shall come upon me and overtake me, because I obey the voice of the Lord my God (Deuteronomy 28:2). I am willing and obedient. I shall eat the good of the land (Isaiah 1:19). The appetite of the sluggard craves and gets nothing, but the appetite of the diligent is abundantly supplied (Proverbs 13:4). You prepare a feast for me in the presence of my enemies. My cup overflows with blessings. (Psalm 23:5). In Jesus' name, AMEN.

day 45

in exchange
for your soul

power promise

*And what do you benefit if you gain the whole world but
lose your own soul? Is anything worth more than your soul?*
Matthew 16:26 (NLT)

Father, I thank You for wisdom. Your Word warns me that
the love of money is a root of all kinds of evil. Some people,
eager for money, have wandered from the faith and pierced
themselves with many griefs (1 Timothy 6:10). What do I
benefit if I gain the whole world but lose my own soul? Is
anything worth more than my soul? (Matthew 16:26). A
person is a fool to store up earthly wealth but not have a
rich relationship with God (Luke 12:21). Therefore Father, I
seek the Kingdom of God above all else, and live righteously,
and You will give me everything I need (Matthew 6:33). For
the sake of the house of the Lord our God, I will seek Your
prosperity (Psalm 122:9). In the name of Jesus, AMEN.

day 46

a double portion

power promise

But you shall be called the priests of the Lord; people will speak of you as the ministers of our God. You shall eat the wealth of the nations, and the glory [once that of your captors] shall be yours. Instead of your [former] shame you shall have a twofold recompense; instead of dishonor and reproach [your people] shall rejoice in their portion. Therefore in their land they shall possess double [what they had forfeited]; everlasting joy shall be theirs. For I the Lord love justice; I hate robbery and wrong with violence or a burnt offering. And I will faithfully give them their recompense in truth, and I will make an everlasting covenant or league with them. And their offspring shall be known among the nations and their descendants among the peoples. All who see them [in their prosperity] will recognize and acknowledge that they are the people whom the Lord has blessed.

Isaiah 61:6-9 (AMP)

Father, thank You for the blessing of the double portion. Even in difficulty and hardship, I shall be blessed. I know You are alert and active, watching over Your Word to perform it (Jeremiah 1:12 AMP). Many are the afflictions of the righteous, but the Lord delivers him out of them all (Psalm 34:19). Father, after Job had prayed for his friends, You restored his fortunes and gave him twice as much as he had before (Job 42:10). For every trial I come through, I shall possess double what I forfeited. Instead of my shame I will receive a double portion, and instead of disgrace I will rejoice in my inheritance. And so I will inherit a double portion in my land, and everlasting joy will be mine (Isaiah 61:7).

I shall be called the priest of the Lord; people will speak of me as a minister of my God. I shall eat the wealth of the nations, and the glory, once that of my captors, shall be mine. Instead of my former shame I shall have a twofold recompense; instead of dishonor and reproach I shall rejoice in my portion. Therefore in my land I shall possess double what I had forfeited; everlasting joy shall be mine. For You, Lord, love justice; You hate robbery and wrong with violence or a burnt offering. And You will faithfully give me my recompense in truth, and You will make an everlasting covenant or league with me. And my offspring shall be known among the nations and my descendants among the peoples. All who see us in our prosperity will recognize and acknowledge that we are the people whom the Lord has blessed (Isaiah 61:6-9 AMP).

Thank You, Father. I receive it now in the name of Jesus, AMEN.

day 47

live long and prosper

power promise

Stay on the path that the Lord your God has commanded you to follow. Then you will live long and prosperous lives in the land you are about to enter and occupy.

Deuteronomy 5:33 (NLT)

Father, I will stay on the path that You have commanded me to follow. Then I will live a long and prosperous life (Deuteronomy 5:33). Wealth is a crown for the wise (Proverbs 14:24 NLT). It is a good thing to receive wealth from God and the good health to enjoy it. This is indeed a gift from God (Ecclesiastes 5:19). True humility and fear of the Lord lead to riches, honor, and long life (Proverbs 22:4). The thief comes only in order to steal and kill and destroy. Jesus came that I may have and enjoy life, and have it in abundance, to the full, till it overflows (John 10:10 AMP). Thank You, Father. I will live a long and prosperous life. My cup overflows with blessings (Psalm 23:5). In Jesus' name, AMEN.

day 48

skip the shortcuts

power promise

Good planning and hard work lead to prosperity, but hasty shortcuts lead to poverty.

Proverbs 21:5 (NLT)

Father, I heed the wisdom of Your Word. Good planning and hard work lead to prosperity, but hasty shortcuts lead to poverty (Proverbs 21:5). A faithful man shall abound with blessings, but he who makes haste to be rich at any cost shall not go unpunished (Proverbs 28:20). I reject the counterfeit shortcuts of the enemy. Father, I follow the divine plan You have set out for my life, to prosper me and not to harm me, plans to give me hope and a future (Jeremiah 29:11). I plan strategically and use my time wisely. I make the most of every opportunity, because the days are evil (Ephesians 5:16). You surround me with Your favor as with a shield (Psalm 5:12). The God of Heaven Himself will prosper me; therefore I will arise and build (Nehemiah 2:20). In Jesus' name, AMEN.

day 49

sevenfold restitution

power promise

Men do not despise a thief if he steals to satisfy himself when he is hungry; But if he is found out, he must restore seven times [what he stole]; he must give the whole substance of his house [if necessary—to meet his fine].

Proverbs 6:30-31 (AMP)

Father, Your Word says the thief does not come except to steal, and to kill, and to destroy. Jesus has come that I may have life, and that I may have it more abundantly (John 10:10). Though I walk in the flesh, I do not war according to the flesh. For the weapons of my warfare are not carnal but mighty in God for pulling down strongholds, casting down arguments and every high thing that exalts itself against the knowledge of God, bringing every thought into captivity to the obedience of Christ, and being ready to punish all disobedience when my obedience is fulfilled (2 Corinthians 10:3-6). I enforce the scriptural punishment of the sevenfold

380

restitution now in the authority of Jesus Christ (Proverbs 6:30-31). I am strong in You, Lord, and in the power of Your might. I put on the whole armor of God, that I may be able to stand against the wiles of the devil. I stand having girded my waist with truth, having put on the breastplate of righteousness, and having shod my feet with the preparation of the gospel of peace; above all, taking the shield of faith with which I will be able to quench all the fiery darts of the wicked one. I take the helmet of salvation, and the sword of the Spirit, which is the Word of God; praying always with all prayer and supplication in the Spirit (Ephesians 6:10-18).

SATAN, it is written, Jesus has given me the keys of the Kingdom of Heaven. Whatever I bind — declare to be improper and unlawful — on earth has already been bound in heaven; and whatever I loose — declare lawful — on earth has already been loosed in heaven (Matthew 16:19). SATAN, I bind you and all principalities, powers, rulers of the darkness of this age, spiritual hosts of wickedness in the heavenly places in the name of JESUS.

I declare ALL demonic activity to steal my provision, kill my physical body, and destroy my relationship with God and my relationships with other people to be improper and unlawful. You cannot cross the blood of Jesus Christ that protects me and my family. I command you to STOP now in the name of Jesus. You are forbidden to steal, to kill, or to destroy anything in my life, in Jesus' name. The blood of Jesus stands against you. Satan, Jesus saw you fall like lightning from heaven. Now I have been given the authority to trample on serpents and scorpions, and over all the power of the enemy, and nothing shall by any means hurt me (Luke 10:18-19). I command you to STOP stealing my provision now. I remind you that I am a tither. My Father — the Lord of Hosts — has rebuked the Devourer for my sake so that you will not destroy the fruit of my ground nor shall the vine fail to bear fruit for me in the field (Malachi 3:11). I cancel all manifestations of debt, lack, shortage, and insufficiency. I cancel all satanic delay, detours, distractions, and diversions sent to steal my provision.

It is written, if the thief is found out, he must restore seven times what he stole; he must give the whole substance of his house if necessary — to meet his fine (Proverbs 6:30-31 AMP). I impose this punishment upon you now. SATAN, I command you to return seven times everything that you have ever stolen from me in the past. I bind the Strongman and plunder all your goods (Matthew 12:29). I command the sevenfold restitution be paid to me now in the name of Jesus Christ. I command you to return and fulfill the sevenfold restitution for all stolen income, stolen employment, stolen promotions, stolen raises, stolen bonuses, stolen property, stolen land, stolen ideas, stolen business income, stolen contracts, stolen clients, stolen business deals, and stolen opportunities. Everything that has ever been stolen from me I command you to make restitution for it now. You must return seven times what you have stolen now in Jesus' name.

The Lord will cause my enemies who rise against me to be defeated before my face; you shall come out against me one way and flee before me seven ways (Deuteronomy 28:7). No weapon formed against me shall prosper (Isaiah 54:17). I triumph over you by the blood of the Lamb and by the word of my testimony (Revelation 12:11). The blood of Jesus protects me, my purpose, my plan, my paternity, my property and possessions, my provision, and my promise. I decree and declare all these things in the authority of Jesus Christ, AMEN.

day 50

a bountiful harvest

power promise

You crown the year with a bountiful harvest; even the hard pathways overflow with abundance.

Psalm 65:11 (NLT)

Father, I thank You I am in my season of harvest. I speak abundance, increase, and overflow over my harvest now. You crown the year with a bountiful harvest; even the hard pathways overflow with abundance (Psalm 65:11). My cup overflows with blessings (Psalm 23:5). I hear the Word, receive, accept, and welcome it, and bear fruit—some thirty times, some sixty times, and some even a hundred times as much as was sown (Mark 4:20). Father, I believe You are commanding the blessing on me in my storehouses and in all to which I set my hand (Deuteronomy 28:8). Yes, Lord, You pour down Your blessings. Our land will yield its bountiful harvest (Psalm 85:12). I am a tither. My harvest is fully protected because You have rebuked the Devourer for my sake (Malachi 3:11). Thank You, Father. In Jesus' name, AMEN.

day 51

pleasure in prosperity

power promise

Let them shout for joy and be glad, Who favor my righteous cause; And let them say continually, "Let the Lord be magnified, Who has pleasure in the prosperity of His servant."

Psalm 35:27 (NKJV)

Bless the Lord, O my soul; and all that is within me, bless His holy name (Psalm 103:1)! I say continually, let the Lord be magnified, Who has pleasure in the prosperity of His servant (Psalm 35:27). Taste and see that the Lord is good. I take refuge in You! I fear the Lord, for those who fear Him will have all they need. Those who trust in the Lord will lack no good thing (Psalm 34:8-10). I trust in the living God, Who gives me richly all things to enjoy (1 Timothy 6:17). Father, I rejoice that You have pleasure in prospering me. You prepare a feast for me in the presence of my enemies. My cup overflows with blessings (Psalm 23:5). I praise Your name! In Jesus' name, AMEN.

day 52

surplus of prosperity

power promise

And the Lord shall make you have a surplus of prosperity, through the fruit of your body, of your livestock, and of your ground, in the land which the Lord swore to your fathers to give you.

Deuteronomy 28:11 (AMP)

Father, I declare that I have a surplus of prosperity. My harvest is abundantly blessed. The blessings of God shall come upon me and overtake me, because I obey the voice of the Lord my God (Deuteronomy 28:2). Whatever I do, I work at it with all my heart, as working for the Lord, not for men. It is the Lord Christ I am serving (Colossians 3:23-24). Thank You, Father, You shall make me have a surplus of prosperity (Deuteronomy 28:11). The blessing of the Lord brings wealth, without painful toil for it (Proverbs 10:22). You crown the year with a bountiful harvest; even the hard pathways overflow with abundance (Psalm 65:11). In the name of Jesus, AMEN.

YOUR 90-DAY FINANCIAL BREAKTHROUGH

day 53

the hundredfold blessing

power promise

Then Isaac sowed in that land, and reaped in the same year a hundredfold; and the Lord blessed him. The man began to prosper, and continued prospering until he became very prosperous; for he had possessions of flocks and possessions of herds and a great number of servants. So the Philistines envied him.

Genesis 26:12-14 (NKJV)

Forever, O Lord, Your Word is settled in Heaven (Psalm 119:89). Father, I speak Your Word over my harvest, and I pronounce the hundredfold blessing over my seed. Isaac sowed in that land, and reaped in the same year a hundredfold; and You blessed him. He began to prosper, and continued prospering until he became very prosperous (Genesis 26:12-13). Father, You are the Lord — You do not change (Malachi 3:6). Just as Isaac sowed and reaped in the same year a hundredfold because You blessed him, I believe

386

I shall receive the hundredfold blessing in this same year on my seed sown. I believe You will command the blessing on me in my storehouses and in all to which I set my hand (Deuteronomy 28:8).

Father, I hear the Word, receive it, accept it, welcome it, and bear fruit—some thirty times, some sixty times, and some even a hundred times as much as was sown (Mark 4:20 AMP). I am a doer of the Word (James 1:22). I will bear fruit from Your Word, a hundred times as much as was sown.

Father, I invest in seven ventures, yes, in eight; I do not know what disaster may come upon the land. I sow my seed in the morning, and at evening my hands are not idle, for I do not know which will succeed, whether this or that, or whether both will do equally well (Ecclesiastes 11:2, 6). Your Word says that Isaac became rich, and his wealth continued to grow until he became very wealthy (Genesis 26:13 NIV). I decree Your blessing over all my effort and every endeavor. I declare that my businesses are highly profitable. I declare a hundredfold increase over my seed sown and over all the work of my hands. I will continue prospering until I become very prosperous. Then the earth will yield its harvests, and God, our God, will richly bless us (Psalm 67:6).

I call in the abundant harvest now in the name of Jesus. Father, I believe that You are dispatching angels — ministering spirits — sent out in the service of God for the assistance of those who are to inherit salvation (Hebrews 1:14). Ministering angels are assisting me now and are bringing in the harvest from the north, south, east, and west. Satan and all demonic forces are bound and cannot delay, detour, or detain my harvest. Praise the Lord! In the name of Jesus, AMEN.

day 54

all things to enjoy

power promise

Command those who are rich in this present age not to be haughty, nor to trust in uncertain riches but in the living God, who gives us richly all things to enjoy.

1 Timothy 6:17 (NKJV)

Father, thank You that every good and perfect gift is from above, coming down from the Father of the heavenly lights, who does not change like shifting shadows (James 1:17). I do not trust in uncertain riches but in You, the living God, who gives me richly all things to enjoy (1 Timothy 6:17). Jesus came that I may have and enjoy life, and have it in abundance — to the full, till it overflows (John 10:10 AMP). It is a good thing to receive wealth from God and the good health to enjoy it. To enjoy my work and accept my lot in life — this is indeed a gift from God (Ecclesiastes 5:19). I thank You, Father. In the name of Jesus, AMEN.

day 55

extravagantly generous

power promise

Let them do good, that they be rich in good works, ready to give, willing to share, storing up for themselves a good foundation for the time to come, that they may lay hold on eternal life.

1 Timothy 6:18-19 (NKJV)

Father, I pray that I will properly steward the rich resources You are entrusting to me. I pray that I may do good, be rich in good works, ready to give, willing to share, storing up a good foundation for the time to come, that I may lay hold on eternal life (1 Timothy 6:18-19). I am extravagantly generous (1 Timothy 6:18 MSG). I am a cheerful giver (2 Corinthians 9:7). Pure and genuine religion in Your sight means caring for orphans and widows in their distress (James 1:27). I open my arms to the poor and extend my hands to the needy (Proverbs 31:20). May Your will be done on earth as it is in Heaven (Matthew 6:10). In Jesus' name, AMEN.

day 56

the hundredfold return

power promise

Jesus said, Truly I tell you, there is no one who has given up and left house or brothers or sisters or mother or father or children or lands for My sake and for the Gospel's who will not receive a hundred times as much now in this time—houses and brothers and sisters and mothers and children and lands, with persecutions—and in the age to come, eternal life.

Mark 10:29-30 (AMP)

Father, I will worship toward Your holy temple and praise Your name for Your loving-kindness and for Your truth and faithfulness; for You have exalted above all else Your name and Your Word and You have magnified Your Word above all Your name (Psalm 138:2 AMP)! Thank You for the promises of Your Word. Thank You for the hundredfold return. Your Word has revived me and given me life (Psalm 119:50). Jesus said, "Truly I tell you, there is no one who has given up and left house or brothers or sisters or mother or father or children or lands for My sake and for the Gospel's who will not receive a hundred times as much now in this time—houses and brothers and sisters and mothers and children and lands, with persecutions—and in the age to come, eternal life." (Mark 10:29-30 AMP). Jesus pronounced the blessing of the hundredfold return. I receive it now. Jesus Christ is the same yesterday and today and forever (Hebrews 13:8).

Father, I have willingly given for the gospel's sake. Lord, You know what I have given and given up to follow You. You know what I have sacrificed for others on Your behalf (Mark 10:28). I believe I receive the hundredfold return now on all that I have given up for Jesus' sake and for the sake of the gospel (Mark 10:29-30). What I have done in secret, Father, I believe You see in secret, and will reward me openly (Matthew 6:4). Every good and perfect gift is from above, coming down from the Father of the heavenly lights, who does not change like shifting shadows (James 1:17). I receive the promise of the hundredfold return, and I believe the blessing is on its way to me now in this time. Father, Your Word will not return to You empty, but will accomplish what You desire and achieve the purpose for which You sent it (Isaiah 55:11).

Remember me, Lord, when you show favor to your people. Let me share in the prosperity of your chosen ones. Let me rejoice in the joy of your people; let me praise You with those who are your heritage (Psalm 106:4-5).

Thank You, Father! In the name of Jesus, AMEN.

day 57

treasures in heaven

power promise

Do not gather and heap up and store up for yourselves treasures on earth, where moth and rust and worm consume and destroy, and where thieves break through and steal. But gather and heap up and store for yourselves treasures in heaven, where neither moth nor rust nor worm consume and destroy, and where thieves do not break through and steal; For where your treasure is, there will your heart be also.

Matthew 6:19-21 (AMP)

Father, I will not copy the behavior and customs of this world (Romans 12:2). I will store treasures in Heaven, where neither moth nor rust nor worm consume and destroy, and where thieves do not break through and steal; for where my treasure is, there my heart will be also (Matthew 6:20-21). I pray that I may be rich in good works, ready to give, willing to share, storing up for myself a good foundation for the time to come, that I may lay hold on eternal life (1 Timothy 6:18-19). In Jesus' name, AMEN.

day 58

a good man

power promise

A good man leaves an inheritance for his children's children, but a sinner's wealth is stored up for the righteous.

Proverbs 13:22 (NIV)

Father, I will establish generational wealth for my family. Your Word declares that a good man leaves an inheritance for his children's children (Proverbs 13:22). Houses and riches are an inheritance from fathers (Proverbs 19:14). Those who fear the Lord will live in prosperity, and their children will inherit the land (Psalm 25:12-13). Blessed are those who fear the Lord, who find great delight in Your commands. My children will be mighty in the land; the generation of the upright will be blessed. Wealth and riches are in my house, and my righteousness endures forever (Psalm 112:1-3). Father, I will leave an inheritance of land, houses, riches, wealth, and righteousness to my children's children. A faithful man shall abound with blessings (Proverbs 28:20). Thank You, Father! In the name of Jesus, AMEN.

day 59

i will restore

power promise

And the floors shall be full of wheat, and the vats shall overflow with wine and oil. And I will restore to you the years that the locust hath eaten, the cankerworm, and the caterpiller, and the palmerworm..."

Joel 2:23-25 (KJV)

Father, I will worship toward Your holy temple and praise Your name for Your loving-kindness and for Your truth and faithfulness; for You have exalted above all else Your name and Your Word and You have magnified Your Word above all Your name (Psalm 138:2 AMP). You are alert and active, watching over Your Word to perform it (Jeremiah 1:12). Thank You, Father, You are restoring to me the years that the locust had eaten, the cankerworm, and the caterpillar, and the palmerworm (Joel 2:25). I declare the destruction of the canker has been reversed. Financial cancer has been healed in the name of Jesus. Jesus Himself bore my sins in

His own body on the tree, that I, having died to sins, might live for righteousness—by His stripes I was healed (1 Peter 2:24). The full impact of financial cancer is reversed now. My finances are restored. My health is restored. My family is restored. My relationships are restored now in Jesus' name.

Father, I bring all the tithes into the storehouse. Your Word declares "Try Me now in this," says the Lord of hosts, "If I will not open for you the windows of heaven and pour out for you such blessing that there will not be room enough to receive it. And I will rebuke the devourer for your sakes, so that he will not destroy the fruit of your ground, nor shall the vine fail to bear fruit for you in the field." (Malachi 3:10-11). The Devourer is rebuked. My harvest has been restored and doubled. Instead of my shame, I will receive a double portion, and instead of disgrace I will rejoice in my inheritance. And so I will inherit a double portion in my land, and everlasting joy will be mine (Isaiah 61:7). The floors shall be full of wheat, and the vats shall overflow with wine and oil (Joel 2:24).

SATAN, it is written, if the thief is found out, he must restore seven times what he stole; he must give the whole substance of his house if necessary — to meet his fine (Proverbs 6:31 AMP). I impose this punishment on you now. I command you to restore seven times that which you have ever stolen from me. I bind the Strongman and plunder all your goods (Matthew 12:29). I command the sevenfold restitution be paid to me now in the name of Jesus Christ.

Father, I praise You for complete healing and restoration now. In the name of Jesus, AMEN.

day 60

abundantly
prosperous

power promise

*And the Lord your God will make you abundantly prosperous
in every work of your hand, in the fruit of your body, of your
cattle, of your land, for good; for the Lord will again delight
in prospering you, as He took delight in your fathers...*
Deuteronomy 30:9 (AMP)

Father, Your Word says whoever gives heed to instruction
prospers, and blessed is the one who trusts in the Lord
(Proverbs 16:20). I trust in You. Holy Spirit, teach me to
profit; lead me in the way that I should go (Isaiah 48:17). I
declare the Lord my God will make me abundantly prosperous
in every work of my hand (Deuteronomy 30:9). Father, I
believe You will make me abundantly prosperous in every
business and in every endeavor I set my hand to do. You
delight in prospering me. I am abundantly prosperous. Let
the Lord be magnified, Who has pleasure in the prosperity
of His servant! (Psalm 35:27). In Jesus' name, AMEN.

day 61

those who work

power promise

Lazy people want much but get little, but those who work hard will prosper.

Proverbs 13:4 (NLT)

Praise the Lord! The fear of the Lord is the beginning of knowledge, but fools despise wisdom and instruction (Proverbs 1:7). Father, open my eyes to see the wonderful truths in Your instructions (Psalm 119:18). Your Word says that lazy people want much but get little, but those who work hard will prosper (Proverbs 13:4). All hard work brings a profit, but mere talk leads only to poverty (Proverbs 14:23). I am hard-working. I am focused. I am disciplined. I am diligent. Faith without accompanying works is dead (James 2:26). I am a doer of the Word (James 1:22). Father, I roll my works upon You — I commit and trust them wholly to You. You will cause my thoughts to become agreeable to Your will - and so shall my plans be established and succeed (Proverbs 16:3 AMP). Thank You, Father. In Jesus' name, AMEN.

day 62

in abundance

power promise

And God is able to make all grace (every favor and earthly blessing) come to you in abundance, so that you may always and under all circumstances and whatever the need be self-sufficient [possessing enough to require no aid or support and furnished in abundance for every good work and charitable donation].

2 Corinthians 9:8 (AMP)

Father, Your way is perfect! The Word of the Lord is tested and tried; You are a shield to all who take refuge and put their trust in You (Psalm 18:30). I stand on Your Word. The Word that You speak is alive and full of power (Hebrews 4:12 AMP). The thief comes only in order to steal and kill and destroy. Jesus has come that I may have and enjoy life, and have it in abundance — to the full, till it overflows (John 10:10). I declare Your Word over my life.

398

Father, You are able to make all grace — every favor and earthly blessing — come to me in abundance, so that I may always, and under all circumstances, and whatever the need, be self-sufficient, possessing enough to require no aid or support and furnished in abundance for every good work and charitable donation (2 Corinthians 9:8 AMP). I know You will liberally supply and fill to the full my every need according to Your riches in glory in Christ Jesus (Philippians 4:19). I believe that You will make me abundantly prosperous in every work of my hand; You delight in prospering me (Deuteronomy 30:9). Let the Lord be magnified, Who has pleasure in the prosperity of His servant (Psalm 35:27).

Father, You shall make me have a surplus of prosperity (Deuteronomy 28:11). I believe that You are commanding the blessing on me now in my storehouses and in all to which I set my hand (Deuteronomy 28:8). You are my Shepherd — to feed, guide, and shield me — I shall not lack (Psalm 23:1). Those who trust in the Lord will lack no good thing (Psalm 34:10). I am debt free. I will let no debt remain outstanding, except the continuing debt to love (Romans 13:8). I will lend and not borrow (Deuteronomy 28:12). My cup overflows with blessings (Psalm 23:5).

Father, out of Your fullness and abundance, I receive one grace after another and spiritual blessing upon spiritual blessing and even favor upon favor and gift heaped upon gift. Grace — unearned, undeserved favor and spiritual blessing —and truth have come through Jesus Christ (John 1:16-17 AMP). Hallelujah! Father, I praise Your name! I believe You are able to do exceedingly abundantly above all that I ask or think, according to the power that works in me. To You be glory in the church by Christ Jesus to all generations, forever and ever! AMEN (Ephesians 3:20-21).

day 63

cherish understanding

power promise

To acquire wisdom is to love oneself; people who cherish understanding will prosper.

Proverbs 19:8 (NLT)

Father, fill me with the wisdom of Your Word. Wisdom is the principal thing; therefore I get wisdom. And in all my getting, I get understanding (Proverbs 4:7). To acquire wisdom is to love oneself; people who cherish understanding will prosper (Proverbs 19:8). I cherish the understanding of Your Word. Blessed are those who find wisdom, those who gain understanding, for she is more profitable than silver and yields better returns than gold. She is more precious than rubies; nothing I desire can compare with her. Long life is in her right hand; in her left hand are riches and honor (Proverbs 3:13-16). Whoever gives heed to instruction prospers, and blessed is the one who trusts in the Lord (Proverbs 16:20). I seek wisdom, cherish understanding, and heed the instruction of Your Word. In Jesus' name, AMEN.

day 64

a crown for the wise

power promise

Wealth is a crown for the wise; the effort of fools yields only foolishness.

Proverbs 14:24 (NLT)

Father, thank You for the ability to produce wealth (Deuteronomy 8:18). Wealth is a crown for the wise; the effort of fools yields only foolishness (Proverbs 14:24). I get wisdom! I get understanding! I will not forget, nor turn away from the words of Your mouth (Proverbs 4:5). I am crowned with wealth and prosperity (Proverbs 14:24). The wise have wealth and luxury, but fools spend whatever they get (Proverbs 21:20). I am wealthy, and a good steward of my wealth. Lazy hands make for poverty, but diligent hands bring wealth (Proverbs 10:4). I am diligent. I am disciplined. My family is abundantly blessed. All who see us in our prosperity will recognize and acknowledge that we are the people whom the Lord has blessed (Isaiah 61:9 AMP). Thank You, Father. In the name of Jesus, AMEN.

day 65

in times of trouble

power promise

The Lord also will be a refuge and a high tower for the oppressed, a refuge and a stronghold in times of trouble (high cost, destitution, and desperation).

Psalm 9:9 (AMP)

Father, You are my Strong Tower and my Help in difficult times. You are a refuge and a high tower for the oppressed, a refuge and a stronghold in times of trouble — high cost, destitution, and desperation (Psalm 9:9). You are my Refuge and Strength, mighty and impenetrable to temptation, a very present and well-proved help in trouble (Psalm 46:1). Father, Your Word declares that the eyes of the Lord are on the righteous, and Your ears are attentive to my cry (Psalm 34:15). Yes, the righteous cry out, and the Lord hears. You will deliver me out of all my troubles (Psalm 34:17). Many are the afflictions of the righteous, but You, Lord, deliver me out of them all (Psalm 34:19).

I will be anxious for nothing, but in everything by prayer and supplication, with thanksgiving, I will let my requests be made known to You, God; and the peace of God, which surpasses all understanding, will guard my heart and mind through Christ Jesus (Philippians 4:6-7).

I shall not fear or fret over any circumstances in my employment or in my businesses. I shall not have any anxiety over conditions in the economy, or the cost of living. No matter what the natural circumstances look like, I trust in You. I walk by faith; not by sight (2 Corinthians 5:7). I cast all of my cares — all anxieties, all worries, all concerns, once and for all — on You, for I know You care for me affectionately, and You care about me watchfully (1 Peter 5:6 AMP).

So I do not worry about my life saying, "What will I eat? What will I drink? What will I wear?" These things dominate the thoughts of unbelievers, but You are my Heavenly Father, and You already know all my needs. I seek the Kingdom of God above all else, and live righteously, and You will give me everything I need (Matthew 6:31-33).

Father, Your Word promises that the blameless spend their days under the Lord's care, and my inheritance will endure forever. In times of disaster I will not wither; in days of famine I will enjoy plenty (Psalm 37:18-19). It is not by my might nor by my power, but by Your Spirit (Zechariah 4:6). When the enemy comes in like a flood, the Spirit of the Lord will lift up a standard against him and put him to flight, for You will come like a raging flood tide driven by the breath of the Lord (Isaiah 59:19). Hallelujah! I praise You, Lord! In the mighty name of Jesus, AMEN.

day 66

give heed to instruction

power promise

Whoever gives heed to instruction prospers, and blessed is the one who trusts in the Lord.

Proverbs 16:20 (NIV)

Father, Your Word declares that whoever gives heed to instruction prospers, and blessed is the one who trusts in the Lord (Proverbs 16:20). The fear of the Lord is the beginning of knowledge, but fools despise wisdom and instruction (Proverbs 1:7). To acquire wisdom is to love oneself; people who cherish understanding will prosper (Proverbs 19:8). Open my eyes to see the wonderful truths in Your instructions (Psalm 119:18). You are my Redeemer, the Holy One of Israel. Holy Spirit, teach me to profit, lead me in the way that I should go (Isaiah 48:17). I heed Your instruction. I am a doer of the Word (James 1:22). Father, command the blessing on all to which I set my hand (Deuteronomy 28:8). Wealth is a crown for the wise (Proverbs 14:24). I declare I am crowned with wealth and prosperity. In Jesus' name, AMEN.

day 67

stand before kings

power promise

Do you see a man diligent and skillful in his business? He will stand before kings; he will not stand before obscure men.
Proverbs 22:29 (AMP)

Father, I declare I am positioned for promotion. I am diligent and skillful in business. I will stand before kings. I will not stand before obscure men or officials of low rank (Proverbs 22:29). Your Word says the hand of the diligent will rule (Proverbs 12:24). Father, I distinguish myself above others, because an excellent spirit is in me (Daniel 6:3). I let my light so shine before men, that they may see my good works and glorify my Father in heaven (Matthew 5:16). I humble myself under Your mighty power, and at the right time, you will lift me up in honor (1 Peter 5:6). Promotion comes from You, Lord. You are Judge! You put down one and lift another up (Psalm 75:6-7). I have divine favor now for promotion, advancement, and abundance. In the name of Jesus, AMEN.

day 68

good news

power promise

He went to Nazareth, where he had been brought up, and on the Sabbath day he went into the synagogue, as was his custom. He stood up to read, and the scroll of the prophet Isaiah was handed to him. Unrolling it, he found the place where it is written: "The Spirit of the Lord is on me, because he has anointed me to proclaim good news to the poor. He has sent me to proclaim freedom for the prisoners and recovery of sight for the blind, to set the oppressed free, to proclaim the year of the Lord's favor." Then he rolled up the scroll, gave it back to the attendant and sat down. The eyes of everyone in the synagogue were fastened on him. He began by saying to them, "Today this scripture is fulfilled in your hearing."

Luke 4:16-22 (NIV)

Praise the Lord! Father, I thank You for the good news of the gospel of Jesus Christ! For You so loved the world that You gave Your only begotten Son, that whoever believes in Him should not perish but have everlasting life (John 3:16). The thief comes only in order to steal and kill and destroy. Jesus came that I may have and enjoy life, and have it in abundance — to the full, till it overflows (John 10:10). Jesus declared: "The Spirit of the Lord is on me, because he has anointed me to proclaim good news to the poor. He has sent me to proclaim freedom for the prisoners and recovery of sight for the blind, to set the oppressed free, to proclaim the year of the Lord's favor." (Luke 4:16-22). Thank You, Jesus, the poor receive prosperity, prisoners are free, the blind now see, and the oppressed are freed. Father, I receive Your divine favor.

Lord Jesus, You disarmed the powers and authorities, and made a public spectacle of them, triumphing over them by the cross (Colossians 2:15). I am free from sin. I have eternal life. I am free from poverty and lack, sickness and disease, and sexual immorality and relationship fracture. I am free from the oppression of debt, debt slavery, lack, and shortage. Chains are broken. I am debt free. I am free from all bondage of the enemy. So if the Son liberates me and makes me free, then I am really and unquestionably free! (John 8:36).

Thank You, Father! You give prosperity to the poor and protect those who suffer. You frustrate the plans of schemers so the work of their hands will not succeed (Job 5:11-12). You are a Father of the fatherless and a Judge and Protector of the widows. You place the solitary in families and give the desolate a home in which to dwell; You lead the prisoners out to prosperity (Psalm 68:5-6). I am coming into my prosperity and abundance now. I receive it in Jesus' name. AMEN.

day 69

richly blessed

power promise

Then the earth will yield its harvests, and God, our God, will richly bless us.

Psalm 67:6 (NLT)

Father, today I enter my season of abundant harvest. I command my harvest to come forth, in the name of Jesus. The earth will yield its harvests, and God, my God, will richly bless me (Psalm 67:6). Yes, the Lord pours down His blessings. My land will yield its bountiful harvest (Psalm 85:12). I am richly blessed. Father, You crown the year with a bountiful harvest; even the hard pathways overflow with abundance (Psalm 65:11). I honor You, Lord, with my possessions, and with the firstfruits of all my increase; so my barns will be filled with plenty, and my vats will overflow with new wine (Proverbs 3:9-10). I am a tither. The Devourer is rebuked for my sake. Satan, you will not destroy my harvest (Malachi 3:11). I cancel every demonic scheme to delay, detain, or disrupt my harvest. I am richly blessed! In Jesus' name, AMEN.

day 70

pours down blessings

power promise

Yes, the Lord pours down his blessings. Our land will yield its bountiful harvest.

Psalm 85:12 (NLT)

Father, I call forth the harvest You have destined for me. Every good gift and every perfect gift is from above, and comes down from the Father of lights, with whom there is no variation or shadow of turning (James 1:17). Yes, Lord, pour down Your blessings. My land will yield its bountiful harvest (Psalm 85:12). Father, I believe You are opening the heavens, the storehouse of Your bounty, to bless all the work of my hands (Deuteronomy 28:12). Just as Isaac sowed in that land, and reaped in the same year a hundredfold because You blessed him, I believe a hundredfold blessing is on its way to me now in this same year. I will prosper, and continue prospering until I become very prosperous (Genesis 26:12-14). I give You all the honor, Lord. In the name of Jesus, AMEN.

day 71

for your sake

power promise

For you are becoming progressively acquainted with and recognizing more strongly and clearly the grace of our Lord Jesus Christ (His kindness, His gracious generosity, His undeserved favor and spiritual blessing), [in] that though He was [so very] rich, yet for your sakes He became [so very] poor, in order that by His poverty you might become enriched (abundantly supplied).

2 Corinthians 8:9 (AMP)

Father, thank You for Your grace that is upon my life through the sacrifice Jesus Himself made for my sake. I am becoming progressively acquainted with and recognizing more strongly and clearly the grace of my Lord Jesus Christ — His kindness, His gracious generosity, His undeserved favor and spiritual blessing — in that though He was so very rich, yet for my sake, He became so very poor, in order that by His poverty I might become enriched and abundantly supplied (2 Corinthians 8:9

AMP). Father, for my sake, You made Him who knew no sin to be sin for me, that I might become the righteousness of God in Christ (2 Corinthians 5:21).

Now Father, I will let this same attitude and purpose and humble mind be in me which was in Christ Jesus. I let Him be my example in humility. The Lord Jesus, although being essentially one with God and in the form of God, did not think this equality with God was a thing to be eagerly grasped or retained, but stripped Himself of all privileges and rightful dignity, so as to assume the guise of a servant and slave, in that He became like men and was born a human being. And after He had appeared in human form, He abased and humbled Himself still further and carried His obedience to the extreme of death, even the death of the cross! Therefore, because He stooped so low, You have highly exalted Him and You have freely bestowed on Him the name that is above every name, that at the name of Jesus every knee must bow, in heaven and on earth and under the earth, and every tongue frankly and openly must confess and acknowledge that Jesus Christ is Lord, to the glory of God the Father (Philippians 2:5-11 AMP).

Therefore, Father, since I am surrounded by so great a cloud of witnesses, I will lay aside every weight, and the sin which so easily ensnares, and I will run with endurance the race that is set before me, looking unto Jesus, the Author and Finisher of my faith, who for the joy that was set before Him endured the cross, despising the shame, and has sat down at the right hand of the throne of God (Hebrews 12:1-2). For the sake of the house of the Lord my God, I will seek Your prosperity (Psalm 122:9). In the name of Jesus, AMEN.

day 72

true humility

power promise

True humility and fear of the Lord lead to riches, honor, and long life.

Proverbs 22:4 (NLT)

Father, Your Word says if My people who are called by My name will humble themselves and pray and seek My face and turn from their wicked ways, I will hear from Heaven and will forgive their sins and restore their land (2 Chronicles 7:14). I am forgiven. I am restored. I humble myself under Your mighty power, and at the right time, you will lift me up in honor (1 Peter 5:6). I am sober and vigilant; because my adversary the devil walks about like a roaring lion, seeking whom he may devour. I resist him, steadfast in the faith (1 Peter 5:8-9). Lord, You take delight in Your people; You crown the humble with victory (Psalm 149:4). True humility and fear of the Lord lead to riches, honor, and long life (Proverbs 22:4). I receive Your blessing. In Jesus' name, AMEN.

412

day 73

your chosen ones

power promise

Remember me, Lord, when you show favor to your people;
come near and rescue me. Let me share in the prosperity of
your chosen ones. Let me rejoice in the joy of your people;
let me praise you with those who are your heritage.

Psalm 106:4-5 (NLT)

Remember me, Lord, when you show favor to Your people.
Let me share in the prosperity of Your chosen ones. Let me
rejoice in the joy of Your people; let me praise You with
those who are Your heritage (Psalm 106:4-5). As for me and
my house, we will serve the Lord (Joshua 24:15). We are a
chosen generation, a royal priesthood, a holy nation, Your
own special people, that we may proclaim Your praises, Who
called us out of darkness into Your marvelous light (1 Peter
2:9). Surely, Lord, You bless the righteous; You surround
us with Your favor as with a shield (Psalm 5:12). Through
Christ, we are Your chosen ones! In Jesus' name, AMEN.

day 74

the love of money

power promise

But godliness with contentment is great gain. For we brought nothing into the world, and we can take nothing out of it. But if we have food and clothing, we will be content with that. Those who want to get rich fall into temptation and a trap and into many foolish and harmful desires that plunge people into ruin and destruction. For the love of money is a root of all kinds of evil. Some people, eager for money, have wandered from the faith and pierced themselves with many griefs.

1 Timothy 6:6-10 (NIV)

Father, Your Word says whoever gives heed to instruction prospers, and blessed is the one who trusts in the Lord (Proverbs 16:20). I trust in You alone. I heed Your instruction on the warnings of wealth. I subdue the cravings and impulses of the sin nature. Those who live according to the flesh set their minds on the things of the flesh, but those who live according to the Spirit, the things of the Spirit. For to be carnally minded is death, but to be spiritually minded is life and peace (Romans 8:5-6). Those who are living the life of the flesh, catering to the appetites and impulses of their carnal nature, cannot please or satisfy You, or be acceptable to You (Romans 8:8). Father, I subdue the desires of the sin nature. I am spiritually minded. I heed the warnings of your Word. I follow the instruction of the Holy Spirit.

I will not allow money to become an idol, by serving money. No one can serve two masters; for either he will hate the one and love the other, or he will stand by and be devoted to the one and despise and be against the other. I cannot serve God and mammon — deceitful riches, money, possessions, or whatever is trusted in (Matthew 6:24).

I will not be greedy for gain, loving money. Father, Your Word warns that those who want to get rich fall into temptation and a trap and into many foolish and harmful desires that plunge people into ruin and destruction. For the love of money is a root of all kinds of evil. Some people, eager for money, have wandered from the faith and pierced themselves with many griefs (1 Timothy 6:9-10).

I will not allow pride and arrogance to take root in my heart, boasting of money. Your Word says, let not the wise boast of their wisdom or the strong boast of their strength or the rich boast of their riches, but let the one who boasts boast about this: that I have the understanding to know You, that You are the Lord, Who exercises kindness, justice, and righteousness on earth, for in these You delight (Jeremiah 9:23-24).

I will not be deceived by self-sufficiency, having confidence in money. I will not say to myself, "My power and the strength of my hands have produced this wealth for me." No, I shall remember You, the Lord my God, for it is You who has given me the ability to produce wealth to confirm Your covenant (Deuteronomy 8:17-18).

I will not toil, overworking for money. Unless the Lord builds the house, the builders labor in vain. Unless the Lord watches over the city, the guards stand watch in vain. I will not rise early and stay up late, toiling for food to eat — for You grant sleep to those You love (Psalm 127:1-2). The blessing of the Lord — it makes truly rich, and You add no sorrow with it, neither does toiling increase it (Proverbs 10:22).

I will not squander my wealth, by wasting money or living wildly. The wise have wealth and luxury, but fools spend whatever they get (Proverbs 21:20).

I will not hoard the wealth You give me, stockpiling and withholding money. There is one who scatters, yet increases more; and there is one who withholds more than is right, but it leads to poverty. The generous soul will be made rich, and he who waters will also be watered himself (Proverbs 11:24-25).

I will not oppress others with money, hurting those who are in need or whom I employ. I shall not defraud or oppress my neighbor or rob him; the wages of a hired servant shall not remain with me all night until morning (Leviticus 19:13).

Father, to the contrary, I will seek the Kingdom of God above all else, and live righteously, and You will give me everything I need (Matthew 6:33). I will sow generously, that blessings may come to someone (2 Corinthians 9:6 AMP). I am extravagantly generous (1 Timothy 6:18 MSG). I will extend my hand to the poor, yes, I will reach out my hands to the needy (Proverbs 31:20). Thank You, Father. In the name of Jesus I pray, AMEN.

day 75

an open highway

power promise

A lazy person's way is blocked with briers, but the path of the upright is an open highway.

Proverbs 15:19 (NLT)

Father, Your Word declares that a lazy person's way is blocked with briers, but the path of the upright is an open highway (Proverbs 15:19). Lazy people want much but get little, but those who work hard will prosper (Proverbs 13:4). I am hardworking. I am disciplined. Lazy hands make for poverty, but diligent hands bring wealth (Proverbs 10:4). I am diligent and skillful in business. I will stand before kings; I will not stand before obscure men (Proverbs 22:29). Father, Your Word says You will go before me and level the mountains to make the crooked places straight; You will break in pieces the doors of bronze and cut asunder the bars of iron (Isaiah 45:2). Thank You, Father, my path is an open highway of blessing, increase, overflow, and abundance. In Jesus' name, AMEN.

day 76

in prosperity

power promise

Who, then, are those who fear the Lord? He will instruct them in the ways they should choose. They will spend their days in prosperity, and their descendants will inherit the land. The Lord confides in those who fear him; he makes his covenant known to them.

Psalm 25:12-14 (NIV)

Show me Your ways, Lord, teach me Your paths. Guide me in Your truth and teach me, for You are God my Savior (Psalm 25:4-5). Your Word declares You will instruct me in the ways I should choose. I will spend my days in prosperity, and my descendants will inherit the land. You will confide in me and make Your covenant known to me (Psalm 25:12-14). Holy Spirit, teach me to profit, lead me in the way that I should go (Isaiah 48:17). I can do all things through Christ who strengthens me (Philippians 4:13). I walk in prosperity and complete victory today. In the name of Jesus, AMEN.

day 77

save now! send now!

power promise

This is the day the Lord has made; We will rejoice and be glad in it. Save now, I pray, O Lord; O Lord, I pray, send now prosperity. Blessed is he who comes in the name of the Lord! We have blessed you from the house of the Lord.
Psalm 118:24-26 (NKJV)

Praise the Lord! This is the day the Lord has made; I will rejoice and be glad in it! Save now, I pray, O Lord; O Lord, I pray, send now prosperity. Blessed is he who comes in the name of the Lord! I have blessed You from the house of the Lord (Psalm 118:24-26). I was glad when they said to me, "Let us go into the house of the Lord." (Psalm 122:1). Everyone who calls on the name of the Lord will be saved (Acts 2:21). Save now, I pray O Lord! Send now Your prosperity. For the sake of the house of the Lord my God, I will seek Your prosperity (Psalm 122:9). In the name of Jesus I pray, AMEN.

day 78

be kind to the poor

power promise

Oh, the joys of those who are kind to the poor! The Lord rescues them when they are in trouble. The Lord protects them and keeps them alive. He gives them prosperity in the land and rescues them from their enemies. The Lord nurses them when they are sick and restores them to health.

Psalm 41:1-3 (NLT)

Father, Your Word says he who oppresses the poor shows contempt for their Maker, but whoever is kind to the needy honors God (Proverbs 14:31). I open my arms to the poor and extend my hands to the needy (Proverbs 31:20). Thank You, Father for the seven blessings You have promised for kindness to the poor. You will rescue me when I am in trouble. You will protect me and keep me alive. You give me prosperity in the land, and You rescue me from my enemies. You will nurse me when I am sick, and restore me to health (Psalm 41:1-3). Thank You, Father. In the name of Jesus, AMEN.

420

day 79

lend generously

power promise

Good comes to those who lend money generously and conduct their business fairly.

Psalm 112:5 (NLT)

Father, I believe Your Word that good comes to those who lend money generously and conduct their business fairly (Psalm 112:5). Lord, You demand accurate scales and balances; You set the standards for fairness (Proverbs 16:11). I am generous, honest, and manage my business affairs with integrity. I will lend to many but will borrow from none (Deuteronomy 28:12). When I help another, I will not charge interest on money I lend or make a profit on food I sell. For You are the Lord my God, who brought me out of bondage to be my God (Leviticus 25:35-38). The generous will prosper; those who refresh others will themselves be refreshed (Proverbs 11:25). When the righteous prosper, the city rejoices (Proverbs 11:10). I am blessed and highly favored of the Lord (Luke 1:28). In the name of Jesus, I pray. AMEN.

day 80

no poor among you

power promise

However, there need be no poor people among you, for in the land the Lord your God is giving you to possess as your inheritance, he will richly bless you, if only you fully obey the Lord your God and are careful to follow all these commands I am giving you today. For the Lord your God will bless you as he has promised, and you will lend to many nations but will borrow from none.

Deuteronomy 15:4-6 (NIV)

Father, the counsel of Your Word stands forever, the thoughts of Your heart through all generations (Psalm 33:11). Your Word declares, "There need be no poor people among you." You will richly bless us, if we fully obey Your Word and are careful to follow Your commands. You will bless us as You have promised. We will lend to many nations but will borrow from none (Deuteronomy 15:4-6). You give prosperity to the poor and protect those who suffer. You frustrate the plans of schemers so the work of their hands will not succeed (Job 5:11-12). Father, Your Word declares, "For I am the Lord, I do not change." (Malachi 3:6).

Jesus said, "The Spirit of the Lord is on me, because he has anointed me to proclaim good news to the poor. He has sent me to proclaim freedom for the prisoners and recovery of sight for the blind, to set the oppressed free, to proclaim the year of the Lord's favor." (Luke 4:18-19). I am free indeed (John 8:36). Father, I receive Your divine favor. The thief comes only in order to steal and kill and destroy. Jesus came that we may have and enjoy life, and have it in abundance — to the full, till it overflows (John 10:10 AMP). Jesus Christ is the same yesterday and today and forever (Hebrews 13:8).

SATAN, I break every generational curse and demonic assignment of poverty, lack, debt, debt slavery, and shortage over my family now, in the name of Jesus. I declare over my family, extended family, children, and children's children: there will be no poor among us, for the Lord our God will richly bless us as He has promised. We shall receive our inheritance. We shall lend and not borrow (Deuteronomy 15:4-6). My children will be mighty in the land; the generation of the upright will be blessed (Psalm 112:2).

SATAN, I am a tither. The Devourer is rebuked in the name of Jesus (Malachi 3:10-11). I cancel every fiery dart and wicked scheme to steal my provision and block my blessings. My God has given the command to bless me, and no one can reverse it (Numbers 23:20).

There will be no poor among us. My family is DEBT FREE, prosperous, and abundantly supplied. In the authority of Jesus Christ I pray. AMEN.

day 81

abounding with blessings

power promise

A faithful man shall abound with blessings, but he who makes haste to be rich [at any cost] shall not go unpunished.
Proverbs 28:20 (AMP)

Father, Your Word says a faithful person shall abound with blessings, but he who makes haste to be rich at any cost shall not go unpunished (Proverbs 28:20). Good planning and hard work lead to prosperity, but hasty shortcuts lead to poverty (Proverbs 21:5). I am hard-working. I am strategic. I am abounding with blessings! I am not deceived by the devil's hasty shortcuts. Greedy people try to get rich quick but don't realize they're headed for poverty (Proverbs 28:22). Wealth not earned but won in haste or unjustly or from the production of things for vain or detrimental use will dwindle away, but he who gathers little by little will increase his riches (Proverbs 13:11 AMP). I am wealthy. I am abounding with blessings! In Jesus' name, AMEN.

day 82

the diligent will rule

power promise

The hand of the diligent will rule, but the lazy man will be put to forced labor.

Proverbs 12:24 (NKJV)

Father, I am made in Your image and in Your likeness. I walk in Kingdom dominion (Genesis 1:26). Your Word declares the hand of the diligent will rule, but the lazy man will be put to forced labor (Proverbs 12:24). I am diligent and skillful in business. I will stand before kings. I will not stand before obscure men or officials of low rank (Proverbs 22:29). My diligent work gets a warm commendation (Proverbs 14:35 MSG). I am the head and not the tail; I shall be above only, and not be beneath, because I heed the commandments of the Lord (Deuteronomy 28:13). Father, Your Word declares that wealth is a crown for the wise (Proverbs 14:24). I am crowned with wealth and prosperity. Father, I give You all the honor and glory. In the name of Jesus, AMEN.

day 83

render unto caesar

power promise

Jesus said to them, "Pay to Caesar the things that are Caesar's and to God the things that are God's." And they stood marveling and greatly amazed at Him.

Mark 12:17 (AMP)

Yours, O Lord, is the greatness, the power, the glory, the victory, and the majesty. Everything in the heavens and on earth is Yours, O Lord, and this is Your Kingdom. I adore You as the One who is over all things. Wealth and honor come from You alone, for You rule over everything. Power and might are in Your hand, and at Your discretion people are made great and given strength (1 Chronicles 29:11-12). Open my eyes to see the wonderful truths in Your instructions (Psalm 119:18).

Father, I seek the Kingdom of God above all else, and live righteously, and You will give me everything I need (Matthew 6:33). I pay to God the things that are God's. Father, Your

426

Word says all the tithe of the land is Yours. It is holy to the Lord (Leviticus 27:30). I will not rob You in tithes and offerings. I bring all the tithes into the storehouse, that there may be food in Your house. I believe You have opened for me the windows of Heaven and You are pouring out for me such blessing that there will not be room enough to receive it. And You have rebuked the Devourer for my sake so that he will not destroy the fruit of my ground, nor shall the vine fail to bear fruit for me in the field (Malachi 3:8-11).

Father, I pay to Caesar the things that are Caesar's (Mark 12:17). I pay my taxes with honesty and integrity, as a matter of principle and for the sake of conscience. I pay my taxes, for the civil authorities are official servants under God, devoting themselves to attending to this very service. I render to all men their dues. I pay taxes to whom taxes are due, revenue to whom revenue is due, respect to whom respect is due, and honor to whom honor is due (Romans 13:5-7).

Father, I repay my debts, for Your Word says the wicked borrow and do not repay, but the righteous give generously (Psalm 37:21). It is better that I should not vow than that I should vow and not pay (Ecclesiastes 5:5). I will let no debt remain outstanding, except the continuing debt to love one another, for whoever loves others has fulfilled the law (Romans 13:8). I will get out and stay out of debt. The rich rule over the poor, and the borrower is slave to the lender (Proverbs 22:7). I AM DEBT FREE. I will lend and not borrow (Deuteronomy 28:12).

Praise the Lord! I pray all these things in the name of Jesus. AMEN.

day 84

wealth and health

power promise

And it is a good thing to receive wealth from God and the good health to enjoy it. To enjoy your work and accept your lot in life—this is indeed a gift from God.

Ecclesiastes 5:19 (NLT)

Father, Your Word says it is a good thing to receive wealth from God and the good health to enjoy it. To enjoy my work and accept my lot in life—this is indeed a gift from You, God (Ecclesiastes 5:19). Thank You, Father, for rewarding work, abundant wealth, and divine health. I pray that I may prosper in every way and that my body may keep well, even as my soul keeps well and prospers (3 John 2). Thank You, Father, the blessing of the Lord — it makes truly rich, and You add no sorrow with it, neither does toiling increase it (Proverbs 10:22). I am healthy and wealthy. I am abounding with blessings (Proverbs 28:20). In the name of Jesus, AMEN.

day 85

enduring wealth and prosperity

power promise

I love those who love me, and those who seek me find me. With me are riches and honor, enduring wealth and prosperity. My fruit is better than fine gold; what I yield surpasses choice silver. I walk in the way of righteousness, along the paths of justice, bestowing a rich inheritance on those who love me and making their treasuries full.

Proverbs 8:17-21 (NIV)

Father, I seek Wisdom. With Wisdom are riches and honor, enduring wealth and prosperity. Her fruit is better than fine gold; what she yields surpasses choice silver. Wisdom walks in the way of righteousness, along the paths of justice, bestowing a rich inheritance on those who love her and making their treasuries full (Proverbs 8:17-21). Wisdom is the principal thing (Proverbs 4:7). With Wisdom, I receive riches, honor, enduring wealth, prosperity, righteousness, justice, and a rich inheritance. My treasuries are full (Proverbs 8:17-21). Thank You, Father. In Jesus' name, AMEN.

day 86

storehouse of his bounty

power promise

The LORD will open the heavens, the storehouse of his bounty, to send rain on your land in season and to bless all the work of your hands. You will lend to many nations but will borrow from none.

Deuteronomy 28:12 (NIV)

Father, I will worship toward Your holy temple and praise Your name for Your loving-kindness and for Your truth and faithfulness; for You have exalted above all else Your name and Your Word and You have magnified Your Word above all Your name! (Psalm 138:2 AMP). I confidently stand on Your Word that You will open the heavens, the storehouse of Your bounty, to send rain on my land in season and to bless all the work of my hands. I will lend to many but will borrow from none (Deuteronomy 28:12). I AM DEBT FREE. From the storehouse of Your bounty, I declare You are blessing all the work of my hands, including my employment, my businesses, my income streams, and my creative works. I am abundantly supplied and blessed to the overflow. Yes, the Lord pours down His blessings. Our land will yield its bountiful harvest (Psalm 85:12). I receive my full harvest now in Jesus' name. I am abounding with blessings (Proverbs 28:20).

I am a tither and a cheerful giver. Father, Your Word declares to try You now in this, and see if You will not open for me the windows of Heaven and pour out for me such blessing that there will not be room enough to receive it (Malachi 3:10). I believe You are alert and active, watching over Your Word to perform it (Jeremiah 1:12). Father, You will liberally supply and fill to the full my every need according to Your riches in glory in Christ Jesus (Philippians 4:19). My cup overflows with blessings (Psalm 23:5). You are able to make all grace — every favor and earthly blessing — come to me in abundance, so that I may always, and under all circumstances, and whatever the need, be self-sufficient, possessing enough to require no aid or support and furnished in abundance for every good work and charitable donation (2 Corinthians 9:8 AMP).

Father, You thwart the plans of the crafty, so that their hands achieve no success (Job 5:12). My provision is protected by the blood of Jesus. I cancel all demonic schemes to delay, detour, detain, or disrupt my provision that is on its way to me from the storehouse of Your bounty. By this I know that You favor and delight in me, because my enemy does not triumph over me (Psalm 41:11). Now thanks be to God who always leads me in triumph in Christ (2 Corinthians 2:14). Let the Lord be magnified, Who has pleasure in the prosperity of His servant (Psalm 35:27). In the name of Jesus, I pray. AMEN.

day 87

wealth and riches

power promise

Praise the Lord. Blessed are those who fear the Lord, who find great delight in his commands. Their children will be mighty in the land; the generation of the upright will be blessed. Wealth and riches are in their houses, and their righteousness endures forever.

Psalm 112:1-3 (NIV)

Praise the Lord! Blessed are those who fear the Lord, who find great delight in Your commands. My children will be mighty in the land; the generation of the upright will be blessed. Wealth and riches are in my house, and my righteousness endures forever (Psalm 112:1-3). Father, I establish multi-generational wealth for my family. Your Word says a good man leaves an inheritance to his children's children (Proverbs 13:22). Houses and riches are an inheritance from fathers (Proverbs 19:14). I establish an inheritance of righteousness, houses, wealth, and riches for my children. The generation of the upright will be blessed! In the name of Jesus, AMEN.

day 88

wealth and luxury

power promise

The wise have wealth and luxury, but fools spend whatever they get.

Proverbs 21:20 (NLT)

Father, Your Word warns that he who loves pleasure will be a poor man; he who loves wine and oil will not be rich (Proverbs 21:17). Yes, the wise have wealth and luxury, but fools spend whatever they get (Proverbs 21:20). To acquire wisdom is to love oneself; people who cherish understanding will prosper (Proverbs 19:8). I acquire wisdom. I cherish understanding. I enjoy wealth and luxury. I am a good and faithful steward over the resources You have entrusted to me. As I am faithful over a few things, You will make me ruler over many things (Matthew 25:21). Wealth is a crown for the wise (Proverbs 14:24). I am crowned with wealth and prosperity. My cup overflows with blessings (Psalm 23:5). Thank You, Father. In the name of Jesus, AMEN.

day 89

faith and patience

power promise

God is not unjust; he will not forget your work and the love you have shown him as you have helped his people and continue to help them. We want each of you to show this same diligence to the very end, so that what you hope for may be fully realized. We do not want you to become lazy, but to imitate those who through faith and patience inherit what has been promised.

Hebrews 6:10-12 (NIV)

Father, I am convinced and sure of this very thing, that You Who began a good work in me will continue until the day of Jesus Christ — right up to the time of His return — developing that good work and perfecting and bringing it to full completion in me (Philippians 1:6 AMP). Your Word says that You are not unjust; You will not forget my work and the love I have shown You as I have helped Your people and continue to help them. I will show this same diligence to the very end, so that what I hope for may be fully realized. I will not become lazy, but I will imitate those who through faith and patience inherit what has been promised (Hebrews 6:10-12). I will not grow weary while doing good, for in due season I shall reap if I do not lose heart (Galatians 6:9). I will let endurance and steadfastness and patience have full play and do a thorough work, so that I may be perfectly and fully developed with no defects, lacking in nothing (James 1:4).

Father, I am sober, I am vigilant; because my adversary the devil walks about like a roaring lion, seeking whom he may devour. I resist him, steadfast in the faith, knowing that the same sufferings are experienced by my brotherhood in the world (1 Peter 5:8-9). For though I walk in the flesh, I do not war according to the flesh. For the weapons of my warfare are not carnal but mighty in God for pulling down strongholds, casting down arguments and every high thing that exalts itself against the knowledge of God, bringing every thought into captivity to the obedience of Christ, and being ready to punish all disobedience when my obedience is fulfilled (2 Corinthians 10:3-6). I am strong in the Lord and in the power of Your might. I put on the whole armor of God, that I may be able to stand against the wiles of the devil, withstand in the evil day, and having done all, to stand (Ephesians 6:10-13).

SATAN – it is written, there is no wisdom, no insight, no plan that can succeed against the Lord (Proverbs 21:30). In the name of Jesus, I command you and all demonic forces — all principalities, powers, rulers of the darkness of this age, and spiritual hosts of wickedness in the heavenly places — to STOP all attacks and schemes against my life. It is written, whatever I bind on earth will be bound in heaven, and whatever I loose on earth will be loosed in heaven (Matthew 16:19). I specifically bind all ruling demons and ranked demonic forces, and cancel all attacks, ambushes, schemes, plans, and manifestations of poverty and lack, sickness and disease, sexual immorality and relationship fracture. Cease and desist. The Lord frustrates the devices of the crafty, so that your hands cannot carry out their plans (Job 5:12). I am a tither. The Lord God Almighty has rebuked the Devourer for my sake (Malachi 3:11). All debt is cancelled. I am delivered from debt slavery. The years that the canker had eaten have been restored (Joel 2:25). Financial cancer is stopped now in Jesus' name. The Lord Jesus Christ personally bore my sins in His own body on the tree as on an altar and offered Himself on it, that I might die to sin and live to righteousness. By His wounds I have been healed (1 Peter 2:24).

It is written, if the thief is found out, he must restore seven times what he stole; he must give the whole substance of his house if necessary—to meet his fine (Proverbs 6:30-31 AMP). I impose this punishment upon you now. Satan, I command you to return seven times everything that you have ever stolen from me in the past. I bind the Strongman and plunder all your goods (Matthew 12:29). I command the sevenfold restitution be paid to me now in the name of Jesus Christ. I command you to return what you have stolen and fulfill the sevenfold restitution for all stolen income, stolen employment, stolen promotions, stolen raises, stolen bonuses, stolen property, stolen land, stolen ideas, stolen business income, stolen contracts, stolen clients, stolen business deals, and stolen opportunities. Everything that has ever been stolen from me I command you to make restitution for it now. You must return seven times what you have stolen now in Jesus' name.

I trample on serpents and scorpions, and over all the power of the enemy, and nothing shall by any means hurt me (Luke 10:18-19). The Lord will cause my enemies who rise against me to be defeated before my face; you shall come out against me one way and flee before me seven ways (Deuteronomy 28:7). No weapon formed against me shall prosper, and every tongue which rises against me in judgment I shall condemn. This is the heritage of the servants of the Lord, and my righteousness is from the Lord (Isaiah 54:17). I am of God — I belong to Him — and have already defeated and overcome the agents of the antichrist, because He Who lives in me is greater and mightier than he who is in the world (1 John 4:4 AMP). I command you to go to dry places and I forbid your return.

God has given the command to bless me, and no one can reverse it (Numbers 23:20). I triumph over you by the blood of the Lamb and by the word of my testimony (Revelation 12:11). The blood of Jesus is against you and protects my Person, Purpose, Plan, Paternity, Property and Possessions, Provision, and my Promise.

If God is for me, who can be against me? (Romans 8:31). Yet amid all these things I am more than a conqueror and gain a surpassing victory through Him Who loves me (Romans 8:37). For I am persuaded beyond doubt — I am sure — that neither death nor life, nor angels nor principalities, nor things impending and threatening nor things to come, nor powers, nor height nor depth, nor anything else in all creation will be able to separate me from the love of God which is in Christ Jesus my Lord (Romans 8:38-39).

Now to Him who is able to do exceedingly abundantly above all that I ask or think, according to the power that works in me, to Him be glory in the church by Christ Jesus to all generations, forever and ever (Ephesians 3:20-21). AMEN.

day 90

blessed!

power promise

Blessed shall you be in the city, and blessed shall you be in the country. Blessed shall you be when you come in, and blessed shall you be when you go out. The Lord will cause your enemies who rise against you to be defeated before your face; they shall come out against you one way and flee before you seven ways. And the Lord will make you the head and not the tail; you shall be above only, and not be beneath, if you heed the commandments of the Lord your God, which I command you today, and are careful to observe them.

Deuteronomy 28:3, 6, 7, 13 (NKJV)

Father, I thank You and I praise You for the power of Your Word. You are not a man, so You do not lie. You are not human, so You do not change Your mind. Have You ever spoken and failed to act? Have You ever promised and not carried it through? (Numbers 23:19). As the rain and the snow come down from heaven, and do not return to it without watering the earth and making it bud and flourish, so that it yields seed for the sower and bread for the eater, so is Your Word that goes out from Your mouth: It will not return to You empty, but will accomplish what You desire and achieve the purpose for which You sent it (Isaiah 55:10-11). You are alert and active, watching over Your Word to perform it (Jeremiah 1:12). Father, I declare Your Word as a confession of my faith over my life.

All these blessings shall come upon me and overtake me, because I obey the voice of the Lord my God (Deuteronomy 28:2). Blessed shall I be in the city, and blessed shall I be in the country. Blessed shall I be when I come in, and blessed shall I be when I go out. The Lord will cause my enemies who rise against me to be defeated before my face; they shall come out against me one way and flee before me seven ways (Deuteronomy 28:3, 6, 7). The Lord will command the blessing on me in my storehouses and in all to which I set my hand, and He will bless me in the land which the Lord my God is giving me (Deuteronomy 28:8). The Lord will establish me, along with my family, as a holy people to Himself, just as He has sworn to me, if I keep the commandments of the Lord my God and walk in His ways. Then all peoples of the earth shall see that I am called by the name of the Lord (Deuteronomy 28:9-10).

And the Lord will grant me plenty of goods — a surplus of prosperity — in the land of which the Lord swore to give me (Deuteronomy 28:11). The Lord will open to me His good treasure, the heavens, the storehouse of His bounty, to give the rain to my land in its season, and to bless all the work of my hand. I shall lend to many nations, but I shall not borrow (Deuteronomy 28:12). And the Lord will make me the head and not the tail; I shall be above only, and not be beneath, if I heed the commandments of the Lord my God, and I am careful to observe them (Deuteronomy 28:13). So I shall not turn aside from any of the Word of the Lord, to the right or the left, to go after other gods to serve them (Deuteronomy 28:14). I declare and decree these blessings over my life in the name of Jesus.

Father, Your Word says no one can serve two masters; for either he will hate the one and love the other, or he will stand by and be devoted to the one and despise and be against the other. I cannot serve God and mammon —deceitful riches, money, possessions, or whatever is trusted in (Matthew 6:24). Therefore, I seek first the Kingdom of God and Your righteousness, and all these things shall be added to me (Matthew 6:33).

When I have eaten and I am full, then I shall bless the Lord my God for the good land which You have given me. I will beware that I do not forget the Lord my God by not keeping Your commandments, Your judgments, and Your statutes. When I have eaten and I am full, and I have built beautiful houses and dwell in them; and when my businesses multiply, and my silver and my gold are multiplied, and all that I have is multiplied; I will not forget the Lord my God Who brought me out of the land of debt, debt slavery, lack, and shortage, from the house of bondage; Who led me through that great and terrible wilderness, in which were fiery serpents and scorpions, Who fed me in the wilderness with manna, that You might humble me and that You might test me, to do me good in the end. I will not say in my heart, "My power and the might of my hand have gained me this wealth," (Deuteronomy 8:10-17).

No, Father, I shall remember YOU, the Lord my God, for it is You and You alone Who has given me the power to get wealth, that You may establish Your covenant which You swore to my fathers, as it is this day (Deuteronomy 8:18).

Yours, O Lord, is the greatness, the power, the glory, the victory, and the majesty. Everything in the heavens and on earth is Yours, O Lord, and this is Your Kingdom. I adore You as the one who is over all things. Wealth and honor come from You alone, for you rule over everything. Power and might are in Your hand, and at your discretion people are made great and given strength (1 Chronicles 29:11-12).

Now to You, Lord — Who, by the action of Your power that is at work within me — are able to carry out Your purpose and do superabundantly, far over and above all that I dare ask or think — infinitely beyond my highest prayers, desires, thoughts, hopes, or dreams—

To You, Lord, be glory in the church and in Christ Jesus throughout all generations forever and ever. AMEN. (Ephesians 3:20-21 AMP).

an invitation

AN INVITATION TO ETERNAL LIFE

Every person must be born again to know God and have everlasting life.

Jesus replied, "Very truly I tell you, no one can see the Kingdom of God unless they are born again...Flesh gives birth to flesh, but the Spirit gives birth to spirit."
John 3:3-6

"For God so loved the world that he gave his one and only Son, that whoever believes in him shall not perish but have eternal life."
John 3:16

Every person has sinned and come short of God's standard. This is the reason we must be born again.

"For all have sinned and fall short of the glory of God."
Romans 3:23

The cost of sin is spiritual death and separation from God, but God provides eternal life through Jesus Christ.

"As for you, you were dead in your transgressions and sins."
Ephesians 2:1

"For the wages of sin is death, but the gift of God is eternal life in Christ Jesus our Lord."
Romans 6:23

You cannot earn salvation. You cannot do it on your own. It is God's gift to us.

"For it is by grace you have been saved, through faith—and this is not from yourselves, it is the gift of God— not by works, so that no one can boast."
Ephesians 2:8-9

Being saved, or born again, means accepting Jesus Christ as your personal Lord and Savior, committing to follow His word.

"If you declare with your mouth, 'Jesus is Lord,' and believe in your heart that God raised him from the dead, you will be saved. For it is with your heart that you believe and are justified, and it is with your mouth that you profess your faith and are saved."
Romans 10:9-10

"We know that we have come to know him if we keep his commands."
1 John 2:3

Pray this prayer and declaration of faith to receive Jesus Christ as your personal Lord and Savior.

Lord Jesus,
I repent of my sin. I let go of my past. I ask You to come into my heart. I believe in my heart that You died for my sin, and that You have risen from the dead. By declaring this with my mouth, and believing it in my heart, today I make you my Lord and Savior. I receive a fresh start today. I choose to live for You and follow Your commands from this point forward. I am now a child of God! In Jesus' name,
Amen.

You are now born again and forgiven. You have eternal life. You are a new creation in Christ Jesus!

"Therefore, if anyone is in Christ, he is a new creation; old things have passed away; behold, all things have become new."
2 Corinthians 5:17

Now you will begin the process of renewing your mind and changing the way you think to live a powerful life in Christ.

"Therefore, I urge you, brothers, in view of God's mercy, to offer your bodies as living sacrifices, holy and pleasing to God—this is your spiritual act of worship. Do not conform any longer to the pattern of this world, but be transformed by the renewing of your mind. Then you will be able to test and approve what God's will is—his good, pleasing and perfect will."
Romans 12:1-2

Begin to study God's word daily.

"So then faith comes by hearing, and hearing by the word of God."
Romans 10:17

Jesus answered, "It is written: 'Man does not live on bread alone, but on every word that comes from the mouth of God.'"
Matthew 4:4

Get involved with a strong Bible-based church so that you can connect with other positive Christian men and women who will help you with your walk with Christ.

"Let us not give up meeting together, as some are in the habit of doing, but let us encourage one another—and all the more as you see the Day approaching."
Hebrews 10:25

You will need to be baptized in water as a believer as an outward sign of your confession of faith in Jesus Christ.

"And Jesus came and spoke to them, saying, 'All authority has been given to Me in heaven and on earth. Go therefore and make disciples of all the nations, baptizing them in the name of the Father and of the Son and of the Holy Spirit, teaching them to observe all things that I have commanded you; and lo, I am with you always, even to the end of the age.' Amen."
Matthew 28:16-20

Peter replied, "Repent and be baptized, every one of you, in the name of Jesus Christ for the forgiveness of your sins. And you will receive the gift of the Holy Spirit."
Acts 2:38

If you would like to contact me, you can reach me at info@madelinealexander.com.

contact us

To schedule a speaking engagement or breakthrough conference for your church, corporation, association, leadership team, university, college, or youth organization, please email us at: info@madelinealexander.com.

The Power Coach™ Madeline Alexander

Madeline Alexander International, LLC

P.O. Box 62243

Houston, TX 77205

Email: info@madelinealexander.com

www.madelinealexander.com

www.thepowercoach.com

www.youtube.com/thepowercoach

www.facebook.com/thepowercoach

www.twitter.com/thepowercoach

www.linkedin.com/in/madelinealexander

I WISH YOU GREAT SUCCESS!
YOU ARE MORE THAN A CONQUEROR!

engagements

LET THE POWER COACH™ M POWER YOUR CHURCH OR LEADERSHIP TEAM!

The Power Coach™ Madeline Alexander is the ideal speaker for your next conference, seminar, meeting, or event! Madeline delivers dynamic keynotes and transformational seminars for churches, corporations, businesses, colleges, universities, youth organizations, and faith-based organizations. To confirm your event date, email us at: info@madelinealexander.com.

The following keynote topics are available for churches for weekend services or conferences. For entrepreneur, corporate, association, or college keynote topics, please visit www.madelinealexander.com. Custom topics will also be prepared for any audience group. Please submit your topic request to info@madelinealexander.com.

YOUR 90-DAY FINANCIAL BREAKTHROUGH

Launch your congregation into a life-changing journey to transform their finances with the Word of God. This call to WAR will challenge you to renew your money mindset, conquer debt, restore your health, and create wealth. Don't tolerate the trespass of the enemy through financial lack, shortage, debt, and debt slavery! Defeat the enemy's Trifold Attack. Learn God's cycle of blessing, and the powerful wealth generation strategies in the Word. It's time to live in the abundance and overflow the Lord has destined for you.

THE URGENCY OF ENTREPRENEURSHIP

This message reveals God's masterful plan for economic recovery, wealth creation, and financial freedom through business ownership. We will uncover God's strategies for biblical, economic health that are clearly outlined in the scriptures. God wants you free from bondage, lack, and debt, thoroughly equipped for every good work! Provide for your family, prepare for the future, pass on wealth to future generations, and provide generously for the needs of others. This is the strategy that will set you free.

THE THIRD REVOLUTION

All great civil movements of liberation that free societies and nations begin with a liberated mind in a leader who will stand up and lead the people of God. This powerful, progressive, and prophetic word will present to your congregation a deeper understanding of the present revolution in which we live, and provoke a stirring call to leadership in those with the revolutionary mindset of Christ.

RELEASING THE POWER OF GOD WITHIN YOU

Our Heavenly Father has equipped us with self-control, free will, and His amazing power and might, but we must know how to release His power to experience God's best in our lives. You are a complex creation and an engineering marvel, but if you do not understand how to manage and control all of the components of your amazing human make-up, you will never fully reach your potential! This message is a game-changer for your congregation....you will NEVER be the same!

STRONGHOLDS OF SEPARATION

Romans 8:35 promises that NOTHING shall be able to separate us from the love of God in Christ Jesus. So why do so many believers struggle with a distant relationship with the Lord...not experiencing His continual loving presence, power, and promises? We will demolish five strongholds of separation that will keep you from the intimacy God desires to have with you, and the abundant promises He has for you!

MASTERFULLY MADE FOR A MISSION

Fulfilling your mission assignment is the key to your extraordinary life. Learn how to answer the two questions every believer must face to unlock and embrace God's specific calling on your life. We will study the heroes of faith to understand God's faithful pattern of calling and equipping even reluctant leaders to stand strong in the will of God! Learn the master keys to unlocking your personal mission, overcoming the "Who, Me?" Syndrome, and stepping out to powerfully fulfill His plan for your life.

YOU ARE GOD'S MASTERPIECE

Learn to uncover and defeat the two most damaging mental barriers that almost all believers face that keep them on the outskirts of their divine destiny! Understand the strategies the enemy uses to implant limiting beliefs in your thinking, and banish them forever. Use the powerful tools God has given you through His Word to truly renew your mind! Change your mindset and change your life.

become a partner

PARTNERS WITH THE POWER COACH™

Partners with The Power Coach™ is a monthly partnership program whereby you can co-labor with me to change lives around the world. You will receive the highest quality instruction available to break through barriers, increase financially, and create holistic success. Every month, you will receive a 70-min Power Coach™ Audio CD with Action Guide, and special incentives for Partners only, including the generous Partner Rewards Program! As an official Partner, you will help me to empower many others in very difficult situations. Through Partners, we are helping many to get a fresh start — we are elevating the lives of the unemployed, and those in drug and alcohol treatment, alternative education, juvenile detention, and the US prison system. To become a Partner, visit www.madelinealexander.com.

POWER COACH™ AUDIO

Whether you want to advance your career, rapidly grow your business, increase financially, expand your leadership influence, improve your health and fitness, or enhance your relationships, it's never been easier to get the actionable strategies you need to succeed! With Power Coach™ Audio, we can coach together any time — listen at home, in your car, at the office, or while you travel! Banish negative thinking, remove self-sabotaging habits, super-charge your success strategies, and fuel up your follow-through. Build the daily success habits that will transform your life! Visit www.madelinealexander.com.

POWER COACH™ FINANCIAL NETWORK (PCFN)

The national Power Coach™ Financial Network (PCFN) business consortium is dedicated to bringing economic recovery and financial empowerment to one million families nationwide through business ownership. With careful vetting and business selection, strong leadership, personal mentoring, and detailed training from skilled professionals who adhere to biblical principles, a relationship marketing or network marketing micro-franchise can be an extraordinarily profitable addition to your wealth generation plan. If you are ready to join a strong, professional, faith-based cooperative micro-franchise team for wealth creation, PCFN is for you!

PCFN provides hands-on entrepreneurship education, business-building training, group coaching, and mentoring to help motivated individuals overcome the single source of income limitation, and develop multiple business income streams, leading to financial stability, wealth creation, and time freedom. PCFN also provides unbiased, 3rd-party business assessments and recommendations, as well as talent portfolio assessments to help you discover your best gifts.

Through PCFN, you will identify your strongest gifts and talents for business building, learn the professional skills needed to build a network marketing micro-franchise, select the micro-franchise that is appropriate for you, and build to sustained profitability. We believe in helping others diversify their income through business ownership, teamwork, and personal development. Leveraging the micro-franchise business model, we will work together to build successful businesses, and become wealthy, healthy, and free. For more information, please visit www.madelinealexander.com or email info@madelinealexander.com.

events

YOUR 90-DAY FINANCIAL BREAKTHROUGH BOOTCAMP

During this power-packed 2-day Breakthrough Bootcamp, I will help your congregation take action to transform their finances now. We will implement the Financial Wellness Action Plan to radically renew their money mindset, conquer debt, restore health, and create wealth. We will focus on specific strategies for economic recovery, debt reduction, wealth creation, and financial freedom through business ownership. Your congregation will be encouraged, energized, and equipped to bring down every financial barrier, and enter into God's promise of abundance with a responsible, generous, and Kingdom-focused mindset. To schedule, please email info@madelinealexander.com.

THE BREAKTHROUGH EXPERIENCE WORSHIP CONFERENCE

This is the 3-day breakthrough event you do not want to miss! Powerful praise & worship, anointed prayer ministry, breakthrough teaching, and practical strategies you can apply immediately to empower you to truly break through! You will be inspired, empowered, ignited, and challenged for change through a personal encounter with God that will liberate your mind and spirit, and transform your life...for good. For upcoming dates and registration, email info@madelinealexander.com.

resources

BOOKS

Your 90-Day Financial Breakthrough; $29.95
90 Power Promises and the Weapons of Our Warfare
To WIN in Your Finances Now

How to Break Through Barriers and Achieve Power Results; .. $24.95
POWER MINDSET II – CHOOSE TO BE A CHAMPION

How to Break Through Barriers and Achieve Power Results; $17.95
Create Your Power Mindset for Success in 30 Days or Less
Inspirational Edition

How to Break Through Barriers and Achieve Power Results; $17.95
Create Your Power Mindset for Success in 30 Days or Less
Motivational Edition

POWER COACH™ AUDIO – CD AND MP3

CD1: Healthy Frustration & Your This Is It Moment $24.97
Harnessing the Power of NOW

CD2: Change Your Words; Change Your World $24.97
Banishing the Language of Limits

CD3: Mission Mapping & Goal Setting — Part 1 .... $24.97

CD4: Mission Mapping & Goal Setting — Part 2 .... $24.97

CD5: From Sabotage to Success $24.97
Harness the Power of Habits to Transform Your Life

CD6: The Truth About Barriers $24.97
The Five Big Secrets of Lasting Breakthrough

additional books

Contains breakthrough Power Coaching on the Champion Mindset, and captures over 60 of the most powerful encouragements from "Today's Power Tip for Success." If you are ready to fulfill your mission assignment, this book is a MUST READ! Comes with a bonus CD of the dynamic, new word single, "RELEASE THE POWER"!

The ideal motivational resources for corporations, colleges, universities, public schools, and associations. Includes over 60 Power Tips for Success in a power-packed, 30-day positive mental conditioning program that will empower both leaders and students to achieve!

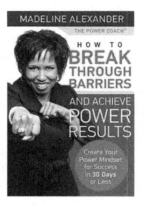

Includes over 60 Power Tips for Success in a power-packed, 30-day positive mental conditioning program that will transform your thinking beginning Day 1, empowering you to achieve optimal success, achievement, and fulfillment! Annotated with power principle scripture verses for each day.